Integration of Natural Language and Vision Processing

(Volume II)

Intelligent Multimedia

Edited by

Paul Mc Kevitt

Dept. of Computer Science, University of Sheffield, U.K.

Reprinted from Artificial Intelligence Review
Volume 9, Nos. 2–3, 1995

Springer Science+Business Media, B.V.

A C.I.P. Catalogue record for this book is available from the Library of Congress.

ISBN 978-94-010-4199-7 ISBN 978-94-011-0445-6 (eBook)
DOI 10.1007/978-94-011-0445-6

Printed on acid-free paper

Originally published by Kluwer Academic Publishers in 1995
Softcover reprint of the hardcover 1st edition 1995

Table of Contents

About the Authors

Elisabeth André received her diploma degree in Computer Science from the University of Saarbrücken, Germany. During her studies, she was concerned with the generation of natural language scene descriptions in the project VITRA (VIsual TRAnslator) that is funded by the German Science Foundation (DFG). Since 1988, she has been working as a full-time researcher in the Intelligent User Interfaces group at the German Research Center for Artificial Intelligence (DFKI). Her current research focuses on computer-based multimedia communication, intelligent user interfaces and knowledge-based presentation systems. In her Ph.D., she is concerned with the development of a plan-based approach for the generation of multimedia presentations. In January 1994, she was elected European Representative of the ACL Special Interest Group on Multimedia Language Processing (SIGMEDIA).

Yigal Arens is a Project Leader on the research staff of the University of Southern California's Information Science Institute, located in Marina del Rey, California, USA. He received his Ph.D. from the University of California at Berkeley, working in the area of natural language understanding, as part of the UNIX Consultant system. In 1983, he joined the faculty of the Computer Science Department at the University of Southern California. He joined USC/ISI in 1987 and first worked there on the Integrated Interfaces project, a multimedia briefing system combining text, tables, maps, and other graphics. Yigal's work on the II project evolved into the work described here. He currently leads the SIMS project at ISI, researching issues involved in intelligent access to multiple distributed data- and knowledge-bases. Yigal's primary research interests are human-machine communication, knowledge representation, and planning in the domain of information servers.

Colin Beardon started working with computers in 1966. He was awarded a BA in Philosophy from the University of Bristol in 1972, a Ph.D. in Artificial Intelligence from the University of Essex in 1976 and an MA in History & Philosophy of Science from the University of New South Wales in 1980. Since 1976 he has worked in industry and higher education in Britain, Australia and New Zealand, specialising in artificial intelligence and natural language processing. For the past four years he has been managing a multimedia research centre within a faculty of art, design and humanities. He is currently involved in projects on iconic communication, the use of multimedia in education and museums, and computer animation environments. He is currently Reader in Computer Graphics in the Rediffusion Simulation Research Centre, Faculty of Art, Design & Humanities at the University of Brighton.

Dominique Béroule is 35 and from the French National Scientific Research Agency (CNRS). He is currently member of the Human-Machine Communication Department at LIMSI, where he is responsible for the "connectionist systems" theme. The main project of this theme is to develop a multimodal system based on Guided Propagation Networks, a computational model inspired by psychophysiological data and initiated at LIMSI in 1983. He defended his dissertation about this model at the University of Orsay in 1985 and since then participated in its application to speech processing, reading modelling, natural language parsing, hardware and control aspects. The reading model has been started in 1987 during a one-year fellowship position at IPO (Institute for Perception Research) in Eindhoven, and then continued in the framework of a cooperation on "connectionism and Man-Machine Dialogue". His current interest concerns the interpretation of natural language and the generation of action in relation to perceptual modalities.

Lindsey Ford lectures on Object-Oriented Programming and Human-Computer Interaction at the University of Exeter, UK. His early research background was in AI-related areas, notably ICAI. He now researches in Human-Computer Interaction, where his interests include visualisation, virtual reality, and media computing. His visualisation research is in visual programming and program visualisation... and the implications for learning and teaching programming. His aim is to make computer programming a productive and pleasurable activity, one in which programs are best made through the application of engineering and artistic skills in an environment (part real, part artificial) that provides novel ways of "navigating" around the program and "travelling" on execution journeys. He likes working closely with undergraduate, masters, and postgraduate research students, from home and abroad, who have a zest for research in HCI.

Eduard Hovy is a Project Leader on the research staff of the University of Southern California's Information Science Institute, and a Research Assistant Professor in USC's Computer Science Department. He has performed research in the area of natural language generation and machine translation for nearly a decade. He currently heads the Pangloss machine translation project (including the Penman language generation system) and the MEDTRANS medical information distribution project at USC/ISI. After completing his Ph.D. at Yale University in 1987 on the topic of user- and situation-oriented language generation, Eduard joined USC/ISI and developed text planning methods for multisentence text within the Penman effort. Subsequently, he has helped develop techniques and resources required to build large robust machine translation and natural language processing systems. He has also elaborated the work on multisentence text to multimedia dialogue planning and management.

Darrel Manuel has a B.Sc. in Computer Science and an M.Sc. (with Distinction) in New Generation Computing, both from the Department of Computer Science at the University of Exeter. He is currently in his first year of Ph.D. study, and his research topic is concerned with techniques and systems for data visualisation.

Jean-Claude Martin is 28 and from France. He is a Temporary Assistant for Teaching and Research at Paris-XI University. He is completing his thesis at LIMSI-CNRS in the field on multimodal human-computer interfaces. His engineer Degree in Computer Science was obtained from the National Engineer School of Telecommunications (ENST), Paris, in 1989. His primary research interests are the study of the interactions between modalities and connectionist networks.

Mark Maybury is Director of the Bedford Artificial Intelligence Center at the MITRE Corporation, a group which performs research in intelligent human computer interaction, natural language processing, knowledge based software and intelligent training. Mark received a BA in Mathematics from the College of the Holy Cross, Worcester, MA in 1986, an M.Phil. in Computer Speech and Language Processing from Cambridge University, England in 1987, an MBA from Rensselaer Polytechnic Institute in Troy, NY in 1989, and a Ph.D. in Artificial Intelligence from Cambridge University, England in 1991 for his dissertation, "Generating Multisentential Text using Communicative Acts". Mark has published over fifty articles in the area of language generation and multimedia presentation. He chaired the AAAI-91 Workshop on Intelligent Multimedia Interfaces and edited the resulting international collection, *Intelligent Multimedia Interfaces* (AAAI/MIT Press, 1993). Mark's research interests include communication planning, tailored information presentation, and narrated animation.

Paul Mc Kevitt is 31 and from Dun Na nGáll (Donegal), Ireland on the Northwest of the EU. He is a British EPSRC (Engineering and Physical Sciences Research Council) Advanced Fellow in the Department of Computer Science at the University of Sheffield in Sheffield, England, EU. The Fellowship, commencing in 1994, releases him from his tenured Lecturership (Associate Professorship) for 5 years to conduct full-time research on the integration of natural language, speech and vision processing. He is currently pursuing a Master's Degree in Education at the University of Sheffield. He completed his Ph.D. in Computer Science at the University of Exeter, England, EU in 1991. His Master's Degree in Computer Science was obtained from New Mexico State University, New Mexico, USA in 1988 and his Bachelor's Degree in Computer Science from University College Dublin, Dublin, Ireland, EU in 1985. His primary research interests are in Natural Language Processing including the processing of pragmatics, beliefs and intentions in dialogue. He is also interested in Philosophy, Multimedia and the general area of Artificial Intelligence.

Stuart Mealing holds a BA(Hons) in Fine Art from the Cardiff College of Art and an MA for Computing in Design from the Centre for Advanced Study of Computer Aided Art and Design, Middlesex Polytechnic. He is the author of *The Art and Science of Computer Animation and Mac 3D* (Intellect) and has exhibited widely to international audiences, both as a practising artist and as a designer.

Ajit Narayanan has written many journal and conference papers in computational linguistics, artificial intelligence and philosophy of AI as well as edited and authored books in these subjects. His first degree was in Communication Science and Linguistics at the University of Aston, and his Ph.D. was in Philsophy at the University of Exeter. He joined the Department in 1980 and was Head of Department from 1987–89. His current research interests, apart from language animation, include nonmonotonic inheritance structures, connectionist models of how we change our minds, and philosophical aspects of neuroscience. He is Senior Lecturer in Computer Science.

Thomas Rist studied computer science and mathematics at the University of Saarbrücken, Germany. As a student, he worked on event recognition in visual image sequences in the project VITRA (VIsual TRAnslator) that is funded by the German Science Foundation (DFG). After he received a diploma degree in Computer Science in 1988, he became a member of the Intelligent User Interfaces Group at the German Research Center for Artificial Intelligence (DFKI) in Saarbrücken. His research interests include issues of multimedia communication, particularity, automated graphics generation.

Jim Spohrer received a B.S. in Physics from MIT in 1978, and a Ph.D. in Computer Science/Artificial Intelligence from Yale in 1989. He was a research scientist at Dialog System/Verbex, a speech recognition company in the Boston area, from 1978 to 1982. After a brief period as a visiting scholar at the University of Rome in Italy, he joined Apple Computer's Advanced Technology Group in 1989. He co-edited *Studying the Novice Programmer* (Lawrence Erlbaum Associates) with Elliot Soloway. His second book is titled *Simulating the Novice Programmer* and is published by Ablex. Jim's research interests lie at the intersection of cognitive science, artificial intelligence, software engineering, and intelligent tutoring systems.

Oliviero Stock is the head of the Natural Language Group at IRST, the Institute for Scientific and Technological Reseach, in Trento, Italy. His research interests include also computer-human interaction and knowledge representation. Before being at IRST, he worked with the Italian National Council for Research. Educated at University of Florence and University of Pisa, Dr. Stock is the author of about 80 scientific papers. Currently, he is the President of AI*IA, the Italian AI association, and the Chairman of the European Coordinating Committee for AI. He has been co-chairman of the Third Applied Natural Language Processing Conference of the ACL.

Dan Tallis graduated in 1992 with a degree in Computer Science at the University of Exeter and is currently in his final year as a Ph.D. student. His Ph.D. research is concerned with the use of software visualisation techniques to aid software comprehension.

Masoud Yazdani joined Exeter University in 1981 as a Lecturer in Computer Science. He is the founding editor of two international journals, *Artificial Intelligence Review* and *Intelligent Tutoring Media* and a past Committee Secretary (1985–88) of the Society for the Study of Artificial Intelligence and Simulation of Behaviour (AISB). His research deals with the common concerns of Artificial Intelligence and Education – the knowledge sources and processes involved in teaching and learning. More recently this has been broadened to consider other kinds of computer mediated interaction and knowledge transfer – Computer Assisted Language Learning, Language Visualisation and Electronic Publishing. In addition to numerous technical articles he has authored or edited 11 books, the most recent entitled *Multilingual Multimedia: Bridging the language barrier with intelligent systems* (Intellect, 1993).

Artificial Intelligence Review **9**: 77–80, 1995.

Editorial

Integration of Natural Language and Vision Processing: Intelligent Multimedia

There has been a recent move towards integration of Natural Language and Vision Processing (NLP and VP) in the field of Artificial Intelligence (AI) (see Denis and Carfantan 1993, Dennett 1991, Mc Kevitt 1994a, 1994b, Pentland 1993, and Wilks and Okada (in press)). The focus here is intelligent multimedia and as such involves the integration of models and systems from the fields of AI and multimedia. The founding of this field is well described in Maybury (1993)[1] and Mark provides an appendix to his paper here which acts as a very useful quick guide to the current literature. This issue is the third of a Special Volume to focus on the Integration of Natural Language and Vision Processing, the others concentrating on models, systems and theory. Issues consist of site descriptions, papers and book reviews. Here, we have four site descriptions, seven papers and one book review.

In this issue there are site descriptions from the DFKI (Germany), Apple Computer (USA), the University of Brighton (England), and LIMSI-CRNS (France). These site descriptions discuss some of the recent developments in intelligent multimedia and they provide lists of interesting publications. The span of countries here indicates that intelligent multimedia is certainly of international interest. Work spans from Apple's *Pupeteer* system which enables designers to build simulations of interactions with people to the DFKI's WIP system for generation of multimedia documents from a formal description of the communicative intent of a planned presentation.

The set of papers here broadly falls into three categories: (1) general issues and multimedia interfaces, (2) multimedia presentation, and (3) multimedia communication. First, we look at two papers which give general overviews on intelligent multimedia and discuss multimedia interfaces. Mark Maybury gives a general overview of current techniques for parsing and generating multiple media. He discusses systems that have integrated parsing and generation to enable multimedia dialogue in the context of intelligent interfaces and he outlines fundamental problems which require further research. Mark also gives an appendix which provides a very useful quick guide to the current literature. Oliviero Stock discusses the integration of NLP with other media such as gestures and graphics and points out that previously NLP was in the form of the *teletype* approach where interaction is limited to typed text. He describes the ALFRESCO system which is an interactive natural language centred system incorporating touchscreen that provides information on Italian frescoes. Also described is MAIA a system which integrates speech recognition, natural language, knowledge representation, vision and reasoning and which consists of a mobile part (a robot) and a fixed part (a "concierge"). Oliviero's group are tackling some of the fundamental problems in integration and intelligent multimedia and the IRST is one of the leading centres in this area.

Next, we have two papers discussing multimedia presentation. Elisabeth André and Thomas Rist discuss the development of a system called WIP for generating coherent presentations employing textual and visual material to provide information on assembling, using, and maintaining physical devices like espresso machines, lawnmowers and modems. They use speech acts, rhetorical relations and referring expressions as a methodological basis for their work. The work at the DFKI, which we have already seen in the first issue, is tackling fundamental issues in language and vision integration. Yigal Arens and Eduard Hovy discuss the design of a multimedia interaction manager called *Cicero* which performs run-time media coordination and allocation. Cicero adapts to the presentation context and knows what it is presenting in order to provide coherent extended human-machine dialogues. Intelligent multimedia presentation will definitely be important in the future as the generation of material for SuperInformationHighways becomes more prevalent.

The next three papers look at the possibility of communication from the point of view of icons and animation. Colin Beardon centres on the fact that the syntactic and semantic structure of language can be retained while iconic images are used instead of words. He is particularly interested in capturing pragmatic aspects of communication such as conveying the intentions of authors. He describes his earlier work on *CD-Icon*, a general purpose graphical language based on Conceptual Dependency theory (see Schank 1972, Schank and Abelson 1977) and discusses his new iconic language called *IconText*. Masoud Yazdani and Stuart Mealing discuss visual communication from the point of view of foreign language speakers. They focus on the possibility of using electronic mail to provide an environment where foreign language users could communicate using icons. They built a system in hypercard which enables hotel booking where there is a dialogue between a potential guest and a hotel manager. Narayanan *et al.* discuss the possibility of developing visual primitives for language primitives where Schank's Conceptual Dependency is used for the latter. They show an example story and how it can be mapped into visual primitives and animation sequences and point to the fact that such sequences will fill in gaps in case-based and frame-based language structures. Beardon, Yazdani and Narayanan *et al.* are onto something here with iconic communication and we shall see a lot more on that in years to come. In fact work on more advanced communication devices including animated faces with speech interaction is being conducted by researchers such as Naoko Tosa at Musashino Art University who has already developed, *Neuro Baby*, a 3-D digital child which simulates emotional patterns based on those of humans (see Graves 1993). Pentland (1993) contains work by a number of researchers on systems which can recognise body language, gaze and eye movement.

Maybury's book *Intelligent Multimedia Interfaces*, reviewed here, is a foundation stone for work in intelligent multimedia and should be read in conjunction with the papers herein. As I scan the papers here once more I see a number of names reoccurring: André, Arens, Beardon, Feiner, Hovy, Maybury, Schank, Stock and Wahlster.

The articles here are in response to a call by Masoud and myself which went out in December '93. I note that the USA and the EU (France, Germany, Britain, Italy) are represented here showing up the fact that intelligent multimedia integration is an international issue. All of the papers have been reviewed by at least one reviewer other than myself and have been subsequently revised. Reviewers Colin Beardon, Andrew Csinger, Debbie Dahl, Steve Feiner, Mark Maybury, Roger Schank, Rohini Srihari, Yorick Wilks, and Masoud Yazdani are to be thanked for the time and effort they have put into this process and I shall not say which reviewers reviewed which papers! The development of this third (and other) issue(s) on language and vision would not be possible without Bill George (Desk Editor, Editorial Department), Polly Margules (Kluwer In-House Editor, Humanities and Social Sciences), Melanie Willow (Journals Editorial Office), and Masoud Yazdani (the Editor of AI Review), and they are to be thanked for all their cooperation. Melanie has worked very hard with authors and reviewers to enable this to happen.

That's the papers for this third issue which should give a good feel for intelligent multimedia which I believe will be crucial in the development of SuperInformationHighways. We move on to look at Theory in the next issue. I'm looking forward . . . :)

Slan leat,

Paul Mc Kevitt*
Dún Na nGáll (Donegal)
Ireland, EU

and

EPSRC Advanced Fellow in Information Technology
[1994–2000]
Department of Computer Science
University of Sheffield
England, EU

NOTES

* Paul Mc Kevitt is currently funded for five years on an Engineering and Physical Sciences Research Council (EPSRC) Advanced Fellowship under grant B/94/AF/1833 for the Integration of Natural Language, Speech and Vision Processing.

[1] This book is reviewed in this special issue by Elisabeth Maier of the DFKI, Germany.

REFERENCES

Denis M. & Carfantan, M. (eds.) (1993). *Images et langages: Multimodalité et modelisation cognitive.* Actes du Colloque Interdisciplinaire du Comité National de la Recherche Scientifique, Salle des Conférences, Siège du CNRS, Paris, April.

Dennett, D. (1991). *Consciousness Explained.* Penguin: Harmondsworth.

Graves, G. (1993). *This Dignital Baby Responds to Coos and Goos.* Tech Watch, Computer Graphics World **16**, July.

Maybury, M. (ed.) (1993). *Intelligent Multimedia Interfaces.* AAAI Press: Menlo Park, CA.

Mc Kevitt, P. (1994a). Visions for language. In *Proceedings of the Workshop on Integration of Natural Language and Vision Processing, Twelfth American National Conference on Artificial Intelligence (AAAI-94)*, Seattle, Washington, U.S.A., August, 47–57.

Mc Kevitt, P. (ed.) (1994b). *Proceedings of the Workshop on Integration of Natural Language and Vision Processing.* Twelfth American National Conference on Artificial Intelligence (AAAI-94), Seattle, Washington, U.S.A., August.

Pentland, A. (ed.) (1993). *Looking at People: Recognition and Interpretation of Human Action.* IJCAI-93 Workshop (W28) at the 13th International Conference on Artificial Intelligence (IJCAI-93), Chambéry, France, E.U., August.

Schank, R. (1972). Conceptual Dependency: A Theory of Natural Language Understanding. *Cognitive Psychology* **3**(4): 552–631.

Schank, R. & Abelson, R. (1977). *Scripts, Plans, Goals and Understanding: An Inquiry into Human Knowledge Structures.* Lawrence Erlbaum Associates: Hillsdale, NJ.

Wilks, Y. & Okada, N. (eds.) (in press). *Computer Language & Vision Across the Pacific.* Ablex: Norwood, NJ.

Artificial Intelligence Review **9**: 81–84, 1995.

Research in Multimedia Systems at DFKI

ELISABETH ANDRÉ and THOMAS RIST

German Research Center for Artificial Intelligence (DFKI), Stuhlsatzenhausweg 3, D-66123 Saarbrücken; Email: {andre,rist}@dfki.uni-sb.de

Abstract. The German Research Center for Artificial Intelligence (Deutsches Forschungszentrum für Künstliche Intelligenz, DFKI) is a non-profit organization that conducts application-oriented basic research in the field of Artificial Intelligence and other related subfields of computer science. One of its current research areas is devoted to Intelligent User Interfaces. The group, headed by Prof. Dr. Wolfgang Wahlster, is concerned with issues of multimedia/multimodal communication. In this paper, an overview of two projects carried out by the group is given.

Key words: multimedia communication, presentation systems, intelligent user interfaces.

1. WIP (KNOWLEDGE-BASED PRESENTATION OF INFORMATION)

In 1989, our group started work with the project WIP. WIP aimed at the development of a presentation system that is able to generate a variety of multimedia documents from input consisting of a formal description of the communicative intent of a planned presentation. In the implemented system, the generation process is controlled by a set of generation parameters such as target group, presentation objective, resource limitations, and target language (see Figure 1).

WIP has been designed for interfacing with heterogeneous back-end systems such as expert systems, tutoring systems, intelligent control panels, on-line documentation and help systems, which supply the presentation system with the necessary input. Since WIP's internal processing schemes are independent of any particular back-end system it requires only a limited effort to adapt the system to a new application. In order to validate WIP's transportability the system was tested in three different application domains (generating illustrated explanations and instructions on using an espresso machine, assembling a lawn-mower, and maintaining a modem). Starting from the original espresso-machine domain we did not have to change a single line of code in going to the two new domains. Only the declarative knowledge sources coded in RAT (Representation of Actions in Terminological Logics), the lexicon and the geometric information are different. While for each domain the application knowledge and the wireframe model are fixed, the presentation goal and the generation parameters can be varied. The benefit of the WIP system lies in its ability to present the same information in a variety of ways depending on the generation parameters. Thus WIP

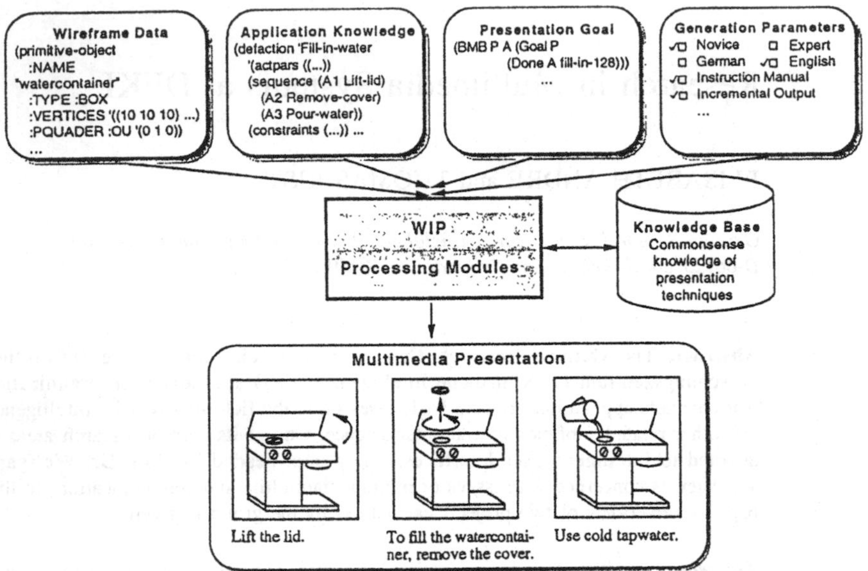

Fig. 1. Functional view of the system.

allows for tailoring presentations for individual users in particular communicative situations.

One of the important insights we gained from building the WIP system is that it is actually possible to extend and adapt many of the fundamental concepts developed to date in AI and computational linguistics for the generation of natural language in such a way that they become useful for the generation of graphics and text-picture combinations as well. This means that an interesting methodological transfer from the area of natural language processing to a much broader computational model of multimedia communication seems possible. In particular, semantic and pragmatic concepts like coherence, speech acts, anaphora, and rhetorical relations take on an extended meaning in the context of text-picture combinations. For a more detailed description of this approach we refer to the paper by André and Rist in this volume.

The WIP project was supported by the German Ministry of Research and Technology under grant ITW 8901 8. The project team, headed by Prof. Dr. Wolfgang Wahlster, was divided into three subgroups for presentation planning (PP), language generation (TAG-GEN) and knowledge representation (KR). The presentation planning group focused on problems of context-directed selection of contents, automated graphics design, coordination of text and graphics (Elisabeth André and Thomas Rist), and constraint-based layout (Winfried Graf). The language generation group worked on the incremental and parallel generation of text using lexicalized tree-adjoining grammars with feature unification (Dr. Karin Harbusch, Anne Kilger and Wolfgang Finkler). The knowledge representation group extended the expressiveness of the terminological logic used in WIP with regard to the representation of temporal relations, action structures, default values and exceptions (Prof. Dr. Bernhard Nebel, Prof. Dr. Jochen Heinsohn and Hans Jürgen Profitlich).

2. PPP (PERSONALIZED PLAN-BASED PRESENTER)

In February 1994, the members of the PP and the KR group started with the project PPP (under grant ITW 9400). The PPP project continues work done in WIP by adding three fundamental extensions:

- *Planning Multimedia Presentation Acts*
  In contrast to WIP, the PPP system not only synthesizes multimedia documents, but also plans how this material is to be presented to various users. One particular objective of the PPP project is to emulate more natural and efficient presentations by the use of an animated character as a presenter who will show and explain the generated material.
- *Interactive Multimedia Presentations*
  Since it is impossible to anticipate the needs and requirements of each potential user, a presentation system should allow for interaction. The PPP system responds to follow-up questions concerning the domain as well as to meta comments on the act of presentation. Furthermore, PPP allows for user interaction, i.e., PPP responds to follow-up questions concerning the domain as well as to meta comments on the act of presentation.
- *Monitoring the Effectiveness of a Presentation*
  In order to find out whether a user really understood an instruction, the presentation system must keep track of the user's behavior in the world. Given such an additional source of feedback, the system is able to monitor the effectiveness of its presentations and can continuously adapt the instruction strategies to the current situation.

Furthermore, in PPP we aim at a firm representational foundation to allow for easy adaptations of new domains. This includes the development of representational techniques which are flexible and powerful enough to support a wide range of applications.

SELECTED PAPERS FROM THE WIP AND PPP PROJECTS

André, E. & Rist, T. (1990). Synthesizing Illustrated Documents: A Plan-Based Approach. In Proceedings of *InfoJapan '90* **2**: 163–170. Tokyo. Also as DFKI Research Report RR-91-06.

André, E. & Rist, T. (1990b). Towards a Plan-Based Synthesis of Illustrated Documents. In Proceedings of *The Ninth ECAI*, 25–30. Stockholm. Also as DFKI Research Report RR-90-11.

André, E. & Rist, T. (1993). The Design of Illustrated Documents as a Planning Task. In Maybury, M. (ed.) *Intelligent Multimedia Interfaces*, 94–116. AAAI Press. Also as DFKI Research Report RR-92-45.

André, E. & Rist, T. (1994). Generating Coherent Presentations Employing Textual and Visual Material. *Artificial Intelligence Review* (this volume).

André, E. & Rist, T. (1994). Multimedia Presentations: The Support of Passive and Active Viewing. In *Working Notes of the AAAI Spring Symposium on Intelligent Multi-Media Multi-Modal Systems*, 22–29. Stanford University.

André, E. & Rist, T. (1994). Referring to World Objects with Text and Pictures. In Proceedings of *The Fifteenth COLING* **1**: 530–534. Kyoto, Japan.

André, E., Finkler, W., Graf, W., Rist, T., Schauder, A. & Wahlster, W. (1993). WIP: The Automatic Synthesis of Multimodal Presentations. In Maybury, M. (ed.) *Intelligent Multimedia Interfaces*, 75–93. AAAI Press. Also as DFKI Research Report RR-92-46.

André, E., Graf, W., Heinsohn, J., Nebel, B., Profitlich, H.-J., Rist, T. & Wahlster, W. (1993). *PPP – Personalized Plan-Based Presenter*. Document D-93-5, DFKI, Saarbrücken.

André, E., Herzog, G. & Rist, T. (1994). Multimedia Presentation of Interpreted Visual Data. In *AAAI-94 Workshop on the Integration of Natural Language and Vision Processing*, 74–82. Seattle, USA.

Butz, A. (1994). Betty: Planning and Generating Animations for the Visualization of Movements and Spatial Relations. In *Advanced Visual Interfaces* (Proc. of AVI '94, Bari, Italy) (to appear).

Graf, W. & Neurohr, S. (1994). *Using Graphical Style and Visibility Constraints for a Meaningful Layout in Visual Programming Interfaces*. Report, DFKI, Saarbrücken (to appear).

Graf, W. (1992). Constraint-Based Graphical Layout of Multimodal Presentations. In *Advanced Visual Interfaces* (Proc. of AVI '92, Rome, Italy), 365–385. Singapore: World Scientific Press. Also as DFKI Research Report RR-92-15.

Harbusch, K., Finkler, W. & Schauder, A. (1991). Incremental Syntax Generation with Tree Adjoining Grammars. In Brauer, W. & Hernandez, D. (eds.) *Verteilte Künstliche Intelligenz und kooperatives Arbeiten: 4. Internationaler GI-Kongreß Wissensbasierte Systeme, Proc.*, 363–374. Springer: Berlin, Heidelberg.

Heinsohn, J., Nebel, B., Profitlich, H.-J., Rist, T. & Wahlster, W. (1992). *RAT: Representation of Actions Using Terminological Logics*. Document, DFKI, Saarbrücken.

Kilger, A. (1994). Using UTAGs for Incremental and Parallel Generation. *Computational Intelligence* (to appear).

Rist, T. & André, E. (1992a). From Presentation Tasks to Pictures: Towards a Computational Approach to Graphics Design. In Proceedings of *The Tenth ECAI*, 764–768. Wien. Also as DFKI Research Report RR-92-44.

Rist, T. & André, E. (1992b). Incorporating Graphics Design and Realization into the Multimodal Presentation System WIP. In Costabile, M. F., Catarci, T. & Levialdi, S. (eds.) *Advanced Visual Interfaces* (Proc. of AVI '92, Rome, Italy), 193–207. World Scientific Press: Singapore.

Rist, T. & André, E. (1992b). Designing Coherent Multimedia Presentations. In Salvendy, G. & Smith, M. J. (Hrsg.) *Human-Computer Interaction: Software and Hardware Interfaces* (Proc. of HCI–93), Volume 19B, 434–439. Elsevier: Amsterdam, London.

Rist, T., Krüger, T., Schneider, G. & Zimmermann, D. (1994). AWI – A Workbench for Semi-Automated Illustration Design. In *Advanced Visual Interfaces* (Proc. of AVI '94, Bari, Italy) (to appear).

Wahlster, W., André, E., Graf, W. & Rist, T. (1991). Designing Illustrated Texts: How Language Production is Influenced by Graphics Generation. In Proceedings of *The Fifth EACI*, 8–14. Berlin, Germany.

Wahlster, W., André, E., Bandyopadhyay, S., Graf, W. & Rist, T. (1991). WIP: The Coordinated Generation of Multimodal Presentations from a Common Representation. In Ortony, A., Slack, J. & Stock O. (eds.) *Communication from an Artificial Intelligence Perspective: Theoretical and Applied Issues*, 121–144. Berlin, Heidelberg: Springer. Also as DFKI Research Report RR-91-08.

Wahlster, W., André, E., Finkler, W., Profitlich, H.-J. & Rist, T. (1991). Plan-Based Integration of Natural Language and Graphics Generation. *AI Journal* **63**: 387–427. Also as DFKI Research Report RR-93-02.

Wazinski, P. (1992). Generating Spatial Descriptions for Cross-Modal References. In Proceedings of *The Third Conference on Applied Conference on Applied Natural Language Processing*, 56–63. Trento, Italy.

Artificial Intelligence Review 9: 85–89, 1995.

Apple Computer's Authoring Tools & Titles R&D Program

JAMES C. SPOHRER

Apple Computer, Inc., Advanced Technology Group, 1 Infinite Loop Drive, Cupertino, CA 95014; e-mail: spohrer@applelink.apple.com

Key words: authoring tools, intelligent multimedia, tool building, extensible simulations, interpersonal simulations, end-user programming, learning architectures

This site description reports on four projects that are part of Apple Computer's Authoring Tools & Titles R&D Program. Our charter is to empower people to build, extend, and maintain interactive multimedia software by lowering barriers to entry for non-programmers and improving the productivity of professional programmers. In addition, we partner with design teams to create software titles that illustrate the potential of intelligent multimedia applications, especially in the areas of education and training.

INTERPERSONAL SIMULATIONS PROJECT (PUPPETEER)

Arthur James and Enio Ohmaye

Puppeteer is a tool designed to empower instructional designers and subject matter experts to build simulations of interactions with people. For example, second language learning simulations allow users to practice their language skills by interacting with native speakers. Puppeteer's interface uses a comic strip metaphor extended with multiple storylines and control annotations (see Figure 1). The grammar editor allows users to define the language patterns that simulated people will respond to as well as generate. Puppeteer supports user input in various forms: selecting from a fixed set of options, typing in natural language statements, or speaking statements into the Apple speech recognition system. Puppeteer combines animation with speech synthesis to produce talking heads that greatly speeds up the authoring process. Puppeteer is designed to develop apprenticeship based models of instruction and can support learning techniques such as scaffolding, modelling, and coaching.

EXTENSIBLE SIMULATION PROJECT (KIDSIM)

Allen Cypher and David Canfield Smith

KidSim is a tool designed to empower kids and teachers to build extensible simulations. Simulations are imaginary worlds populated with programmed characters. In KidSim, users can define their own characters and modify existing

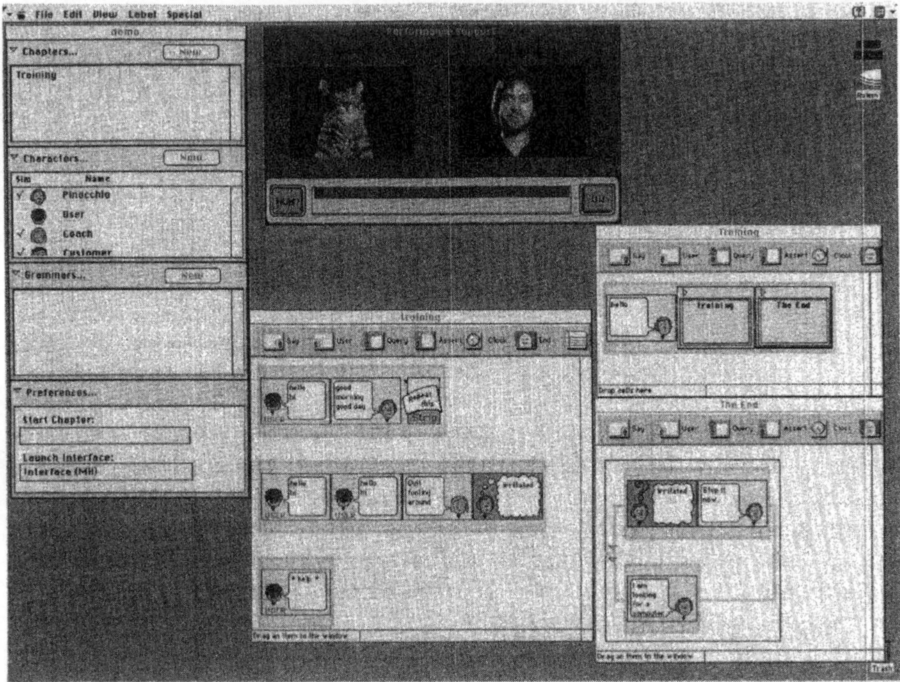

Fig. 1. Puppeteer: comicstrip strip script editor, chapters, and cast.

ones. KidSim allows kids with no programming experience to build simulations quickly. Kids can draw characters, place them on a game board, and give them rules of behavior (see Figure 2). Instead of using a programming language, the rules of behavior are defined in terms of screen snapshots. Creating a rule is done via direct manipulation, by specifying the relevant context for the rule and then demonstrating the desired actions to reach an end state.

TOOL CONSTRUCTION ENVIRONMENT PROJECT (TOOLBUILDER)

Ruben Kleiman, Adam Chipkin, Hernan Epelman-Wang, Brian Roddy, Lori Leahy, Sidney Markowitz, Dave Yost, Stephanie Houde

ToolBuilder is a next generation software development environment designed to empower professional programmers and advanced scripters to build intelligent multimedia applications and derivative tools. Derivative tools are tools designed for specific markets. For example, one might want to build a derivative tool that could be used by real estate agents to put together an interactive sales brochure complete with home walking tours and floor plans. Alternatively, one might want to build a tool that authors can use to build interactive mathematics or science titles, or empower kids and teachers to build simulations. In

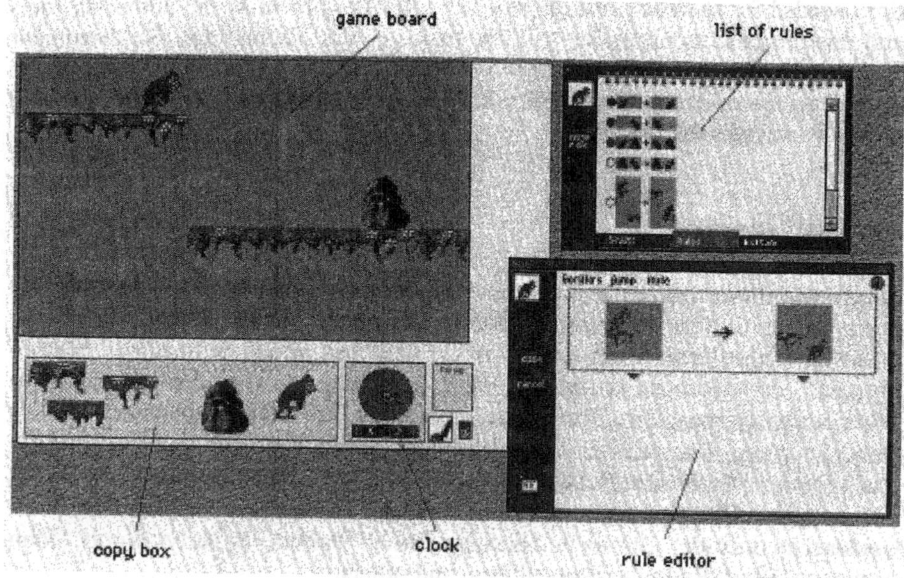

Fig. 2. KidSim game board, copy box, clock, rule editor, list of rules.

fact, KidSim is an example of a derivative tool constructed with ToolBuilder. The ToolBuilder architecture has several major aspects: dynamic prototype-instance object system, scripting language with complex data structures and full featured debugging environment, graphics systems optimized for thousands of objects and programmable renderers, application framework/object libraries, and a project builder interface. ToolBuilder provides an application framework that allows many types of derivative tools to be built very rapidly. ToolBuilder was designed to liberate some of the ideas for great software that have remained trapped on white boards for too long.

EAST/WEST CONSORTIUM PROJECT (E/W)

James C. Spoher and other Consortium Members

Apple Computer and its partners in the East/West Authoring Tools Group have won an award from the Advanced Research Projects Agency (ARPA) of the Department of Defense to develop authoring tools and instructional software. Together Apple Computer, Houghton Mifflin Company, PWS Publishing, the University of Massachusetts Amherst, Carnegie Mellon University, the University of Colorado, and Stanford University Medical School, the founding members of the Group, will work to develop new tools to empower the authors of next generation educational and training software. The authoring tools will enable teams skilled in education, but not in programming, to design educational software that will be effective and user friendly, and will dramatically reduce the time needed for students to learn new skills. Development of the authoring tools and instructional applications will be part of the Technology Reinvestment Project, a government-wide collaborative effort to focus commercial attention on technology innovation, infrastructure, and training of importance to the national economy and national security.

ACKNOWLEDGEMENTS

Many others have played an important role in these projects. We would like to acknowledge the contributions of Phyllis Lewcock, Julaine Salem, and B. J. Allen-Conn (the three teachers who work with us), Dana Schockmel, Marian Djurovic (our two area associates), Mark L. Miller and members of the User Solutions group (especially Rachel Bellamy), Alan Kay and members of Learning Concepts group, and members of the ATG staff, Mike Wirth and members of PIE, Alan Peterson, Mark Loughridge and other contractors, many summer interns, as well as other colleagues too numerous to mention. Colleagues from the East/West Consortium include: Elizabeth Hacking, David Parker, Beverly Woolf, John Anderson, David Redmiles, Parvati Dev, and others.

SELECTED PUBLICATIONS

Cook, C., Scholtz, J. & Spohrer, J. C. (eds.) (1993). *Empirical Studies of Programmer Workshop 5*. Ablex Publishers: N.J.

Cypher, A. (ed.) (1993). *Watch What I Do: Programming by Demonstration*. MIT Press: Boston, MA.

James, A. & Spohrer, J. C. (1992). Simulation-Based Learning Systems: Prototypes and Experiences. Demonstration. Proceeding of the *ACM/SIGCHI Human Factors in Computing Systems*, 523–524. May 3–7. Monterey, CA.

Kay, A. (1991). Computers, Networks, and Education. *Scientific American* **265**(3).

Houde, S. & Sellman, Royston (1994). In Search of Design Principals for Programming Environments. In Proceedings of *CHI'94*, Boston, MA. April 24–28.

Nardi, B. A. (1993). *A Small Matter of Programming: Perspective on End User Computing*. MIT Press: Cambridge, MA.

Norman, D. (1993). *Things that Make Use Smart*. Addison-Wesley Publishing Company: Reading, MA.

Ohmaye, E. (1992). *Simulation-based Language Learning: An Architecture and a Multimedia Authoring Tool*. Technical Report # 30, June 1992. Northwestern University, Institute for Learning Sciences: Evanston, IL.

Smith, D. C. (1977). *Pygmalion: A Computer Program to Model and Stimulate Creative Thought*. Birkhauser Verlag Basel: Stuttgart.

Smith, D. C., Cypher, A. & Sophrer J. C. (1994). *KidSim: Programming Agents without a Programming Language*. CACM: New York, NY.

Soloway, E. & Spohrer, J. C. (eds.) (1989). *Studying the Novice Programmer*. Lawrence Erlbaum Associates, Inc.: Hillsdale, N.J.

Spohrer, J. C. (1990). Integrating Multimedia and AI for Training: Examples and Issues. Proceedings of *The IEEE Systems, Man, and Cybernetics Conference*. Los Angeles, CA.

Spohrer, J. C., James, A., Abbott, C. A., Czora, G. J., Laffey, J. & Miller, M. L. (1991). A role

Playing Simulator for Needs Analysis Consultations. Proceedings of *The World Congress on Expert Systems*. Pergamon Press: Orlando, FL.

Spohrer, J. C., Vronay, D. & Kleiman, R. (1991). Authoring Intelligent Multimedia Applications: Finding Familiar Representations for Expressing Knowledge. Proceedings of *The IEEE Systems, Man, and Cybernetics Conference*. Charlottesville, VA.

Spohrer, J. C. (1992). *MARCEL: Simulating the Novice Programmer*. Ablex Publishers: N.J.

Spohrer, J. C., Hacking, E., Parker, D., Woolf, B., Anderson, J., Fischer, G. & Dev, P. (1993). *Proposal for an Authoring Tools Consortium*. Unpublished Manuscript.

Vronay, D. & Spohrer, J. C. (1993). Pins, Grooves, and Sockets: An Interface for Graphical Constraints. Proceedings of *INTERCHI '93*.

Artificial Intelligence Review **9**: 91–93, 1995.

Research into Iconic Communication at the University of Brighton

COLIN BEARDON

Rediffusion Simulation Research Centre, Faculty of Art, Design & Humanities, University of Brighton, Grand Parade, Brighton BN2 2JY, England; e-mail: ceb7@vms.brighton.ac.uk

Key words: icons, iconic languages, animated help.

The Rediffusion Simulation Research Centre is located in the Faculty of Art, Design & Humanities at the University of Brighton and is devoted to research into multimedia and related issues. It has strong links with traditional areas of art and design, such as graphic design, animation and fine art, as well as with major areas of computing, such as artificial intelligence and computational linguistics.

One of the major research areas of the Centre is iconic communication which explores the potential of graphical images in systems of communication. The development of multimedia environments, which are much richer than the pencil-and-paper context in which previous iconic languages were developed, gives rise to both new possibilities and new problems. Such computer-based systems allow us to use two-dimensional layout, animation and interactivity for communicative purposes, but we are currently confronted with an environment that seriously lacks effective communicative rules. There is great potential for more sophisticated graphical languages to enable users to communicate complex ideas without the restriction to alphabetic text.

Our work in this area began in 1991 with some initial experiments in the design of an interactive, real-time iconic language based loosely upon Schank's Conceptual Dependency structures (Schank 1973). A system was developed, called CD-Icon, that is based around four types of interactive graphical window which can be used to refer to different kinds of entity: simple concepts, objects, conceptualisations (actions or states), and messages. Fuller descriptions of the system can be found in Beardon (1992, 1993). Prototype software was developed to allow messages to be built by selecting items from in an iconic dictionary, and for completed messages to be read by first watching an animation and then interacting with its static frames. A limited amount of testing took place in which users unfamiliar with the system were presented with eight iconic messages developed in CD-Icon without any introduction to the system. They were asked to explore the messages and write down the nearest English equivalent to what they thought was being said. The resulting sentences were generally accurate but were sometimes incomplete.

While meaning representation in both CD and CD-Icon is a network of nodes and links (or, more strictly, a partitioned network) the requirement to present it as a sequential animation raises some important research questions. Most complex messages result in multi-stage animations which are composed of single stages that reflect different parts of the message. Heuristics need to be developed to order the stages in which a message is displayed. Different heuristics are required, for example, depending whether the message is declarative or interrogative.

A second issue concerns the set of relations that are available to form complex messages. Our work on CD-Icon suggests that, while CD may provide a good basis for conveying information about single events, the set of conceptual relations it offers is too weak to allow the expression of a significant range of complex messages. It seems advisable to separate the particular static meaning representation language embodied in CD-Icon from the more general mechanisms of animated iconic representation. While the former relate to the semantic content of the message, the latter are concerned more with discourse issues. This has led us to consider discourse and rhetorical issues that need to be faced by these types of iconic language (Beardon 1994).

A third issue concerns the set of primitive actions (ACTs) that are proposed with Conceptual Dependency. Whilst the reduction of all verbs to fourteen or so ACTs may appear breathtaking in its reductionism, even greater reduction seems possible in iconic languages as the two basic activities one can represent in an animation involve changing the properties of an object or changing its location. Most of Schank's proposed ACTs can be presented as variations of 'physical_transfer' (PTRANS) using different metaphorical backgrounds.

A separate part of our research is concerned with the development of animated help sequences, the intention being to produce animated help for application software that would eliminate the need for translation into different natural languages. Much of this work is carried out by Claire Dormann who utilises semiotics in order to classify the principles and techniques of visual rhetorics and to relate them to different help situations. Of particular interest has been a recent investigation into the use of humour in animations and the particular advantages it may have to offer. Apart from the more obvious use in making readers more well-disposed, we found some situations where humour could be seen as providing solutions to specific problems: for example in assisting identification, and in the provision of explanations that are commensurate with the experiences of users (Dormann and Beardon, forthcoming). More recent work has involved design experiments which aim to see whether there are common approaches to developing animated explanations among groups of users.

REFERENCES

Beardon, C. (1992). CD-Icon: An Iconic Language Based on Conceptual Dependency. *Intelligent Tutoring Media* 3(4): 111–116.

Beardon, C. (1993). Computer-Based Iconic Communication. In Ryan, K. & Sutcliffe, R. (eds.) *AI and Cognitive Science '92.*, 263–276. Springer-Verlag: London.

Beardon, C. (1994). Discourse Structures in Iconic Communication. *Artificial Intelligence Review* **8**(3).

Dormann, C. & Beardon, C. (forthcoming, 1994). Animated Icons and Visual Help. In Earnshaw, R. & Vince, J. (eds.), *Multimedia Systems & Applications.* Academic Press: London.

Schank, R. C. (1973). Identification of Conceptualisations Underlying Natural Language. In Schank, R. & Colby, M. (eds.), *Computer Models of Thought and Language*, 187–247. W. H. Freeman: San Francisco.

Artificial Intelligence Review **9**: 95–102, 1995.

Temporal Codes within a Typology of Cooperation Between Modalities

JEAN-CLAUDE MARTIN[1, 2] and DOMINIQUE BÉROULE[1]

[1] *LIMSI (Laboratoire d'Informatique et de Mécanique pour les Sciences de l'Ingénieur) bat. 508, BP 133, F-91403 Orsay Cedex, France, E-mail: martin@limsi.fr,domi@limsi.fr*; [2] *ENST (Ecole Nationale Supérieure des Télécommunications) 46 rue Barrault, F-75634 Paris Cedex 13, France*

Key words: multimodality, transfer, equivalence, specialisation, redundancy, complementarity, Guided Propagation networks, binding through synchrony.

The Human-Machine Communication Department of LIMSI (LIMSI Report 1994), a laboratory of the French National Scientific Research Agency (CNRS), conducts research in the field of Pattern Recognition, Artificial Intelligence and Pattern Generation. Several approaches are currently investigated there for studying interactions between modalities: studies about the cognitive processes involved in human intermodal tasks (Denis and Cocude 1992; Gryl 1994; Daniel *et al.* 1994), image and language interactions for learning (Bordeaux 1993), human factors (Castaing and Truc 1993), symbolic approaches for designing multimodal human-computer interfaces (Bellik and Teil 1993; Barès *et al.* 1992), spatial reasoning (Ligozat 1992; Briffault 1992).

The project reported in this paper is concerned with the development of a connectionist architecture for multimodal human-machine communication within the "connectionist systems" research team. A conceptual framework for studying multimodal interactions is presented, followed by a description of temporal codes which are aimed at being used in various and deep interactions between modalities.

1. TYCOON: A FRAMEWORK BASED ON TYPES OF COOPERATION

There is a wide range of interactions between language and vision and several approaches for studying them (AAAI-NLP-VP 1994; Image and Language 1993). In order to gain a significant understanding of multimodality, researchers tend to propose conceptual frameworks for studying multimodal human-computer interfaces (Nigay and Coutaz 1993). We have developed TYCOON, a framework based on TYpes and goals of COOperatioN (Martin and Béroule 1993; Martin 1994) (Figure 1).

According to the "types" dimension of TYCOON, two modalities may cooperate through:

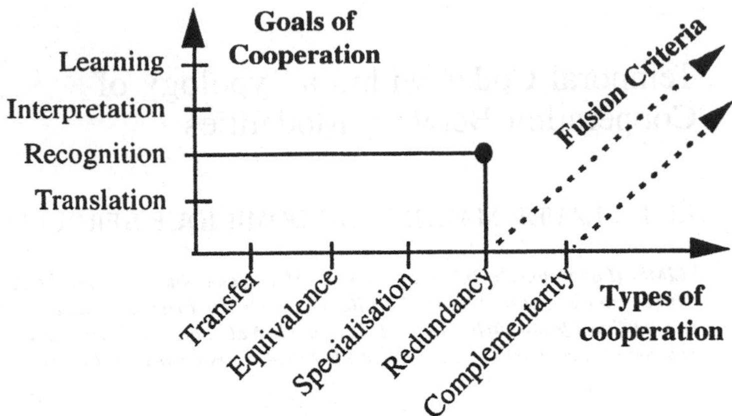

Fig. 1. TYCOON, a conceptual framework for studying multimodal interactions. Types of cooperation (redundancy) may be involved in several goals (recognition). Both redundancy and complementarity ask for the fusion of monomodal messages (dotted arrows).

- *transfer*: a message obtained by one modality is used by the other modality,
- *equivalence*: a single message may be conveyed by either modality,
- *specialisation*: a specific type of message is always conveyed by the same modality,
- *redundancy*: the same message is conveyed by both modalities,
- *complementarity*: distinct messages concerning a single entity are transmitted by both modalities and have to be merged so as to reach a specific goal.

Members of a French working group (GDR-PRC-CHM 1993) are working on multimodal concepts such as these types of cooperation introduced in (Faure and Arnold 1993; Martin and Béroule 1993).

According to the second dimension of TYCOON, each type of cooperation can be used to achieve several "goals". These goals are thereafter illustrated by examples on image and language interactions taken from literature.

• *Translation.* The visual description of a scene can be used to generate a corresponding linguistic description (Jackendoff 1987; Gryl 1994; Daniel *et al.* 1994). Similarly, a graphical description can be generated from a linguistic description (Arnold 1993; Ó Nualláin and Smith 1994). In (Nenov and Dyer 1988), a linguistic description of objects generates a sequence of graphical pictures and vice versa.

• *Recognition.* Intramodal recognition can be improved thanks to multimodality: equivalence enables us to choose the modality having the highest recognition results, complementarity induces simplification of monomodal messages, and redundancy induces increased attention (Huls *et al.* 1994), and may also increase noise resistance and summation of monomodal recognition results.

• *Interpretation.* The analysis carried out by one modality can be guided by a transfer of information from another modality. In (Béroule *et al.* 1994), a reading model simulates a word frequency effect by skipping parts of the most frequent words, thus using linguistic knowledge to actively guide a window scanning the text to be read. Furthermore, interpretation of multimodal messages asks for the fusion of complementary monomodal information concerning the same object (each modality being specialised in specific features or values). In (Novak and Bulko 1990) constraints supplied by the text and diagram mutually reduce ambiguity by using co-references. Interpretation can also be modified by redundancy pointing out the significance of a feature.

• *Learning.* In (Nenov and Dyer 1988; Bordeaux 1993), during learning, both modalities cooperate by complementarity to bind a word to its corresponding visual features, allowing language to ground symbols in visual experience. In (Grumbach 1994), words are specialised in learning rules that associate a symbolic representation of the visual perception to an action and pictures are specialised in the rules directly associating pictures to actions.

TYCOON provides a global view of the interactions between modalities and the advantages of using multimodality. It may be used to classify and specify multimodal systems. A dimension which should also be taken into account is the degree of complexity of interaction between modalities. Complementarity and redundancy may need a binding process between several levels of abstraction: visual speech recognition (Robert-Ribes *et al.* 1994) calls for binding low-level events in both modalities. As a matter of fact, in a multimodal system, each type and each goal of cooperation should be allowed at any level of abstraction. The next sections describe time-based representations which are currently investigated with this purpose in mind.

2. GUIDED PROPAGATION NETWORKS

The integration of existing monomodal systems not only implies their assembling, but also the effort required to make them compatible and work together accurately. The load on this adjustment process may vary in proportion with the dissimilarity between the representations and mechanisms to be integrated. For this reason, the same computational model is proposed here to approach both vision and language, with the project of combining these modalities according to the above types of interaction in mind (Section 1).

This model involves a *topological* memory, in which every piece of information is represented by a relative location in both time and space. Data retrieval shows itself in the activation of a given position in memory, at a certain time. *Guided Propagation* is a parallel processing principle thanks to which such characteristic locations can be retrieved, from a sequence of input events. The implementation of this principle brings into play a network of elementary processing units (Figure 2) organised in a specific way (Béroule 1989, 1990). We now outline features related to the goals of cooperation specified in the previous section.

• *Learning*: The network is built and modified in the course of processing, depending on the familiarity of the current input, in a non-supervised manner.

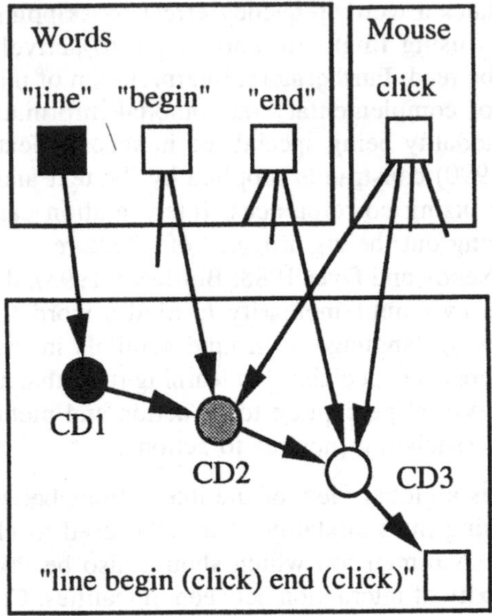

Fig. 2. Representation of a multimodal command in a Guided Propagation Network. A module "Multimodal expressions" detects combinations of sequences and coincidences between signals sent by detectors (squares). It therefore uses Context Dependent (CD) cells. For instance, the recognition of the word "line" induces the activation of the detector associated to this word; this sends a signal to the context cell CD1 which becomes activated; CD1 sends a contextual signal to unit CD2 which means that the remainder of the command is expected; CD2 will be fully activated if the word "begin" and a mouse click then occur.

New combinations of multi-modal events can thus give rise to permanent structures (*memory pathways*), which are then reinforced whenever used (Béroule 1988). This on-line adaptativity at the lowest level of processing is a source of robustness for a multi-modal system oriented towards learning tasks, since unexpected events can give rise to new representations, not only during a preliminary "learning phase".

• *Recognition*: Pattern Recognition involves comparisons to be carried out between an input pattern and internal references. Instead of a series of comparisons between input parameters and arrays of reference parameters, Guided Propagation Networks (GPN) implement a parallel comparison between the memory locations activated by input stimuli (input patterns) and the locations (references) reached at the same time by an internal flow of activation. This comparison is carried out by the memory units, which may receive both types of activation at the same time, possibly originating from several modalities. They detect rough coincidence between delayed inputs, allowing a certain degree of temporal distortion, and variability. The discrete input required by this real-time mechanism is robust to noise, in particular when significant events occur simultaneously within a given modality such as speech (Escande *et al.* 1991).

• *Interpretation*: A group of memory pathways stemmed from the same origin (*root-unit*) deals with the same kind of events (i.e.: *letters*, or *spoken words*, or *syntactic structures* . . .). These groups, referred to as *modules*, can be organised in both hierarchical and multi-modal ways, reflecting respectively the different levels of abstraction inside any modality, the parallel analyses performed at any knowledge level. Due to this parallel representation, every piece of information concerned with a complex situation participates simultaneously in the interpretation process. The internal flow that propagates in a module implements predictions concerning the next events to possibly occur, and results in the selective facilitation of their activation.

• *Translation*: Since modalities share the same type of representations, no problem of translation between modalities may occur at the lowest level. Notably, the Pattern Generation modules of the network own the same tree-like structure as recognition modules.

Current monomodal applications of GPN include: speech recognition (Lainé and Béroule 1994), strategies of syntactic learning (Roques 1994), robust parsing (Westerlund *et al.* 1994), hand-written character recognition, modelling of reading (Béroule *et al.* 1994), and control of the global architecture (Nioche *et al.* 1994). The next section illustrates how the dynamic nature of the signals exchanged by the processing units in GPN is used for multimodal binding.

3. BINDING THROUGH SYNCHRONY

The basic principle of binding through synchrony in neural networks is that internal signals emitted by processing units are synchronised if they code for the same object. It may allow efficient processing by dynamically creating bindings between the internal representations of objects in a given scene without cross-talk.

This code has been used to model both low level perceptual processes in several modalities and high level tasks: segmenting superposed auditory signals (von der Malsburg and Schneider 1986), visual shape recognition (Hummel and Biedermen 1990) and reflexive reasoning (Shastri and Ajjanagadde 1993). Figure 3 illustrates how synchrony can code several types of bindings in an elementary example of graphics and words integration.

We have integrated this binding principle within GPN. In current simulation, synchronisation allows the establishment and short-term memorisation of a dynamic binding between a variable (word "begin") and an associated value (a 2D location).

4. PERSPECTIVES

On the one hand, the adaptation of temporal codes to processes occurring within each modality will be continued. On the other hands, these codes are now applied to elementary multimodal tasks in relationship with the types and goals of

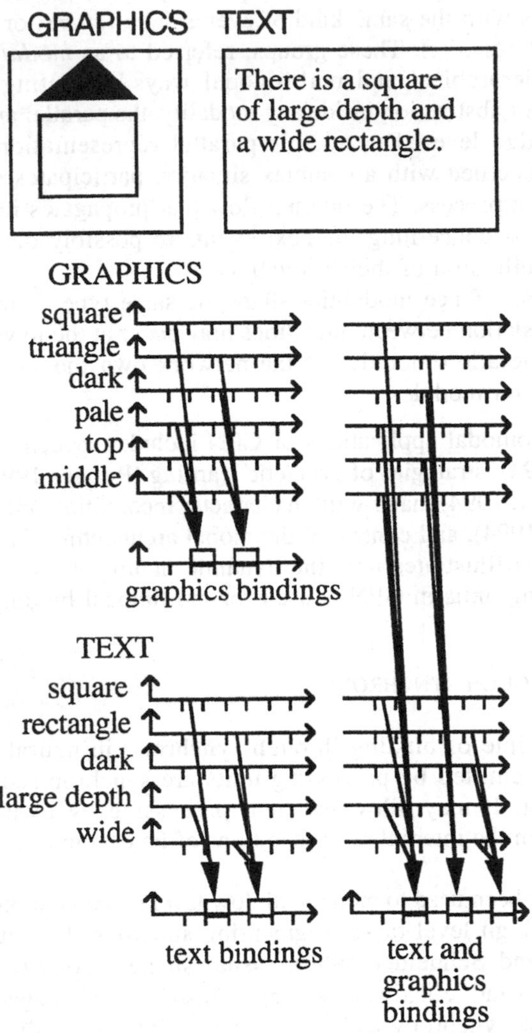

Fig. 3. In the elementary example of multimodal scene (to the top), text is specialised in the description of invisible object (wide rectangle); the square shape is transmitted redundantly in both text and graphics; complementary features such as the depth and luminosity of the square are transmitted on separate modalities. Some objects which appear in the graphics such as the dark triangle amy not be mentioned in the text. The histograms below show how this scene is coded by the synchrony of internal signals emitted by labelled processing units ("square", "triangle" . . .). Synchrony can code for graphics binding (top left histogram): graphical features concerning the same object (square, pale, middle) send synchronised signals to a unit which codes graphics bindings. Synchrony can also code text (to the bottom left) and graphics/text bindings (right). Monomodal binding processes are currently simulated, providing an output that can be used to study their interaction.

cooperation defined in our conceptual framework. On a longer-term scale, it is planned to apply this formalism to multimodal tasks of increasing complexity, involving spatial reasoning and semantic representations.

ACKNOWLEDGEMENTS

J. C. Martin was financed by a DRET/CNRS grant.

REFERENCES

AAAI-NLP-VP (1994). Working notes of the workshop on the Integration of Natural Language and Vision Processing. Chair P. Mc Kevitt. Twelfth National Conf. on Artificial Intelligence, august, 2nd/3rd, Seattle.

Arnold, M. (1993). Linguistic and Spatial Representation of a Scene: An Experiment in Image Synthesis. *Sémiotiques* **4**: 7–29. In French.

Barès, M., Nèel, F., Teil, D. & Martin, J.-C. (1992). Conceptual Approach to Man-Machine Interaction: Application to Pilote's Assistance. In Proceedings of *The Interface Between Real and Virtual Worlds Conference*, 571–590. Montpellier, France. In French.

Bellik, Y. & Teil, D. (1993). A Multimodal Dialogue Controller for Multimodal User Interface Management System Application: A Multimodal Window Manager. Adjunct proceedings of *INTERCHI'93*, 93–94. ACM Press: Amsterdam.

Béroule D. (1990). Guided Propagation: Current State of Theory and Application. In Soulié, F. Fogelman & Hérault, J. (eds.) *Neurocomputing*, Vol. F 68, 241–260. NATO ASI Series; Berlin Heidelberg: Springer-Verlag.

Béroule, D. (1988). The Never-Ending Learning. In Eckmiller, R. & Malsburg, C.v.d. (eds.) *Neural Computers*, 219–230. NATO ASI Series vil F41, Berlin: Springer-Verlag.

Béroule, D. (1989). The Adaptive, Dynamic and Associative Memory Model: A Possible Future Tool for Vocal Human-Computer Communication. In Taylor, M., Néel, F. & Bouwhuis, D. G. (eds.) *The Structure of Multimodal Dialogue*, 189–202. Elsevier Science Publisher B.V.: North Holland.

Béroule, D., Von Hoe, R. & Ruellan, H. (1994). A Guided Propagation Model of Reading, Instituut voor Perceptie Onderzoek (IPO), Annual Progress Report NB0228, Eindhoven, The Netherlands.

Bordeaux, F. (1993). Building Categories from Visual Experiences. In Proceedings of *The IEEE International Conference on Systems, Man and Cybernetics*. October, Le Touquet, France.

Briffault, X. (1992). Computer Modelisation of the Expression of Localisation in Natural Language. Ph.D. diss. Paris VI University. 255 pp. In French.

Castaing, M. F. & Truc-Martini, D. (1993). Constraints in the Recording of Speech Data Bases. In Proceedings of *The Internat. Symp. on Spoken Dialogue*, 29–31. Tokyo, Japon.

Daniel, M. -P., Carité, L. & Denis, M. (1994). Modes of Linearization in the Description of Spatial Configurations. In Portugali, J. (ed.) *The Construction of Cognitive Maps*. Kluwer: Dordrecht, The Netherlands.

Denis, M. & Cocude, M. (1992). Structural Properties of Visual Images Constructed form Poorly or Well-structured Verbal Descriptions. *Memory and Cognition* **20**: 497–506.

Escande, P., Béroule, D. & Blanchet, P. (1991). Speech Recognition Experiments with Guided Propagation. Proc. of IJCNN'91, Singapour.

Faure, C. & Arnold, M. (1993). Man-Machine Interaction and Minimum Principle. In Proceedings of *The IHM'93*, 3–8 Lyon. In French.

GDR-PRC-CHM (1993). Activity Report About Multimodal Human-Computer Interfaces, CNRS-MESR, Coutaz, J. & Caelen, J. In French. In 1994: C. Faure is at the head of the CHM Pôle, F. Poirier at the head of the multimodal working group.

Grumbach, A. (1994). *Artificial Cognition*. Addison-Wesley France. In French.

Gryl, A. (1994). Cognitive Approach of Route Descriptions. In Pre-proceedings of *The Fith European Workshop on Imagery and Cognition (EWIC)*, 6–8 Saarbrücken, Germany, Univ. of the Saarland.

Huls, C., Bos, E. & Dijkstra, A. (1994). Talking Pictures. An Empirical Study into the Usefulness of Natural Language Output in a Graphical Interface. *Working notes of the AAAI-94 workshop on the Integration of Natural Language and Vision Processing*, 83–90. Chair P. McKevitt. Twelfth National Conf. on Artificial Intelligence, Seattle, Washington.

Hummel, J. E. & Biederman, I. (1990). Dynamic Binding: A Basis for the Representation of Shape by Neural Networks. *12th Annual Meeting of the Cognitive Science Society*. Cambridge, MA.

Images and Languages. (1993). Proceedings of *The Interdisciplinary Workshop "Image and Language: Multimodality and Cognitive Modelisation"*. M. Denis and M. Carfantan (eds.) CNRS, Paris, 1993. In French.

Jackendoff, R. (1987). On Beyond Zebra: The Relation of Linguistic and Visual Information. *Cognition* **26**(2): 89–114.

Lainé, A. & Béroule, D. (1994). Towards Active Perception for Automatic Speech Recognition. In Proceedings of *The NSI'94* Chamonix, 23–26. In French.

Ligozat, G. (1992). Strategies for Route Description: An Interdisciplinary Approach. ECAI'92 workshop W19, Spatial Concepts: Connecting Cognitive Theories with Formal Representations. Vienna, Austria.

LIMSI, Scientific Report, Human-Machine Communication Department, Orsay, 1994.

Martin, J. C. (1994). A Study Based on Several Types of Coorperation between Modalities and Binding through Synchrony. *Working notes of the AAAI-94 workshop on the Integration of Natural Language and Vision Processing* 181–184. Chair P. Mc Kevitt. Twelfth National Conf. on Artificial Intelligence, Seattle, Washington.

Martin, J. C. & Béroule, D. (1993). Types and Goals of Co-Operation Between Modalities. Proceedings of *The IHM'93*, 17–22. Lyon. In French.

Nenov, V. I. & Dyer, M. G., (1988). DETE: Connectionist/Symbolic Model of Visual and Verbal Association. In Proceedings of *The Connexionnist Models Summer School 1988*. CMU.

Nigay, L. & Coutaz, J. (1993). A Design Space For Multimodal Systems: Concurrent Processing and Data Fusion. conf. Proceedings of *The INTERCHI'93*, 172–178. ACM Press: Amsterdam.

Nioche, C., Tassin, J-P. & Béroule, D. (1994). Towards a Functional Modelisation of Neuromodulation. In Proceedings of *The NSI'94*, 231–234. Chamonix, In French.

Novak, G. S. & Bulko, W. C. (1990). Understanding Natural Language with Diagrams. In Proceedings of *The 8th National Conf. on Artificial Intelligence* Vol. 1, 465–470, AAAI Press/MIT Press.

Ó Nualláin, S. & Smith, A. G. (1994). *Artificial Intelligence Review* **8**(2–3): 113–122 (this volume).

Robert-Ribes, J., Schwartz, J. L. & Escudier, P. (1994). *Artificial Intelligence Review* **9** (this volume).

Roques, M. (1994). Dynamic Grammatical Representations in Guided Propagation Networks. In Lecture Notes in Artificial Intelligence 862, Carrasco, R. C. , Oncina, J. (eds.) *Grammatical Inference and Applications*, 189–202. Second International Colloqium, ICGI-94, Alicante, Spain.

Shastri, L. & Ajjanagadde, V. (1993). From Simple Associations to Systematic Reasoning: A Connectionist Representation of Rules, Variables and Dynamic Bindings Using Temporal Synchrony. *Behavioral and Brain Sciences* **16**: 417–494.

von der Malsburg, C. & Schneider, W. (1986). A Neural Cocktail-Party Processor. *Biol. Cybern.* **54**: 29–40.

Westerlund, P., Béroule, D. & Roques, M. (1994). Experiments of Robust Parsing Using a Guided Propagation Network. In Proceedings of *The International Conference on New Methods in Language Processing (NEMLAP)*, Manchester.

Artificial Intelligence Review 9: 103–127, 1995.

Research in Multimedia and Multimodal Parsing and Generation

MARK T. MAYBURY

The MITRE Corporation, Artificial Intelligence Center, Mail Stop K331, 202 Burlington Road, Bedford, MA 01730, U.S.A.; e-mail: maybury@mitre.org

Abstract. This overview introduces the emerging set of techniques for parsing and generating multiple media (e.g., text, graphics, maps, gestures) using multiple sensory modalities (e.g., auditory, visual, tactile). We first briefly introduce and motivate the value of such techniques. Next we describe various computational methods for parsing input from heterogeneous media and modalities (e.g., natural language, gesture, gaze). We subsequently overview complementary techniques for generating coordinated multimedia and multimodal output. Finally, we discuss systems that have integrated both parsing and generation to enable multimedia dialogue in the context of intelligent interfaces. The article concludes by outlining fundamental problems which require further research.

Key words: multimedia interfaces, multimodal interfaces, parsing, generation, intelligent interfaces.

1. INTRODUCTION

When humans converse with one another, we utilize a wide array of media to interact including written and spoken language, gestures, and drawings. We exploit multiple human sensory systems or modes of communication including vision, audition, and taction. Some media and modes of communication are more efficient or effective than others for certain tasks, users, or contexts (e.g., the use of maps to convey spatial information, the use of speech to control devices in hand and eyes-busy contexts). In other cases, some combination of media supports more natural, efficient, or accurate interaction (e.g., 'put that there' interactions which mix speech and gesture). Whereas humans have a natural facility for managing and exploiting multiple input and output media and modalities, computers do not. Hence, the ability of machines to interpret multimedia input and generate multimedia output would be a valuable facility for a number of key applications such as information retrieval and analysis, training, and decision support. While significant progress has been made developing mechanisms for parsing and generating single media, less emphasis has been placed on the integration and coordination of multiple media and multiple modalities. The purpose of this article is to introduce techniques for building multimedia and multimodal interfaces, that is, those interfaces that parse and generate some combination of spoken and written natural language, graphics, maps, gesture, non-speech audio, animation, and so on.

The primary motivation for this line of research is the premise that human abilities should be amplified, not impeded, by using computers. While there has been much research focused on developing user, discourse, and task models to improve human computer interaction (Kobsa and Wahlster 1989), here we focus on intelligent *multimedia* interaction. If appropriate media are utilized for human computer interaction, there is the potential to (1) increase the bandwidth of information flow between human and machine (that is, the raw number of bits of information being communicated), and (2) improve the signal-to-noise ratio of this information (that is, the amount of useful bits conveyed). To achieve these potential gains, however, requires a better understanding of information characteristics, how they relate to characteristics of media, and how they relate to models of tasks, users, and environments. This goal is exacerbated by the proliferation of new interactive devices (e.g., datagloves and body suits, head mounted displays, eye-trackers, three dimensional sound), the lack of standards, and a poor or at least ill-applied knowledge of human cognitive and physical capabilities with respect to multimedia devices (see Figure 1). For example, some empirical studies (Krause 1993) provide evidence that even well accepted applications of multimedia (e.g., the use of check marks and graying out in menus) can exacerbate rather than improve user performance. This motivates the need to understand the principles underlying multimedia communication. Understanding these principles will not only result in better models and interactive devices, but also lead to new capabilities such as context-sensitive multimedia

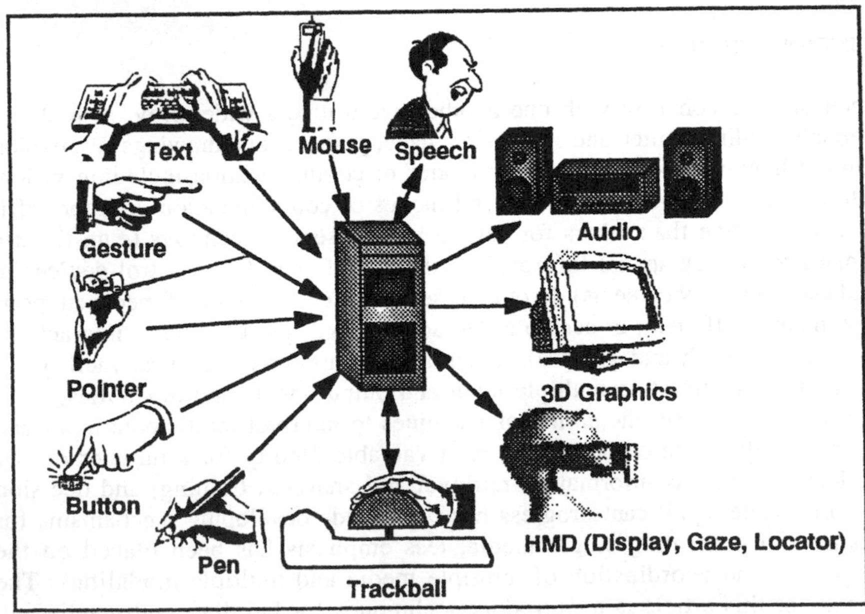

Fig. 1. Device proliferation.

help, tools for (semi-)automated multimedia interface construction, and intelligent agents for multimedia information retrieval, processing, and presentation. This article first outlines research in parsing multimedia input, next mechanisms for generating multimedia output, and finally methods for integrating these together to support multimedia dialogue between computer and user. The article concludes by indicating directions for future research.

2. MULTIMEDIA PARSING (INPUT)

While there has been significant previous research in parsing and interpreting spoken and written natural languages (e.g., English, French), the advent of new interactive devices has motivated the extension of traditional lines of research. There has been significant investigation into processing isolated media, especially speech (Rabiner and Schafer 1978, Fallside and Woods 1985, Waibel and Lee 1990, Roe and Wilpon 1994), natural language (Grosz *et al.* 1986, Allen 1987, ARPA 1993) and, to a lesser degree, handwriting (IWFHR III 1993). Other research has focused on parsing equations (e.g., a handwritten '5 + 3'), drawings (e.g., flow charts), and even face recognition (e.g., lip, eye, head movements) (Pentland 1993). Wittenburg (1993) overviews techniques for parsing handwriting, math expressions, and diagrams, including array grammars, graph grammars (node and hyper-edge replacement), and constraint-based grammars. In contrast, integrating multiple input media presents even greater challenges, and yet the potential benefits are great. For example, adding a visual channel to a speech recognizer provides visual information (e.g., lip movements, body posture) that can help resolve ambiguous speech as well as convey additional information (e.g., about attitudes). Figure 2 illustrates the notion of integrating multiple channels of input. As with natural language processing, there are many distinct repre-

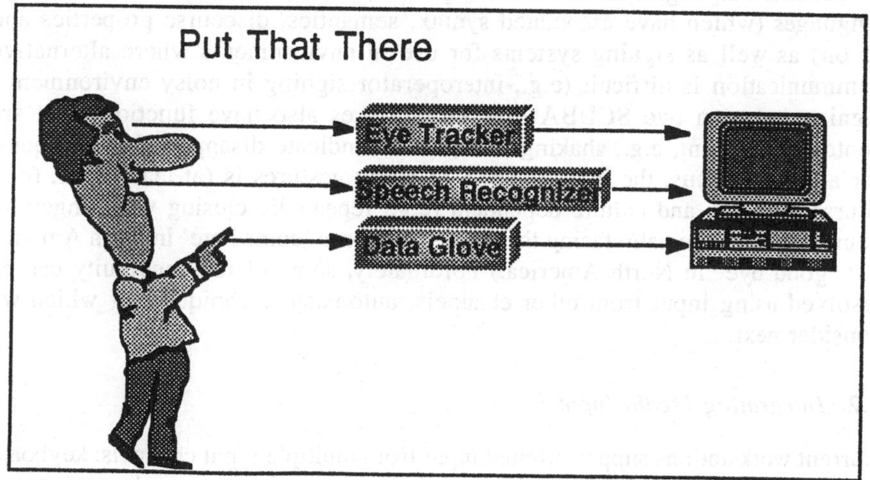

Fig. 2. Multimedia parsing.

sentation and processing problems with multimedia parsing including the need to segment the input into discrete elements, syntactically parse them, semantically interpret them, and exploit discourse and contextual information to deal with input that is ungrammatical, ambiguous, vague and/or impartial. Input media need to be represented at many levels of abstraction (at least morphology, lexicosyntactic, semantic, pragmatic, and discourse) to enable cross media constraint, correlation, and, ultimately, media integration.

2.1. *Interpreting Gesture*

Some of these representational and processing complexities manifest themselves in gesture. Gestural input can come in a variety of forms from a variety of interactive devices (e.g., mouse, pen, dataglove). Just as (spoken and written) natural language can be used to perform various communicative functions (e.g., identify, make reference to, explain, shift focus), so too gestures can perform multiple functions and/or be multifunctional. Analogously, whereas gaze has been traditionally used as a replacement for mouse or deictic input (Jacob 1990), it can also be used to track user interest and focus of attention, to regulate turn taking, to indicate emotional state (e.g., eyes dropping), to indicate interpersonal attitudes (e.g., winking, rolling eyes), and even indicate level of expertise (e.g., by correlating movement with task accomplishment). Rimé and Schiaratura (1991) characterize several classes of gesture. *Symbolic* gestures are conventional, context-independent and typically unambiguous expressions (e.g., an OK or peace sign). In contrast, *deictic* gestures are pointers to entities, analogous to natural language deixis (e.g., "this not that"). *Iconic* gestures are used to display objects, spatial relations, and actions (e.g., illustrating the orientation of two cars at an accident scene). Finally, *pantonimic* gestures display an invisible object or tool (e.g., making a fist and moving to indicate a hammer).

Gestural languages, or rather sublanguages, exist as well. These include sign languages (which have associated syntax, semantics, discourse properties and so on) as well as signing systems for use in environments where alternative communication is difficult (e.g., interoperator signing in noisy environments, signing between two SCUBA divers). Gestures also have functions that are context dependent, e.g., shaking a finger can indicate disapproval or a request for attention. Thus, the interpretation of many gestures is (at least) task, (discourse) context, and culture dependent (e.g., repeatedly closing your fingers to your palm with the palm facing the addressee means 'come here' in Latin America but 'good bye' in North America.) Fortunately, some of this ambiguity can be resolved using input from other channels, automated techniques for which we consider next.

2.2. *Integrating Media Input*

Current workstations support limited input from multiple input channels: keyboard (textual), mouse (graphical), and, increasingly, microphone (speech, non-speech audio) and video. Unfortunately, for most users and applications these channels are severely restricted to independent, sequential, and, in the case of gesture, two-dimensional input. Despite, or perhaps because of, the daunting range and complexity of gestural input, there have been many computational investigations of gesture. The first was Carbonell's (1970) SCHOLAR system for geography tutoring, whose intelligent interface allowed for natural language interaction with simple pointing gestures to a map. Like many subsequent investigations, referent objects had pre-defined, unambiguous screen regions associated with them to enable a direct (one-to-one) mapping between screen location and referent.

Such was not the case in Kobsa *et al.* (1986) TACTILUS subcomponent of the XTRA (eXpert TRAnslator) system, an expert system interface to an electronic tax form (Wahlster 1991). TACTILUS contained no pre-defined screen areas, and graphical objects were composites, thus there was no one-to-one correspondence between a visual region and referent. Moreover, the user could choose from a menu of deictic gestures of varying 'granularity' (pencil, index finger, hand, region encircler). The ambiguity of regions combined with the vagueness of gesture required the system to resolve inexact and pars-pro-toto (part-for-the-whole) pointing. It did so by computing 'plausibility values' of each *demonstratum*, an object being pointed to, by measuring the portion of the demonstratum covered by the pointer. Candidates were then pruned using the semantics of any associated language or dialogue. When referents were determined, no visual feedback was given to the user (following human communication conventions), although the authors recognized this risked possible false user implicature regarding the success of their identification. Also, as in other systems that integrated language and deixis (e.g., CUBRICON, which we consider next), language and pointing input had to occur sequentially, and yet they often temporally overlap in human-human communication. Interestingly, their implementation investigated two-handed input, as did (Buxton and Myers 1986), in which one hand could be used to indicate a region of focus of attention while the other could perform a selection.

The CUBRICON (Calspan-UB Research Center Intelligent CONversationalist) system (Neal and Shapiro 1991) permitted not only the use of gestures to resolve ambiguous linguistic input, but also the use of linguistic input to resolve ambiguous gestures. CUBRICON addressed the interpretation of speech, keyboard and mouse input using an Augmented Transition Net work grammar of natural language that included gestural constituents (in noun phrase and locative adverbial positions). Thus a user could, in natural language, query 'Is this ⟨point-using-the-mouse⟩ a Surface to Air Missile?' or command 'Enter this ⟨point-map-icon⟩ here ⟨point-form-slot⟩.' or state 'Units from this ⟨point-1⟩ airbase will strike these targets ⟨point-2⟩ ⟨point-3⟩ ⟨point-4⟩.' The system allowed either spoken or written input, although the natural language and deictic input had to occur sequentially. Interestingly, when semantically interpreting combined linguistic and gestural input, ambiguous point gestures were resolved by exploiting a class or property expressed in the natural language. Moreover, when the natural language and gesture were inconsistent, the system applied a heuristic that started at the display position indicated by point gesture and performed an incremental bounded search to find at least one object consistent with the semantic features expressed in the natural language.

An interesting issue investigated in CUBRICON, parallel to the integration of linguistic and gestural input, was the coordination of gesture and language upon output. CUBRICON generated natural language with coordinated gestures in two cases: (1) when referents were visible on a display, e.g., 'The mobility of these SAMs ⟨point-1⟩ ⟨point-2⟩ is low and the mobility of this SAM ⟨point-3⟩ is high' and (2) when the referent was a component of an object that is visible on a display, e.g., 'The target of OCA001 is the 3-L-runway of the Merseberg Airbase ⟨point-to-airbase⟩.' We will return more fully to the issue of coordinating multimedia output in a subsequent section.

Like CUBRICON, the Intelligent Multimedia Interface (AIMI) system (Burger and Marshall 1993) also investigated multimedia dialogue including natural language and graphical deixis in the context of a mission planning system. For example, a user might first query in natural language 'What aircraft are appropriate for the rescue mission?', to which the system might respond by automatically generating a table of appropriate aircraft. If the user then pointed to an item on the generated table, this would be introduced into the discourse context so that she could subsequently simply ask 'What is its speed?'. Similarly, if a window containing a graphic was in focus in the dialogue, the user could anaphorically say 'Print that chart'. In contrast to CUBRICON's Augmented Transition Network grammar representation, AIMI parsed input (including menu and windows interactions) into expressions in a sorted first-order language (with generalized quantifiers) whose predicates are drawn from the terms in a subsumption hierarchy, as in KL-ONE (see Brachman and Schmolze (1985)). Like CUBRICON, AIMI included a detailed model of the discourse context, including the user's focus of attention, but also incorporated a rich model of the (mission planning) task which enabled cooperative interaction. We return to multimedia dialogue in a subsequent section.

Two of the fundamental problems with interpreting heterogeneous input are integrating temporally asynchronous input from different channels and parsing and interpreting the input to an appropriate level of abstraction so that these multiple channels can be integrated. For example, Koons *et al.* (1993) investigated integrating simultaneous speech, gestural, and eye movement for reference resolution in map and blocks world interactions. Whereas the previously described systems focused on (two dimensional) pointing in which gestures are typically terminals in the grammar (e.g., in CUBRICON), Koon's *et al.* (1993) application required parsing three dimensional and time varying gestures. For processing, they found it necessary to capture gesture features such as the posture of the hand (straight, relaxed, closed), its motion (moving, stopped), and its orientation (up, down, left, right, forward, backward – derived from normal and longitudinal vectors from the palm). Over time, a stream of gesture features is then abstracted into more general *gestlets* (e.g., Pointing = attack, sweep, end reference). Similarly, low level eye tracking input was classified into classes of events (fixations, saccades, and blinks). The more general levels of representation were then exploited to integrate different channels of information.

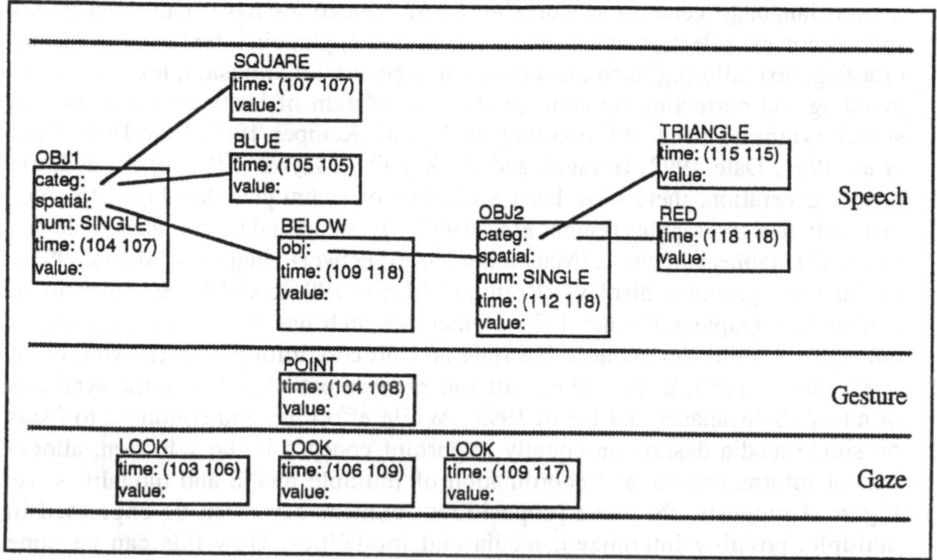

Fig. 3. Idealized input to speech, gesture, gaze parser.

Figure 3 illustrates an idealized example of the frame representation their media parsers produce when a user utters '. . . that blue square below the red triangle' while pointing to and looking at objects on a screen. After parsing, an interpretation component finds values for each frame. Values are either objects for qualitative and categorical expressions such as 'red' or 'square' or regions in a spatial system for input such as gestures, gaze, and spatial expressions, e.g., 'below'. Ambiguous references (e.g., if there are multiple blue squares in the scene) are resolved by methods associated with the frames that find temporally adjacent input events that constrain interpretation.

While ambitious in its integration of three input modalities, many applications will require even richer and deeper representations of input to capture the complexity of language, gaze, and gesture (e.g., selectional restrictions, intentional representations). Equally, this work could be extended to incorporate other modalities (e.g., face recognition, lip reading, body posture). As we consider in the next section, equal challenges apply when coordinating several modalities for output.

3. MULTIMEDIA GENERATION (OUTPUT)

Just as improved human-computer communication requires the ability to interpret multiple media and modalities upon input, so too it requires the selection and coordination of multiple media and modalities upon output. There have been many investigations into single media generation. With respect to language, a number of methods for planning and realizing natural language text have emerged. Several natural language generation workshops and collections have addressed issues such as context selection, intention (i.e., speech act) planning, text structuring and ordering, text tailoring, incremental sentence generation, revision, lexical choice, avoiding and correcting misconceptions, the relation of language generation to speech synthesis, and text formatting and layout (Kempen 1987, Dale 1990, Paris *et al.* 1991, Dale 1992, Horacek and Zock 1993, Maybury 1994b). In addition to text generation, there have been a number of techniques developed to automatically design graphics (Feiner *et al.* 1992). These include techniques to design and realize tables and charts (Mackinlay 1986), network diagrams (Marks 1991a, b), business graphics displays (Roth and Mattis 1991), and three dimensional explanatory graphics (Feiner 1985). Other research has investigated the use of non-speech audio to communicate state and process information (Buxton *et at.* 1985, Garver 1986, Buxton 1989, Buxton *et al.* in press) and even the synthesis of music (Schwanauer and Levitt 1993). While effort has and continues to focus on single media design, an equally important concern is the selection, allocation of information to, and coordination of multiple media and modalities. As Figure 4 suggests, the same propositional content can often be expressed in multiple, possibly intermixed, media and modalities. How this can be done automatically, we consider next.

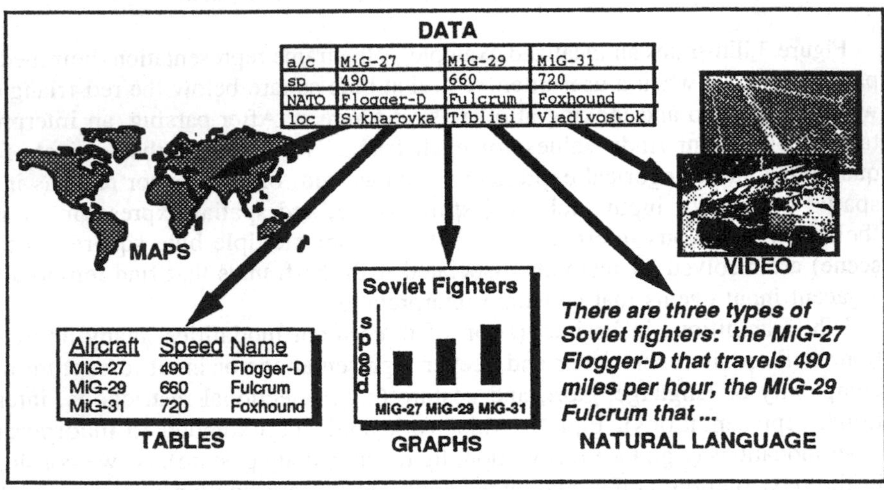

Fig. 4. Multimedia generation (attribute information of aircraft represented in multiple media).

3.1. *Content Selection and Media Representation*

Often the first step in designing a presentation is determining what information to convey. Determining the importance and relevancy of content is a key problem in natural language generation and information retrieval and hence is beyond the scope of this article. Nevertheless, it is important to note that selecting content interacts in non-trivial ways with media design and realization, indeed while it may be the first step, it may be revisited as subsequent realization or layout constraints dictate. For example, selecting particular kinds of context can dictate certain media (e.g., the expression of quantification in natural language).

Related to selecting what to say is the way in which it is represented (and of course what is represented). Hovy and Arens (1993) describe the knowledge required for reasoning about multimedia information, formalizing in systemic networks the context, form, and purpose of the presentation and the characteristics of the producer, perceiver, and communicative situation. Other researchers have extended KL-ONE like knowledge representation schemes to include graphical knowledge and reasoning mechanisms, for example, to support reasoning about layout (Graf 1992) or cross-modal references (e.g., 'the red switch at the bottom of the picture') which requires mapping between spatial and linguistic structures (André *et al.* 1993).

3.2. *Media Allocation*

Once a system has determined (at least initially) what information to convey to an addressee, it must determine in what medium or which media to convey this information. In his APT system, Mackinlay (1986) developed 'expressiveness rules' to relate characteristics of information to encoding techniques (e.g., position, size, orientation, shape, color) for graphical displays. Similarly, the Integrated Interfaces system (Arens *et al.* 1991) used simple 'presentation rules' (e.g., display positions using points on a map, display future actions as text) to design mixed text, graphics, map, and tabular displays of daily reports of the US Navy's Pacific Fleet. Unlike APT, it allowed for preset stereotypical presentations if requested and was based on a KL-TWO knowledge representation scheme to handle a broader range of data. SAGE (Roth *et al.* 1991) also went beyond the graphics focus of APT and employed allocation heuristics (as in COMET, described below) which preferred graphics when there were a large number of quantitative or relational facts but natural language when the information was about, e.g., abstract concepts, or processes or when it contained relational attributes for a small number of data objects (e.g., total budget).

In contrast to these heuristics, the AIMI system (Burger and Marshall 1993) utilized design rules for media allocation which included media preferences (e.g., cartographic displays are preferred to flat lists which are preferred to text) that were governed by the nature of the original query and the resulting information to be presented (e.g., qualitative vs. quantitative, its dimensionality). For example a natural language query about airbases might result in the design of a cartographic presentation, one about planes that have certain qualitative characteristics, a list, ones that have certain qualitative characteristics, a bar chart. One interesting notion in AIMI was the use of non-speech audio to convey the speed, stage or duration of processes not visible to the user (e.g., background computations). AIMI also included mechanisms to tailor the design to the output device.

The WIP knowledge based presentation system (André and Rist 1993) also incorporated media preferences for different information types. These specified:

- graphics over text for concrete information (e.g., shape, color, texture . . . also events and actions if visually perceptible changes)
- graphics over text for spatial information (e.g., location, orientation, composition) or physical actions and events (unless accuracy is preferred over speed, in which case text is preferred)
- text to express temporal overlap, temporal quantification (e.g., 'always'), temporal shifts (e.g., 'three days later') and spatial or temporal layout to encode sequence (e.g., temporal relations between states, events, actions)
- text to express semantic relations (e.g., cause/effect, action/result, problem/solution, condition, concession) to avoid ambiguity in picture sequences; graphics for rhetorical relations such as condition and concession only if accompanied by verbal comment
- text for quantification, especially most vs. some vs. exactly-n
- graphics to express negation (e.g., overlaid crossing bars) unless scope was ambiguous, then use text

Some of these preferences were captured in constraints associated with presentations actions, which were encoded in plan-operators, and used feedback from media realizers to influence the selection of content.

In contrast to WIP's plan-based approach, the COMET (COordinated Multimedia Explanation Testbed) (Feiner and McKeown 1993) system followed a pipe-line approach using rhetorical schema to determine presentation content (logical forms) followed by a 'heuristic' media allocator to select between text and three dimensional graphics (See Figure 5). The media allocation heuristics were (1) realize locational and physical attributes in graphics only, (2) realize abstract actions and connectives among actions (e.g., causality) in text only, and (3) realize simple and compound actions in both text and graphics.

One problem with the above approaches to media allocation is that they map information characteristics onto media classes (e.g., text versus graphics) or media objects (e.g., tables, bar charts). In contrast, in an analytical study, Hovy and Arens (1993) characterize the complexity of media allocation in their investigation of rules that relate more general characteristics of information to

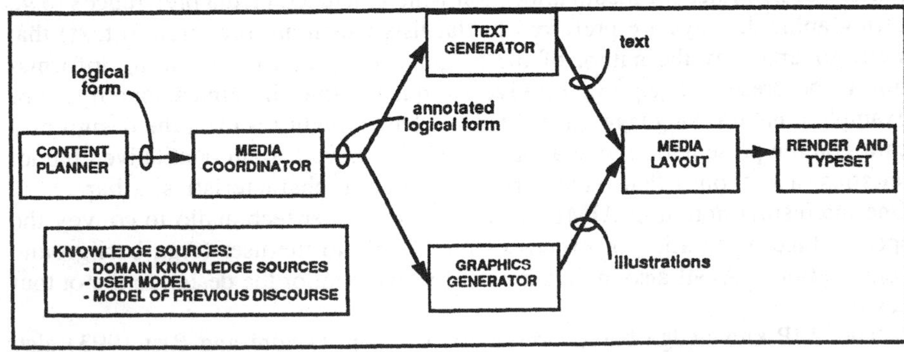

Fig. 5. The COMET Architecture.

characteristics of media. They characterize media allocation as the multistep process:

1. Present data duples (e.g., locations) on planar media (e.g., graphs, tables, maps).
2. Present data with specific denotations (e.g., spatial) on media with same denotations (e.g., locations on maps).
3. 'If more than one medium can be used, and there is an existing presentation, prefer the medium/a that is/are already present . . .'.
4. Choose medium/a that can accommodate the most amount of information to be presented.

They further characterize the complexity of information to media interdependencies by defining rules in a systemic framework. For example, to convey the notion of *urgency* they have two rules:

1. If the information is not yet part of the presentation, use a medium whose default detectability is high (e.g., aural medium) either for substrate (e.g., a piece of paper, a screen, a grid) or carrier (e.g., a marker on a map substrate; a prepositional phrase within a sentence predicate substrate).
2. If information is already displayed, use a present medium but switch one or more of the channels from fixed to the corresponding temporally varying state (e.g., flashing, pulsating, hopping).

What remains to be done is to computationally investigate and (with human subjects) evaluate these and other rules in an attempt to make progress toward a set of principles for media allocation.

3.3. *Media Design and Coordination*

In addition to selecting media appropriate to the information, successful presentations must ensure coordination across media. First, the content must be consistent, although not necessarily equivalent, across media. In addition, the resulting form (layout, expression) should be consistent. The COMET system achieves this, in part, by coordinating sentence breaks with picture breaks, providing cross references from text to graphics, and allowing intergenerator influence (i.e., between text and graphics generators). Feiner *et al.* (1993) later considered incorporating a temporal reasoning mechanism within COMET in order to control the presentation of temporal media (e.g., animation and speech) by managing the order and duration of communicative acts.

Whereas COMET allocates information to media subsequent to content selection, the WIP architecture and that of TEXPLAN (Maybury 1991) perform content selection and media allocation simultaneously using plan operators. This enables declarative encoding of media and content constraints in one formalism which is then used to generate a resulting hierarchical, multimedia presentation plan. Media generators (e.g., for text, graphics) can then interact with this structure, as well as with each other, to provide feedback to the design. Figure 6 illustrates a portion of an illustrated instruction generated by WIP with its underlying presentation plan. In WIP, the text and graphics generators interact, for example, to generate unambiguous linguistic and visual references to objects (André *et*

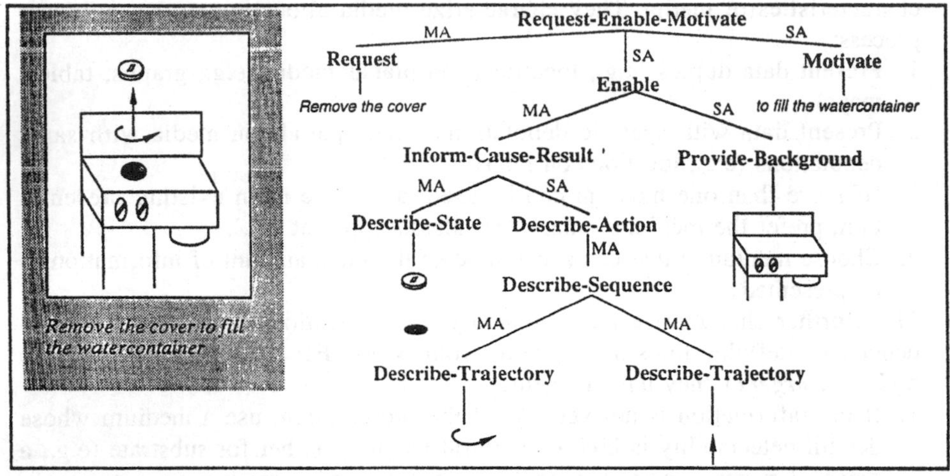

Fig. 6. Intelligent multimedia interfaces.

al. 1993). This interaction enables the text generator to make visual references such as 'The on/off switch is located in the upper left part of the picture.' WIP also includes a grid-based layout system (Graf 1992), described below, that co-constrains the presentation planner.

3.4. *Communicative Acts for Multimedia Generation*

Following a tradition that views language as an action-based endeavor (Austin 1962, Searle 1969), researchers have begun to formalize multimedia communication as actions, in a hope at arriving at a deeper representation of the mechanisms underlying communication. Some systems have gone beyond single media to formalize multimedia actions (e.g., WIP, TEXPLAN), attempting to capture both the underlying structure and intent of presentations using a plan-based approach to communication. For example, as Figure 6 above illustrates, WIP designs its picture-text instructions using a spech-act like formalism that includes communicative (e.g., describe), textual (e.g., S-request), and graphical (e.g., depict) actions.

Maybury (1991, 1993, 1994, in press) details a taxonomy of communicative acts that includes linguistic, graphical, and physical actions. These are formalized as plan operators with associated constraints, enabling conditions, effects, and subacts. Certain classes of actions (e.g., deictic actions) are characterized in a media-independent form, and then specialized for particular media (e.g., pointing or tapping with a gestural device, highlighting a graphic, or utilizing linguistic deixis as in 'this' or 'that'). When multiple design and realization choices are possible, preference metrics, which include media preferences, mediate the choice. Given a choice, the metric prefers plan operators with fewer subplans (cognitive economy), fewer new variables (limiting the introduction of new entities in the focus space of the discourse), those that satisfy all preconditions (to avoid backward chaining for efficiency), and those plan operators that are more common or preferred in naturally-occurring explanations (e.g., certain kinds of communicative acts occur more frequently in human-produced presentations or are preferred by rhetoricians over other methods). Maybury (1991) details its application to the design of narrated, animated route directions.

3.5. *Automated Layout of Media*

The physical format and layout of a presentation often conveys the structure, intention, and significance of the underlying information and plays an important role in the presentation coherency. Most investigations of layout have focused on single media. For example, Hovy and Arens (1991) exploited the rhetorical structure used to generate text to guide the format of the resulting text, realized using the text formatting program, TeX. For example, when their text planner structured text using a SEQUENCE relation, this would be realized using the *bullet* TeX command. Marks (1991a, b) investigated layout and encoding of arc-node diagrams in his ANDD system. ANDD grouped nodes sharing common graphical values (e.g., shape, color, size) to reinforce perception of graphical properties. It was guided by 'pragmatic directives', for example, 'emphasize' certain structural or quantitative values associated with particular modes or groups of nodes. Relatedly, Roth and Mattis (1991) sorted chart objects and tree nodes to support search.

In contrast to these investigations of single media, Feiner's (1988) GRaphical Interface Design (GRID) system investigated text, illustrations, and, subsequently, virtual input devices. Layout was performed in an OPS5-like production system guided by a graphical design grid. In contrast to this rule-based approach, Graf (1992) argues that the design of an aesthetically pleasing layout can be characterized as a constraint satisfaction problem. Graf's LayLab system, the constraint-based layout manager within WIP, achieves coherent and effective output by reflecting certain semantic and pragmatic relations in the visual arrangement of a mixture of automatically generated text and graphics fragments. LayLab incorporates knowledge of document stereotypes (e.g., slides, instruction manuals, display environments), design heuristics (e.g., vertical vs. horizontal alignment), and graphical constraints. Layout includes the mapping of semantic and pragmatic relations (e.g., 'sequence', 'contrast' relations) onto geometrical/topological/temporal constraints (e.g., horizontal and vertical layout, alignment, and symmetry) using specific visualization techniques. For example, two equally sized graphics can be contrasted by putting them beside one another or one under the other. To accomplish this task, LayLab integrates an incremental hierarchy solver and a finite domain solver in a layered constraint solver model in order to position the individual fragments on an automatically produced graphic design grid. Thus, layout is viewed as an important carrier of meaning. This approach could be generalized beyond static text-picture combinations to include dynamic and incrementally presented presentations as well as those that incorporate additional media (e.g., animation, video) (Graf forthcoming). An interesting research issue concerns developing a constraint acquisition component that could infer design constraints from graphical sketches by human experts.

In an interactive setting, the CUBRICON multimedia interface (Neal and

Shapiro 1991) supported multiple monitor/window interaction using an Intelligent Windows Manager (IWM). IWM rated the importance of a window, W, using a weighted importance based on:

- (35%) Recency of creation of W = $e^{\frac{-(\text{time of current interaction} - \text{time of window creation})}{10}}$
- (30%) Content of W = $\frac{\sum \text{weights of objects in window W}}{\text{number of objects}}$
- (15%) Recency of last interaction = $e^{-\text{total \# of interactions after last interaction with window W}}$
- (10%) Frequency of use of W = $\frac{\text{number of interactions with window}}{\text{total number of interactions since creation}}$
- (10%) Context

Window management rules then controlled allocation of generated media to screen real-estate. Accordingly, IWM preferred to place maps on the color monitor, tables on monochrome. Forms were only placed on the monochrome monitor. IWM would place a map windows with a related table on the color monitor if there was space, otherwise the least important window (and any related table) would be removed to make space. If there was space on the monochrome monitor, the table was placed there in a position corresponding to the new map, otherwise if the new table was more important than an existing form, it was placed in the lower right corner of the monochrome monitor. The importance ratings combined with placement heuristics yielded an effective technique for managing high level media objects (e.g., windows, tables) in an interactive setting.

3.6. *Tailoring Multimedia Output*

In addition to selecting and coordinating output, it is important to design presentations that are suited to a particular user's abilities and task. In their research with SAGE, (Roth and Mattis 1990, 1991) characterize a range of information seeking goals for viewing quantitative and relational information. These purposes included accurate value-lookup (e.g., train table times, phone #'s), value-scanning (approximate computations of, e.g., the mean, range, or sum of a data set), counting, n-wise comparison (e.g., product prices, stock performances), judging correlation (e.g., estimating covariance of variables), and locating data (e.g., finding data indexed by attribute values). Each of these goals may be supported by different presentations. Burger and Marshall (1993) capture this task-tailoring when they contrast two (fictional) responses to one natural language query, 'When do trains leave for New York from Washington?' (see Figure 7). If the addressee is interested in trend detection, a bar chart presentation is preferred; if they are interested in exact quantities (e.g., to support further calculations), a table is preferred. Presentations can be tailored to other factors, such as properties of the task, context (e.g., previously generated media), and user (e.g., visual ability, level of expertise).

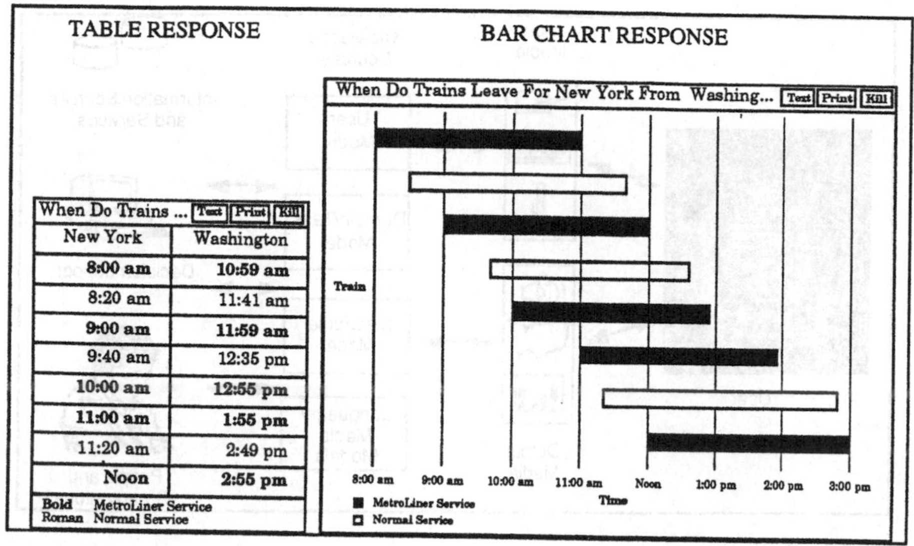

TABLE RESPONSE

When Do Trains ... Text Print Kill

New York	Washington
8:00 am	**10:59 am**
8:20 am	11:41 am
9:00 am	**11:59 am**
9:40 am	12:35 pm
10:00 am	**12:55 pm**
11:00 am	**1:55 pm**
11:20 am	2:49 pm
Noon	**2:55 pm**

Bold MetroLiner Service
Roman Normal Service

Fig. 7. Exactness (table) versus trend analysis (bar chart) (Burger and Marshall 1993).

4. TOWARD INTELLIGENT MULTIMEDIA INTERFACES

The previous two sections consider the integration and coordination of multimedia input and output. What about integrating these into an interactive multimedia interface? As Figure 8 illustrates, supporting multimedia dialogue requires models of the user, task, and discourse as well as models of media. Thus, multimedia interfaces build upon research in discourse and user modeling for interface design and management (Kobsa and Wahlster 1989). Not only must media and its design and interaction be included, but other traditional knowledge sources and processes need to be modified to support a multimedia interaction. For example, discourse models need to incorporate representations of media, for example, to enable media (cross) reference and reuse. Similarly, user models need to be extended to represent media preferences of users.

Examples of multimedia dialogue systems include CUBRICON (Neal and Shapiro 1991), XTRA (Wahlster 1991), AIMI (Burger and Marshall 1993), and AlFresco (Stock *et al.* 1993). Typically, these systems parse integrated input and generate coordinated output, but also worry about concerns such as maintaining coherency, cohesion, and consistency across both multimedia input and output. For example, these systems typically support integrated language and deixis for both input and output. They incorporate models of the discourse, for example, to resolve multimedia references (e.g., 'Send this plane there'). For example, CUBRICON represented a global focus space ordered by recency; AIMI a focus space segmented by the intentional structure of the discourse (i.e., a model of the domain tasks to be completed).

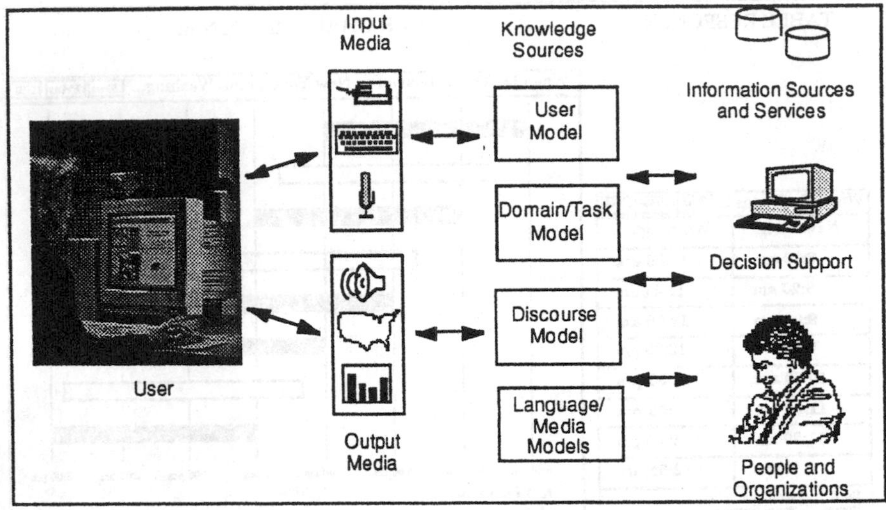

Fig. 8. Intelligent Multimedia Interfaces.

While intelligent multimedia interfaces promise natural and personalized interaction, they remain complicated and require specialized expertise to build. One practical approach to achieving some of the benefits of these more sophisticated systems without the expense of developing full multimedia interpretation and generation components, was achieved in AlFresco (Stock *et al.* 1993), a multimedia information kiosk for Italian art exploration. Figure 9 illustrates a typical multimedia interaction with AlFresco. By adding natural language processing to a traditional hypermedia system, AlFresco achieved the benefits of hypermedia (e.g., organization of heterogeneous and unstructured information via hyperlinks, direct manipulation to facilitate exploration) together with the benefits of natural language parsing (e.g., direct query of nodes, links, and subnetworks

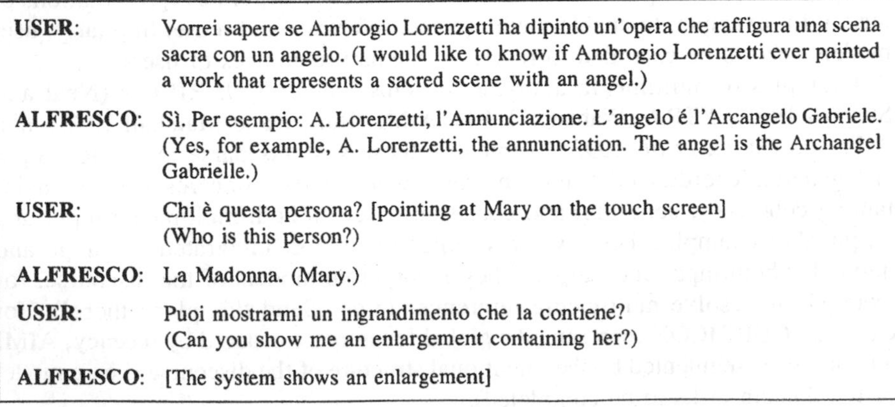

USER:	Vorrei sapere se Ambrogio Lorenzetti ha dipinto un'opera che raffigura una scena sacra con un angelo. (I would like to know if Ambrogio Lorenzetti ever painted a work that represents a sacred scene with an angel.)
ALFRESCO:	Sì. Per esempio: A. Lorenzetti, l'Annunciazione. L'angelo é l'Arcangelo Gabriele. (Yes, for example, A. Lorenzetti, the annunciation. The angel is the Archangel Gabrielle.)
USER:	Chi è questa persona? [pointing at Mary on the touch screen] (Who is this person?)
ALFRESCO:	La Madonna. (Mary.)
USER:	Puoi mostrarmi un ingrandimento che la contiene? (Can you show me an enlargement containing her?)
ALFRESCO:	[The system shows an enlargement]

Fig. 9. Multimedia interaction with AlFresco.

which provides rapid navigation). Parsing helps overcome the indirectness of hypermedia as well as disorientation and cognitive overhead caused by too many links. Also, as in other systems previously described (e.g., CUBRICON, TACTILUS), ambiguous gesture and language can yield a unique referent through mutual constraint. Finally, AlFresco incorporates simple natural language generation which can be combined with more complex canned text (e.g., art critiques) and images.

Reiter *et al.* (1992) also integrated traditional language generation with hypertext to produce hypertext technical manuals. In addition to information kiosks, many other practical applications of intelligent multimedia interfaces have been investigated in domains such as intelligent tutoring (Cornell *et al.* 1993, Goodman 1993), car-driver interfaces (Bonarini 1993), tax-form completion (Kobsa *et al.* 1986, Wahlster 1991), and air pollution analysis (Marti *et al.* 1992). A less investigated but nevertheless important class of applications, which can in part exploit results in multimedia parsing and generation, is multimedia indexing, retrieval (Stein *et al.* 1992, Stein and Thiel 1993), and summarization.

While practical systems are possible today, the multimedia interface of the future may have facilities that are much more sophisticated. These interfaces may include human-like agents that converse naturally with users, monitoring their interaction with the interface (e.g., key strokes, gestures, facial expressions) and the properties of those (e.g., conversational syntax and semantics, dialogue structure) over time and for different tasks and contexts. Equally, future interfaces will likely incorporate more sophisticated presentation mechanisms. For example, Pelachaud (1992) characterizes spoken language intonation and associated emotions (anger, disgust, fear, happiness, sadness, and surprise) and from these uses rules to compute facial expressions, including lip shapes, head movements, eye and eyebrow movements, and blinks. Finally, future multimedia interfaces should support richer interactions, including user and session adaptation, dialogue interruptions, follow-up questions, and management of focus of attention.

5. REMAINING RESEARCH PROBLEMS

While the above systems afford exciting possibilities, there remains a gap between current capabilities and a system that could more fully interact using multiple media and modalities. Many fundamental questions remain unanswered, including issues concerning the architecture and knowledge needed to support intelligent multimedia interaction, techniques for media integration and coordination, and methods for evaluation. With respect to architecture, many questions remain including: What are they key components (knowledge sources, processes) for multimedia interaction? What functionality do they need to support? What is the proper flow of control? How should they interact (e.g., serially, interleaved, co-constraining)? Can we develop infrastructure/tools to support and encourage progress?

5.1. *Models*

Equally important as these architectural concerns is the issue of how systems and system builders can acquire, represent, maintain, and exploit models of the knowledge required for such systems. Knowledge needed includes models of information characteristics, producer characteristics and goals, media and modalities (e.g., their characteristics, strengths and weaknesses), users (e.g., (physical and cognitive) abilities, preferences, attention, and intentions), discourse/dialogue histories, task histories, and models of the situation (e.g., tracking system parameters such as load and available media). What seems evident from the current state of the art is that no single model will suffice, rather, models will have to be represented and reasoned about at multiple levels of abstraction and/or fidelity. For example, media models will have to represent the range from higher level artifacts (e.g., text, tables, graphics) down to their smallest constituent parts (e.g., pixels).

5.2. *Multimedia Parsing and Generation*

In addition to knowledge, expert processes need to be invented, both for the interpretation and generation of media. Fundamental input parsing processing includes segmentation (within and across) of media, parsing and interpretation of (both ill-formed and partial) input, and resolving ambiguous and partial multimedia references. In addition to extended and novel parsing technology, new interactive devices (e.g., those replicating force feedback, those recognizing facial and body expressions) will need to be developed and tested. Finally, techniques for media integration and aggregation need to be further refined to ensure synergistic coupling among multiple media, overcoming asynchronous timing and varying levels of abstraction of input.

In addition to input, output techniques require further extension. Generation advances are required for content selection (i.e., choosing what to say), media allocation (i.e., choosing which media to say what in), modality selection (e.g., realizing language as visual text or aural speech), media realization (i.e., choosing how to say items in a particular media), media coordination (cross modal references, synchronicity), and media layout (size and position). One research issue concerns the degree of module interaction and/or self correction. For example, the WIP system described above required two feedback loops (one after media design and one after realization) to help resolve inter/intra media synthesis problems. Another issue regards the degree of reuse and/or refinement of pre-existing, canned media with dynamically generated media (e.g., AlFresco's integration of hypertext and natural language processing). Related to this is whether or not systems save the history or structure of a presentation and if and how canned artifacts (e.g., an animation) can be connected to representations of abstract knowledge. The need for deep knowledge of designed graphics depends at least upon the intended use of the multimedia presentation (e.g., for teaching versus manual generation) and the environment in which it is used (e.g., interactive, static). Still another issue concerns the degree of automation versus mixed initiative. For example, while many systems attempt to generate a final presentation, COMET (Feiner and McKeown 1993) does support user-controlled camera positions and the InformationKit (IKIT) (Suthers' *et al.* 1993) tutoring environment enables the user to control which 'viewer' a concept is realized in (e.g., text, graphics). Fully automated generation becomes even more difficult if not impossible when aiming for user and context tailored multimedia presentations. Moreover, presentation composition and coordination must be sensitive to the purpose of the communication, the (cognitive) complexity of resulting presentation, its perceptual impact (e.g., clutter), consistency (e.g., of dimensions, sizes, with respect to previous presentations), and ambiguity (overlapping encodings of color, shape, etc.).

5.3. *Multimedia Interfaces*

In addition to better techniques for interpreting and synthesizing media, initial multimedia interface prototypes have uncovered areas for further research. These include moving beyond hypermedia to support multimedia question and answering (including cross modal references and follow-up questions), the ability to post-edit presentations, to critique user designs (both during and after their construction) and, finally, to manage the multimedia dialogue (e.g., turn-taking). Many issues remain to be resolved including dealing with ill-formed and incomplete input and output at multiple levels of abstraction (e.g., syntax, semantics, pragmatics), the utilization of media independent acts (for analysis, generation, and interaction management), and the relationship of models of focus of attention and multimedia acts. We also need to move beyond interfaces incorporating language, graphics, and gesture to consider less explored media (e.g., non-speech audio, facial expressions, body language) and modalities (e.g., taction, olfaction) or even to invent new ones. Finally, the relation of multimedia interfaces and multimedia classification, indexing and retrieval offers interesting research possibilities.

5.4. *Methodology and Evaluation*

A final research area which can help foster progress toward a science of multimedia interaction is methodology and evaluation. A number of different methodological approaches are apparent in current work in the field. Some researchers build systems, guided by reverse-engineering human designs and human-human interactions. Others focus on self-adaptive system, where effective techniques are learned via interaction with users. Still others focus on empirical validation of techniques (through observation of man-machine interactions). Others follow a combination of approaches. Perhaps there are other, equally useful approaches? In all of these cases evaluation metrics and methods to measure progress need to be developed. In some cases, we need to determine the 'goodness' of alternative presentations by measuring presentation well-formedness, consistency, balance, coherency, and cohesion. In other cases it is important to measure the pedagogic benefit, increase in efficiency, or increase in the effectiveness of accomplishing some task (e.g., teaching, fixing) to provide evidence of value-added of additional machinery for input or output. This may involve time/quality tradeoffs among media or processes. It will require both black box and glass box system evaluations. Finally, we also need to judge among possible input and output facilities, matching media to human (physical and cognitive) capabilities such as memory and attention. All of these evaluative endeavors demand standard terms, units of measurement, levels of performance, techniques of use, and so on, to enable comparison and sharing of results.

6. CONCLUSION

This article has described research in parsing simultaneous multimedia input and generating coordinated multimedia output, as well as prototypes that integrate these to support multimedia dialogue. Intelligent multimedia interfaces have the potential to enable systems and people to use media to their best advantage, in several ways. First, they can increase the raw rate of information flow between human and machine (for example, by using the most appropriate medium or mix of media and modalities for information exchange). Second, they can facilitate human interpretation of information by helping to focus user attention on the most important or relevant information. Third, these investigations can provide explicit models of media to facilitate interface design so, for example, future interfaces can benefit from additional aspects of human communication that are currently ignored by current interfaces (e.g., speech inflections, facial expressions, hand gestures). Intelligent multimedia interaction is relevant to a range of application areas such as decision support, information retrieval, education and training, and entertainment. This technology promises to improve the quality and effectiveness of interaction for everyone who communicates with a machine in the future, but we will only reach this state by solving the remaining fundamental problems outlined above.

ACKNOWLEDGEMENTS

I thank all the referenced authors for their ideas, which I have attempted to faithfully represent herein. Particular thanks go to Wolfgang Wahlster, Ed Hovy, and Yigal Arens for their comments on multimedia and multimodal issues. I am grateful to Rich Mitchell for creating Figures 1 and 2.

REFERENCES

Allen, J. (1987). *Natural Language Understanding*. Benjamin Cummings: Reading, MA.

André, E. & Rist, T. (1993). The Design of Illustrated Documents as a Planning Task. In (Maybury 1993), 94–116. Also DFKI Research Report RR-92-45.

André, E., Finkler, W., Graf, W., Rist, T., Schauder, A. & Wahlster, W. (1993). WIP: The Automatic Synthesis of Multimodal Presentations. In (Maybury 1993), 73–90. Also DFKI Research Report RR-92-46.

Arens, Y., Miller, L. & Sondheimer, N. K. (1991). Presentation Design Using an Integrated Knowledge Base. In (Sullivan and Tyler 1991), 241–258.

Proceedings of the *ARPA Human Language Technology Workshop*, March 1993. Morgan Kaufman: San Francisco.

Austin, J. (1962). *How to do Things with Words*, J. O. Urmson (ed.), Oxford University Press: England.

Blattner, M. M. & Dannenberg, R. B. (eds.). (1992). *Multimedia Interface Design*, ACM Press/Addison-Wesley: Reading, MA.

Bonarini, A. (1993). Modeling Issues in Multimedia Car-Driver Interaction. In (Maybury 1993), 353–371.

Brachman, R. J. & Schmolze, J. G. (1985). An Overview of the KL-ONE Knowledge Representation System. *Cognitive Science* **9**(2): 171–216.

Burger, J. & Marshall, R. (1993). The Application of Natural Language Models to Intelligent Multimedia. In (Maybury 1993), 167–187.

Buxton, W. & Myers, B. A. (1986). A Study in Two-Handed Input. Proceedings of *Human Factors in Computing Systems* (CHI-86), 321–326, ACM: New York.

Buxton, W., Bly, S., Frysinger, S., Lunney, D., Mansur, D., Mezrich, J. & Morrison, R. (1985). Communicating with Sound. Proceedings of *The Human Factors in Computing Systems* (CHI-85), 115–119, New York.

Buxton, W. (ed.). (1989). *Human-Computer Interaction 4: Special Issue on Nonspeech Audio*, Lawrence Erlbaum.

Buxton, W., Gaver, W. & Bly, S. *Auditory Interfaces: The use of Non-speech Audio at the Interface*. Cambridge University Press (in press).

Carbonell, J. R. (1970). Mixed-Initiative Man-Computer Dialogues. Bolt, Beranek and Newman (BBN) Report No. 1971, Cambridge, MA.

Cornell, M., Woolf, B. & Suthers, D. (1993). Using 'Live Information' in a Multimedia Framework. In (Maybury 1993), 307–327.

Dale, R., Mellish, C. & Zock, M. (eds.). (1990). *Current Research in Natural Language Generation*. Based on Extended Abstracts from the Second European Workshop on Natural Language Generation, University of Edinburgh, Edinburgh, Scotland, 6–8 April, 1989. London: Academic Press. ISBN 0-12-200735-2, 356 pp.

Dale, R., Hovy, E. Rösner, D. & Stock, O. (eds.). (1992). *Aspects of Automated Natural Language Generation, Lecture Notes in Computer Science, 587*. Proceedings of *The 6th International Workshop on Natural Language Generation*, Trento, Italy, April 5–7, 1992. Springer-Verlag: Berlin.

Fallside, F. & Woods, W. (eds.). (1985). *Computer Speech Processing*. Prentice Hall: Englewood Cliffs, NJ. Contributions by speakers at an advanced course on computer speech processing held at the University of Cambridge in 1983.

Feiner, S. (1985). APEX: An Experiment in the Automated Creation of Pictorial Explanations. *IEEE Computer Graphics and Application* **5**(11): 29–37.

Feiner, S. (1988). A Grid-based Approach to Automating Display Layout. Proceedings of *The Graphics Interface*, 192–197. Morgan Kaufmann: Los Angeles.

Feiner, S. K. & McKeown, K. R. (1993). Automating the Generation of Coordinated Multimedia Explanations. In (Maybury 1993), 113–134.

Feiner, S. K., Litman, D. J., McKeown, K. R. & Passonneau, R. J. (1993). Towards Coordinated Temporal Multimedia Presentations. In (Maybury 1993), 139–147.

Feiner, S., Mackinlay, J. & Marks, J. 1992. Automating the Design of Effective Graphics for Intelligent User Interfaces. Tutorial Notes. *Human Factors in Computing Systems*, CHI-92, Monterey.

Goodman, B. A. (1993). Multimedia Explanations for Intelligent Training Systems. In (Maybury 1993), 148–171.

Gray, W. D., Hefley, W. E. & Murray, D. (eds.). (1993). In Proceedings of *The 1993 International Workshop on Intelligent User Interfaces*. Orlando, FL January, 1993. ACM: New York.

Graf, W. (1992). Constraint-based Graphical Layout of Multimodal Presentations. In (Catarci, Costabile, and Levialdi 1992), 365–385. Also available as DFKI Report RR-92-15.

Graf, W. (1994) Semantik-gesteuertes Layout-Design multimodaler Präsentationen, Ph.D. diss., Technische Fakultät, Universität des Saarlandes, Saarbrücken, Germany.

Grosz, B. J., Sparck Jones, K. & Webber, B. L. (eds.). (1986). *Readings in Natural Language Processing*. Morgan Kaufmann: Los Altos.

Horacek, H. & Zock, M. (eds.). (1993). *New Concepts in Natural Language Generation: Planning, Realization and Systems*. Frances Pinter, London and New York.

Hovy, E. H. & Arens, Y. (1991). Automatic Generation of Formatted Text. In Proceedings of *The Ninth National Conference of the American Association for Artificial Intelligence*, 92–97, Anaheim, CA.

Hovy, E. H. & Arens, Y. (1993). On the Knowledge Underlying Multimedia Presentations. In (Maybury 1993), 280–306.

Jacob, R. J. K. (1990). What You Look at is What You Get: Eye Movement-Based Interaction Techniques. In Proceedings of *The Human Factors in Computing Systems (CHI '90)*, 11–18. ACM Press: New York. Seattle, April 1–5.

Kempen, G. (ed.). (1987). *Natural Language Generation: New Results in Artificial Intelligence, Psychology, and Linguistics*, Martinus Nijhoff. NATO ASI Series: Dordrecht.

Kobsa, A. & Wahlster, W. (eds.). (1989). *User Models in Dialog Systems*. Springer-Verlag: Berlin.

Kobsa, A., Allgayer, J., Reddig, C., Reithinger, N., Schmauks, D., Harbush, K. & Wahlster, W. 1986. Combining Deictic Gestures and Natural Language for Referent Identification. Proceedings of *The 11th International Conference on Computational Linguistics*, 356–361, Bonn, West Germany.

Koons, D. B., Sparrell, C. J. & Thorisson, K. R. (1993). Integrating Simultaneous Output from Speech, Gaze, and Hand Gestures. In (Maybury 1993), 243–261.

Krause, J. (1993). A Multilayered Empirical Approach to Multimodality: Towards Mixed Solutions of Natural Language and Graphical Interfaces. In (Maybury 1993), 312–336.

Mackinlay, J. D. (1986). Automating the Design of Graphical Presentations of Relational Information. *ACM Transactions on Graphics* 5(2): 110–141.

Marks, J. W. (1991). Automating the Design of Network Diagrams. Ph.D. thesis, Harvard University, Cambridge, MA.

Marks, J. (1991). A Formal Specification Scheme for Network Diagrams that Facilitates Automated Design. *Journal of Visual Languages and Computing* 2(4): 395–414.

Marti, P., Profili, M., Raffaelli, P. & Toffoli, G. (1992). Graphics, Hyperqueries, and Natural Language: an Integrated Approach to User-Computer Interfaces. In (Catarci, Costabile, and Levialdi, 1992), 68–84.

Maybury, M. T. (1990). Planning Multisentential English Text using Communicative Acts. Ph.D. diss., University of Cambridge, England. Available as Rome Air Development Center TR 90-411, In-House Report, December 1990 or as Cambridge University Computer Laboratory TR-239, December, 1991.

Maybury, M. T. (1991). Planning Multimedia Explanations Using Communicative Acts. In Proceedings of *The Ninth National Conference on Artificial Intelligence*, 61–66. AAAI: Anaheim, CA.

Maybury, M. T. (ed.). (1993). *Intelligent Multimedia Interfaces*. AAAI/MIT Press: Menlo Park.

Maybury, M. T. (1994). Knowledge Based Multimedia: The Future of Expert Systems and Multimedia. *International Journal of Expert Systems with Applications. Special issue on Expert Systems Integration with Multimedia Technologies* 7(3), 387–396. Ragusa, J. (ed.)., Elsevier Science.

Maybury, M. T. (1994). Automated Explanation and Natural Language Generation. In *Computational Text Generation*. Bibliography. Sabourin, C. (ed.), Montreal: Infolingua, 1–88.

Maybury, M. T. (in press). Communicative Acts for Multimedia and Multimodal Dialogue. In Taylor, M. M., Néel, F. & Bouwhuis, D. G. The *Structure of Multimodal Dialogue*. North-Holland: London. ISSN 1018-4554. Proceedings from workshop at Acquafredda di Maratea, Italy. September 16–20, 1991.

Neal, J. G. & Shapiro, S. C. 1991. Intelligent Multi-Media Interface Technology. In (Sullivan and Tyler 1991), 11–43.

Paris, C. L., Swartout, W. R. & Mann, W. C. (eds.). (1991). *Natural Language Generation in Artificial Intelligence and Computational Linguistics*. Kluwer: Norwell, MA.

Pelachaud, C. (1992). Functional Decomposition of Facial Expressions for an Animation System. In (Catarci, Costabile, and Levialdi 1992), 26–49.

Pentland, A. (ed.). (1993). Proceedings of IJCAI Special Workshop #3, Looking at People: Recognition and Interpretation of Human Action. Held in conjunction with 13th IJCAI, Chambrey, Savoie France, 28 August–3 September, 1993.

Rabiner, L. R. & Schafer, R. W. (eds.). *Digital Processing of Speech Signals*. Prentice Hall: Englewood Cliffs, NJ.

Rimé, B. & Schiaratura, L. (1991). Gesture and Speech. In Feldman, R. S. & Rim, B. (eds.) *Fundamentals of Nonverbal Behavior*, 239–281. New York: Press Syndicate of the University of Cambridge.

Reiter, E., Mellish, C. & Levine, J. (1992). Automatic Generation of on-line Documentation in the IDAS Project. Proceedings of the *3rd Conference on Applied Natural Language Processing*, 31 March–3 April 1992, Trento, Italy. Association of Computional Linguistics: Morristown, NJ.

Roe, D. B. & Wilpon, J. S. (eds). (to appear). Proceedings of *The National Academy of Sciences Colloquium on Human Machine Communication by Voice*, National Academy of Sciences Press: Washington, DC.

Roth, S. F. & Mattis, J. 1990. Data Characterization for Intelligent Graphics Presentation. In Proceedings of *The 1990 Conference on Human Factors in Computing Systems*, 193–200. New Orleans, Louisiana. ACM/SIGCHI.

Roth, S. F. & Mattis, J. 1991. Automating the Presentation of Information. In Proceedings of *The IEEE Conference on AI Applications*, 90–97. Miami Beach, FL.

Roth, S. F., Mattis, J. & Mesnard, X. (1991). Graphics and Natural Language Generation as Components of Automatic Explanation. In (Sullivan and Tyler 1991), 207–239.

Schwanauer, S. & Levitt, D. (eds). (1993). *Machine Models of Music*. MIT Press: Cambridge, MA.

Searle, J. R. (1969). *Speech Acts: An Essay in the Philosophy of Language*. Cambridge University Press: London.

Stein, A., Thiel, U. & Tissen, A. (1992). Knowledge based Control of Visual Dialogues in Information Systems. In Catarci, T., Costabile, M. F. & Levialdi, S. (eds.) 1992. *Advanced Visual Interfaces: Proceedings of the International Workshop AVI'92*, Singapore: World Scientific Series in Computer Science, Vol. 36, 138–155.

Proceedings of the Third International Workshop on Frontiers of Handwriting Recognition (IWFHR III). Buffalo, NY. May 25–27, 1993.

Stein, A. & Tissen, A. (1993). A Conversational Model of Multimodal Interaction in Information Systems. In Proceedings of *The Eleventh National Conference on Artificial Intelligence*, 283–288. AAAI/MIT Press: Washington, DC.

Stock, O. & the ALFRESCO Project Team (1993). ALFRESCO: Enjoying the Combination of Natural Language Processing and Hypermedia for Information Exploration. In Maybury, M. (ed.) *Intelligent Multimedia Interfaces*, 197–224. AAAI/MIT Press: Menlo Park.

Sullivan, J. W. & Tyler, S. W. (eds.). (1991) *Intelligent User Interfaces*. Frontier Series. New York: ACM Press.

Taylor, M. & Bouwhuis, D. G. (eds). (1989) *The Structure of Multimodal Dialogue*. Elsevier Science Publishers: Amsterdam.

Thorisson, K., Koons, D. & Bolt, R. (1992). Multi-modal Natural Dialogue. In Proceedings of *Computer Human Interaction (CHI-92)*, 653–654.

Wahlster, W. (1991). *User and Discourse Models for Multimodal Communication*. In (Sullivan and Tyler, 1991), 45–67.

Waibel, A. & Lee, K. (eds.) (1990). *Readings in Speech Recognition*, Morgan Kaufmann: San Mateo, CA.

Wittenburg, K. (1993). *Multimedia and Multimodal Parsing: Tutorial Notes*. 31st Annual Meeting of the ACL, Columbus, Ohio, 23, June, 1993.

APPENDIX A: QUICK GUIDE TO THE LITERATURE

Relevant intelligent multimedia interfaces literature includes many workshops on individual media (e.g., text generation, graphics generation). Related collections from workshops have focused on intelligent user interfaces in general (Sullivan and Tyler 1991, Gray *et al.* 1993), multimedia interface design (Blattner and Dannenberg 1992, Catarci, Costabile, and Levialdi 1992), and multimedia communication (Taylor and Bouwhuis 1989). (Maybury 1993) focuses specifically on those intelligent interfaces that exploit multiple media and modes to facilitate human-computer communication.

BOOKS

Taylor, M. & Bouwhuis, D. G. (eds.). (1989). *The Structure of Multimodal Dialogue.* Elsevier Science Publishers: Amsterdam.

Sullivan, J. W. & Tyler, S. W. (eds). (1991). *Intelligent User Interfaces.* Frontier Series. ACM Press: New York.

Blattner, M. M. & Dannenberg, R. B. (eds.). (1992). *Multimedia Interface Design.* ACM Press/Addison–Wesley: Reading, MA.

Catarci, T., Costabile, M. F. & Levialdi, S. (eds.). (1992). *Advanced Visual Interfaces:* Proceedings of *The International Workshop AVI'92*, Singapore: World Scientific Series in Computer Science, Vol. 36.

Buxton, W., Gaver, W. & Bly, S. (in press). *Auditory Interfaces: The use of Non-speech Audio at the Interface.* Cambridge University Press.

Maybury, M. (ed.). (1993). *Intelligent Multimedia Interfaces.* AAAI/MIT Press: Cambridge, MA.

WORKSHOP/CONFERENCE PROCEEDINGS

Neches, B. & Kaczmarek, T. (1986). *Working Notes from the AAAI Workshop on Intelligence in Interfaces*, August 14, 1986. AAAI: Menlo Park.

Arens, Y., Feiner, S., Hollan, J. & Neches, B. (eds.). (1989). *Workshop Notes from the IJCAI-89 Workshop on A New Generation of Intelligent Interfaces.* Detroit, MI, 22 August.

Maybury, M. T. (ed.). (1991). *Working Notes from the AAAI Workshop on Intelligent Multimedia Interfaces.* Ninth National Conference on Artificial Intelligence. 15 July, Anaheim, CA. AAAI: Menlo Park.

Taylor, M., Bouwhuis, D. G. & Neél, F. (eds.). (1991) *Pre-proceedings of the Second Venaco Workshop on The Structure of Multimodal Dialogue*, Acquafredda di Maratea, Italy, September, 1991.

Gray, W. D. Hefley, W. E. & Murray, D. (eds.). (1993). Proceedings of *The 1993 International Workshop on Intelligent User Interfaces*, Orlando, FL January, 1993. ACM: New York.

Johnson, P., Marks, J., Maybury, M., Moore, J. & Feiner, S. (organizing committee) Working notes from *The AAAI 1994 Spring Symposium on Intelligent Multimedia and Multimodal Systems*, Stanford, CA, March 21–24, 1994.

TUTORIALS/OVERVIEWS

Wittenburg, K. (1993). Multimedia and Multimodal Parsing: Tutorial Notes. 31st Annual Meeting of the ACL, Columbus, Ohio, 23 June, 1993.

Feiner, S., Mackinlay, J. & Marks, J. (1992). Automating the Design of Effective Graphics for Intelligent User Interfaces. Tutorial Notes. Human Factors in Computing Systems, CHI-92, Monterey, May 4, 1992.

Wahlster, W. (1993). Planning Multimodal Discourse. Invited Talk. Association for Computational Linguistics, Annual Meeting, Ohio State Univ., Columbus, Ohio, 24 June 1993.

APPENDIX B: TERMINOLOGY DEFINITIONS

There is much terminological inconsistency in the literature regarding the use of the terms *media* and *modality*. By mode or modality we refer primarily to the human senses employed to process incoming information, e.g., vision, audition, taction, olfaction. We do not mean mode in the sense of purpose, e.g., word processing mode versus spread sheet mode. Additionally, we recognize medium, in its conventional definition, to refer both to the material object (e.g., paper, video) as well as the means by which information is conveyed (e.g., a sheet of paper with text on it). We would elaborate these definitions to include the possibility of layering so that, for example, a natural language medium might use written text or speech as media even though those media themselves rely on other modes.

Media and mode are related non-trivially. First, a single medium may support several other media or modalities. For example, a piece of paper may support both text and graphics just as a visual display may support text, images, and video. Likewise, a single modality may be supported by many media. For example, the language modality can be expressed visually (i.e., typed or written language) and aurally (i.e., spoken language) – in fact spoken language can have a visual component (e.g., lip reading). Just as a single medium may support several modalities and a single modality may be supported by many media, many media may support many modalities, and likewise. For example, a multimedia document which includes text, graphics, speech, video, effects several modalities, e.g., visual and auditory perception of natural language, visual perception of images (still and moving), and auditory perception of sounds. Finally, this multimedia and multimodal interaction occurs over time. Therefore, it is necessary to account for the processing of discourse, context shifts, and changes in agent states over time.

Artificial Intelligence Review **9**: 129–146, 1995.

A Third Modality of Natural Language?*

OLIVIERO STOCK

IRST – Istituto per la Ricerca Scientifica e Tecnologica, 38050 Povo – Trento, Italy; e-mail: stock@irst.it

Abstract. In the late Eighties the Natural Language Processing community began appreciating the role of multimodality in interactive systems. Intelligent multimodal systems are systems that integrate natural language (generally so far keyboard-based input, shortly also voice) with other media such as gestures in input or graphics in output. The perspective of what can be called visible interactive communication is discussed and considered as a possible new modality of natural language, after the spoken and the written ones. This should not be confused with the type of hypermedia that are now being developed. There, basically, the interface space is finite, even if one dimension may be added. Here the infinite creativity of human language is potentially preserved as the fundamental communication instrument.

Key words: natural language, multimedia, human-computer interaction, communication modalities, dialogue, generation.

1. INTRODUCTION

An observer of the field of Natural Language Processing (NLP) that had left her vantage point fifteen years ago and had come back just a few years ago, would probably have been more disappointed than anything else. Most of the big issues in applied natural language processing are still there, some areas that seemed promising have not delivered. Certainly the situation is not worse than in other areas of AI or perhaps of computer science. And of course the challenge is big: Natural Language is "AI-complete", i.e. a problem as tough as the toughest AI problems. Nonetheless a striking aspect of most of the activity in the field up to very recent times is that of some schizophrenia. On one side it promotes the development of basic formal devices and tries to solve linguistic problems *in vitro*, on the other side it assumes a naive view of what Applied NLP is and what its possible impact can be *in corpore vili*. For instance this is the attitude that lay behind taking for granted the "teletype approach" in natural language-based human-machine interfaces, an approach by which the channel of communication is restricted, as in devices we have known for a long time, such as the telex. It has been very simplistic assuming that in any case the world wants natural language interfaces without qualifying the request more precisely.

Only recently have we begun to understand that the computer offers larger possibilities. I think that human ecology will change in a dramatic way for what concerns humans' interacting with machines in the first place, but in the long run with any human-made objects. We are facing an extraordinary revolution that touches all levels of our life. Computers and telecommunication are really becoming part of our ecological system.

This technology is perceived fundamentally as a two-way interface to an abstract blackbox and is prone to be seen as an extension of our human capacity; this is true both in the sense that it makes distances disappear and information made available and in the sense that we become adapted to the technological features of the interface. What is characteristic of computers, and not of human-human biological interfaces is that: (a) they have a potential large bandwidth of communication with humans, in particular if we consider their dynamic graphical capabilities combined with other, language-based means; (b) they provide a visible context, and external memory, represented on the screen. The form of what is being communicated in both directions is there, on the same medium, and, different from what happens in written paper-based communication, the physical medium can be made active. Things can be selected, changed and used for new input. With the concept of direct manipulation even the distinction between the notions of input medium and output medium is blurred.

I think that our understanding of what a human-computer interface can be and our understanding of natural language processes, if put in a creative context, will eventually lead to a new way of interacting, a way that I would still call natural or ecological, even if not just biologically based. This way of interacting will be centered on natural language, but in a new creative way that exploits the possibilities of the computer and perhaps some of our own, underexploited capabilities.

What we human beings have developed filogenetically and culturally as modalities of language-based communication may not exactly correspond to the new situation: oral language and written language will perhaps be joined by a different, third modality of natural language.

Technically speaking we may talk of different technology-determined modalities, such as telex or telephone language, but they are all limitations imposed upon the two fundamental modalities; the whole class of intelligent interfaces I will talk about may constitute a new communicative and cognitive development.

I would like to show that this is a creative and a very interesting perspective in the core of AI and that we have innovative, though initial, ideas and prototypes to begin experimenting with these concepts, and also, why can something practical not be developed in the near future?

2. BEYOND THE TELETYPE APPROACH

In the late Eighties the NLP community began appreciating the role of multimodality in interactive systems. A larger bandwidth of communication has been proposed for communicating with a computer.

Intelligent multimodal systems are systems that integrate natural language (generally so far keyboard-based input, shortly also voice) with other media such as gestures in input or graphics in output (see Maybury 1993). Systems of this type have been developed for interfacing a user with a dynamic process such as the simulation of the operations inside a factory (Cohen *et al.* 1989), a simulated battlefield (MacLaughlin and Shaked 1989) or the activities of U.S. Navy ships (Arens *et al.* 1988). In such applications, the advantage of integrating multiple media in output is obvious, for instance, to explicitly make clear a sequence of operations or to display the status of a complex process. Similarly for input, pointing to images on a screen may individuate the objects involved in some desired action (Hollan *et al.* 1988; Lemke and Fischer 1990; Wahlster 1992). Among others it is worth recalling the pointing study developed by Wahlster's group (Schmauks 1987). Pointing, perhaps the most natural of communicative actions, may be a highly ambiguous act (with the same gesture one may refer to different things), and the combination with language gives rise to a process of mutual contribution to achieving the overall understanding of the message. So, for instance, to retrieve the correct referent a system may make use of information deriving from the head-noun the deictic adjective is modifying (e.g. "who put this ⟨pointing gesture⟩ computer on the net?", or from features of an identification request (e.g. "who is this ⟨pointing gesture⟩?" entails a person), or from the structure of the selectional restrictions (e.g. "who signed this ⟨pointing gesture⟩?" entails the referent is a document), but it may require also a structured memory of previously cited objects, down to a complex model of the pragmatics of the ongoing dialogue and the intentional state of the user.

Of course having the pointing integrated in the natural language system has begun changing the characteristics of the language used. It has changed it from the limited telex-like communication situation toward a situation that for some aspects is more reminiscent of face-to-face communication where the two agents can refer to a common deictic scene. So for instance in XTRA, one of the best developed prototypes (Allgayer *et al.* 1989), user and system could both refer to regions in a tax form, without a superimposed definition of pointing-sensitive areas. In practice, to refer directly to objects is very convenient, as all mouse friends know . . .

At this point it is worth making clear that pointing could not in general *take the place* of language (I have seen only too often the silly claim that e.g. menus are enough); unless one thinks of an us of menus like Texas Instruments' NLMenu system where menus are used to build exactly a natural language expression: there is an equilibrium among syntheticity, ambiguity and redundance in human thought and language that requires expressive constructs for communicating, when the situation is not trivial. How could quantifiers, negation, qualitative aspects be seriously conveyed, just to mention a few features needed for effective communication? How could a reasonable user model be developed by the system? Of course there are yet situations where graphic signs are better than language communication, as in the case of spatial orientation or spatial relations, and must be integrated in the system capabilities.

Before moving any further it is useful to talk about evaluation of natural language modalities. Even for those modalities that have stayed with us for a long time the history of evaluation is not very long and we could not take much from the outside world: conversation analysis and corpus collection are essentially limited means developed by ethnolinguists, quantitative linguists etc.; only the sensitivity of some people in the NLP community has permitted taking some more complex steps.

One of the key aspects for the studies that are relevant for us is that often we want to understand and evaluate systems that do not yet exist, at least in a complete form. We want to be able to study the modalities diacronically too, understand how a modality or an abstract system can evolve (because of technology advancement, more problems solved in basic NLP etc.), and what is the level necessary for granting desired features of communication quality.

Evaluation so far tends to be made for a single linguistic modality (spoken fact to face, written, telephone-based, teletype-based etc.) and less for a combination of modalities. But there is something general that can be said that seems to differentiate human-computer communication from communication between humans. Utterances tend to be briefer, grammatically simpler and better specified; there is less expectation of a common knowledge, dialogue is more stereotyped and tends to lack confirmatory and explanatory language, fewer pronouns and implicit references are used (Dahlbäck and Jönsson 1989).

To evaluate a system not only linguistic and performance measures are used (Oviatt and Cohen 1989, 1991). Whole task measures are to be considered, such as total time and query number to complete a task, comparison with look-up on a book, dialogue assessment; and also human-computer interactivity measures, such as turnaround time, impact of system error feedback, support of mixed initiative interactions etc. Tradoffs between different answer strategies (e.g. guessing, providing partial answers, no answer at all, initatiting clarification subdialogs) and between system features are also beginning to be examined. Dialogue evaluation is critical but hard: coding illocutionary acts to get at the intentions and beliefs of the user has proved to be very difficult and plan-based theories of dialogues are difficult to apply even for a dialogue concerned with a very restricted task.

On the other side the study of actual human interactions suggests that the various forms of human dialogic communication can be seen as modifications to a single conversation's basic structure. The *organization of conversation* depends in essential ways upon the material and social circumstances of human interaction, i.e. upon those features that characterize dialogue as an example of *situated action*. Suchman (1987) underlines the importance of local control for the success of face-to-face human interaction: we can remedy the troubles that occur during communication not because we can predict all the possible problems, but because the organization of conversation provides a very powerful mechanism for exploiting the contextual information shared by the people taking part in a dialogue. Multimedial interaction offers a way of enlarging the share of the interactional situation that is available both to the user and the system, and may yield a better understanding between them. If both the participants can refer to a rich range of contextual knowledge, having the opportunity of shifting initiative to signal and remedy interactional problems, it should be possible to achieve a satisfactory simulation of the recover mechanisms of human interaction. For instance, if the user fails to understand a natural language description identifying a character represented in a picture, the system might generate a kind of deictic action such as a graphical highlighting of the area of the picture representing the character.

Let us turn our attention to multiple modalities in output generation.

In his Stanford Ph.D Thesis "Automatic Design of Graphical Presentations" (1986) J. Mackinlay says:

> . . . computational linguistics is potentially relevant to the development of computer-based graphical communication. However the work that is most relevant focuses on communication activities that do not deal with the final form of communication, such as modeling the beliefs of the other individuals or deciding when a speech act is required to accomplish a task (Appelt 1985)" and then (ibid., Mackinlay 1986) "Unlike natural language and formal logic, which have substantial expressive power, graphical languages are specialized languages that have limited expressive power. However specialized languages generally have advantages that justify their use in situations where their expressive limitations are unimportant."

The acknowledgment that graphical languages are important for relational information and can be integrated in a natural language-based presentation system have become quite widespread in the NL generation community: one interesting question is how to best coordinate the linguistic and the graphic media to obtain through this combination something that goes beyond the sum of the parts. It is a matter of obtaining a globally more effective communication, tuned to human mental capabilities. Of course graphical analogical images are even more obviously complementary to language: often nothing is more perspicuous than a map if the aim is to provide *geographical* information.

Joint planning of text and diagrams has been addressed for instance, by using presentation rules that hold for several media at once (Arens and Hovy 1990). Rules are generalized to take into account the system's communicative goals, a model of the reader, features characterizing the information to be displayed and features characterizing the media available to the system.

The combination of analogical images and text has been developed in several systems: in Comet (Feiner and McKeown 1990), for instance, a coordinator has the role of negotiating with the different mode specialists. This aspect is even more developed in Maybury's Texplan system (1991), where media realization and layout constraints influence both content selection and the structure of the resulting explanation.

In the WIP system (Wahlster *et al.* 1992), concerned with the presentation of information for the mutual belief between system and audience that the system has the goal that a certain action is performed by the audience) as defined by the back-end application. This is common to other generation systems, but here the main question is then how to best decompose this goal into subgoals to be realized by the mode-specific generators, so that they can complement each other. The interesting consequence is that semantic and pragmatic concepts such as coherence, focus, communicative act, implicature, discourse model, reference etc. acquire an extended meaning. An analogical representation of the technical device is also produced from an internal format. Another relevant aspect of the project is concerned with the capacity of incremental generation,i.e. of starting to produce output even when not all the information to convey is yet available.

One of the aspects treated in Wahlster's (1992) project is layout managing, not a trivial problem: how would a certain multimodal output be best allocated on a medium? In this vein very relevant are R. Dale's remarks (1992) and those by E. Hovy and Y. Arens (1991) on the constraints and the opportunities that come from the medium: for instance acknowledgement of the available space but also,in written text, indentation, the use of different characters such as italics, the use of notes and so on.

The potential of these aspects, the pragmatics of "visible language" needs further study; it will play an important part also in the development of the ideas described in the following sections.

3. HYPERMEDIA AND NLP

Access to information within the NLP community has been traditionally considered from two main points of view:

- the data base tradition, brought into intelligent question answering systems. In applications of this kind, there can be quite sophisticated input, but there is no stress on user modelling and discourse management is accordingly limited: basically the idea is single precise queries;
- the dialogue oriented approach, often employed in connection with an expert system. It takes into account a structure of goals and plans, intention recognition, and more generally a sophisticated user model in the context of some limited task.

Often though, a user would want, in principle at least, to access information directly through precise requests but also to explore information possibilities, to find new elements of interest and so on. In many domains this latter aspect is even more important. Some of the main problems lie in the fact that the user often does not have a clear goal at the beginning, or at least one not tuned to the system capabilities or to the information actually available.

None of the two NLP applied traditions above have answers to this; of course the second one is more promising and important in the long run but is still problematic even for the simplest cases when the goals of the user are clear. Natural language processing may find a strategic counterpart in a non-AI world, hypermedial technology, overcoming limits present in either approach taken individually.

Hypermedia, "a style of building systems for information representation and management around a network of multimedia nodes connected together by typed links" (Halasz 1988), have opened interesting perspectives on the problem of accessing loosely structured information. Hypermedial systems promote a navigational, explorative access to multimodal information: the user, browsing around the network, is at the same time both exploring the network and searching for useful information.

Multimodality and hypermediality open a possibility of realizing intelligent interfaces that amplify capabilities we have in nature (as opposed to trying to reproduce them). In fact, while it is true that people, in face-to-face communication, not only use spoken language but also take into account gestures, the visual environment and more, it is not so easy for people to reproduce or create images, and especially to make an integrated active medium out of the combination of images and language. In particular it is not easy to break the sequentiality of language, both spoken and written.

In substance this vision was already in the work of the first originator of the idea of hypertext, Vannevar Bush (1945) and was emphasized by Ted Nelson in his Xanadu project (Nelson 1981), where the net environment is seen as an empowering of human mind and at the same time a cooperative work, and therefore a sociological revolution.

But hypermedia *per se* are no solution. Without language processing they have obvious limits. So in hypertexts, beside the fact that the technology is very shallow and not based on real understanding, one of the problems underlined by Conklin (1987) is *disorientation*: hypertexts offer more degrees of freedom, more dimensions in which one can move, and hence a greater potential for the user to become lost or disoriented; the user has the problem of having to know where he is and how to get to some other place that he knows (or thinks) exists in the network. One of the proposed solutions to the disorientation problem is the integration of a query facility within the system. Such a facility should provide a way of jumping inside the network without having to follow the predefined paths through it.

Halasz (1988) underlines that it is possible to identify two different types of queries about an hypermedia network:

1) *content queries* allow retrieval of all objects (nodes or links) that satisfy some requirements. All objects in the network "are considered as independent entities and are examined individually for a match to a given query": content search ignores the structure of the network.
2) *structure queries* allow retrieval of a subnetwork matching a given pattern.

Of course by having a natural language interface these queries can be made, if we assume that the system has some information about the knowledge presented by the different nodes and about the semantics of the structure of the network. Beside this, NLP can offer the possibility of integrating not just isolated queries but information access-oriented dialogue.

In sum, integrating NL with hypermedia facilities provides the following advantages: from the NL perspective, a means for organizing heterogeneous and unstructured information, for favouring the direct manipulation of all objects, integrated with language, and for facilitating explorative behaviour; from the hypermedia perspective, a solution to the problems of disorientation and of the cognitive overhead of having too many links. Looking at all this as an independent new approach, its overall characteristics are a high level of interactivity and system habitability where each modality overcomes the constraints of the other, resulting in the whole being more than the sum of the parts. The crucial point is to integrate an exploration modality in the environment. With this a user finds it easy to move around, see what is available here and there, possibly follow some exploration path, without being necessarily constrained by any definite goal.

Conklin (1987) points out that a common difficulty arising in interacting with a hypermedia system is the *cognitive overhead* caused by the number of links that it is possible to follow from each node. Hypermedia have been described as offering *seamless* information. This can be too much for a poor user under stress in his search for the answer or for cues that may be of further interest. It would be very useful to be able to tell which links the specific user is less likely to follow, in order not to display them all (or to display them with a lower degree of relevance). User modelling has a long history and great power in NLP, basically to represent the communicative context in which a sentence is uttered (Kass and Finin 1988; Kobsa 1989). So, for instance in generation, a text can be naturally tailored (at all levels, from the rhetorical to the lexical choices) for the intended reader, yielding an effective communicative act (Hovy 1988; Paris 1987).

The handling of initiative shifts and of different attitudes on the part of the user is of basic importance for the improvement of human-computer interaction. When a user encounters a system that he has never used before he is very unlikely to have a clear idea of how to formulate a problem so that the system understands it. It is also possible that the user does not have enough information about the domain to be able to produce *any* clear problem formulation. I believe that at least in typically "explorative" and "individually creative" domains, a substantial global environment habitability is of utmost importance, and does greatly benefit from a global, even if approximate user model arising through dialogue.

The combination of the relative freedom provided by a natural language interface (with the power of making complex and precise requests and answers) and a visual presentation (with direct manipulation possibility) of some organized subdomains has immense potential impact. And of course the user can interleave precise requests with concrete exploration of "the surroundings".

4. SOME WORK DONE

At IRST we have done work based on the ideas discussed above.

ALFRESCO (Stock 1991) is an interactive, natural-language centered system for a user interested in frescoes, with the aim not only of providing information, but also of promoting other masterpieces that may attract the user. It runs on a workstation connected to a videodisc unit and a touchscreen. The particular videodisc in use includes images about Fourteenth Century Italian frescoes and monuments. The system, besides understanding and using language (Lavelli *et al.* 1992; Lavelli and Stock 1990; Stock 1989; Strapparava 1991), integrates NL and hypermedia both in input and output. In input, our efforts have been focussed on combining the interpretation of NL deictic references with pointing to images displayed on a touch screen (Samek-Lodovici and Strapparava 1990). For instance, the user can ask a question such as: "In what frescoes did Giotto paint this saint?" while touching the image of a person appearing in the currently displayed fresco. Both the linguistic and the graphical deixes may be ambiguous, but usually the correct integration of the information provided by the two channels allows the identification of the intended reference. In output, images and generated text with buttons are yielded that offer entry points for further hypertextual exploration as described in the next section. The result is that the user communicates linguistically and by manipulating various entities, images, and text itself. The system builds a simple model of the user as the linguistic and image-based dialogue proceeds and it uses it for output, while allowing the user to browse around freely without taking particular notice otherwise.

Fourteenth Century frescoes have a content that almost always is centered on a sacred scene. The scene includes an event that can be reasonably well described (for instance the event "annunciation" performed by the angel Gabriel to Mary, where the contents of the message is another event, namely the forthcoming birth of Jesus) and includes a number of well identified recurring characters: humans, animals, saints, angels etc. The contents actually represented (in a hybrid KR system called YAK (Franconi 1990)) are the contents of the foreground of the paintings, while nothing is said about the background in which the artist could have expressed any real world scene. In this particular context the indexabilty of the objects and the related concept of the granularity of internal representation can be made clear to the user quite easily, without spoiling the image. But it can be noted that in other situations where the image global quality is not so essential there are other ways to indicate the pointable areas: shading of excluded areas, colouring, emphasis on lines and edges are among the possible techniques.

A different system has been designed as part of MAIA (Stringa 1990), the overall project at IRST. MAIA is conceived as an integration of components being developed here in different fields of AI (speech recognition, natural language, KR, vision, reasoning, etc.). It consists of both a mobile part (a robot moving in the corridors of the institute) and a fixed part (a kind of "concierge" to which a visitor may, for instance, ask questions about the institute's organization and production). The task of the latter so far has been giving information about researchers' activities and institute organization; as the project evolves natural language dialogues will also include direct interaction with the robot (whose role is to accompany the visitor to some office or deliver parcels) and an integration with speech recognition and synthesis. Within this more complex situation, the NLP component has to increase its capabilities in order to cope with aspects such as the multiple access to information and the interaction with the robot planner.

Also in this case the system includes the possibility of pointing at images (for example "what did this researcher and her roommate write together in 1991" indicating, by touch, someone in a group on a picture on the screen) and includes the possibility of combining access to information in natural language with possible navigation through a hypertextual environment concerned in this case with the documents produced at IRST. Graphical output has also been experimented in combination with linguistic replies. One major long-term aim is to access scenes seen by the robot, and to ask for instance "what was beyond that door", requiring the system to retrieve another recorded fragment, or "go again beyond that door", provoking an action in the physical world. In this case we are referring to an event that has occurred before. The problem of connection between video fragments, relevant internally represented facts, linguistic descriptions and exploration will become a challenging aspect of the project.

5. GENERATION AND HYPERMEDIA

In answering a request for information a system should ideally satisfy two linked output aspects:

a) giving the right, punctual answer to the user; but also
b) providing further optional information readily accessible to the user.

Examples of this are seen in the following situations: (1) the user may want to see individually presented information as immersed in a more standard information base that can be directly explored if linked to the given presentation; (2) the user may want to see more specific details connected to the output presented by the system.

Often there is no other vehicle than generated natural language if complex information is to be conveyed, tailored for the particular user in a dynamic context. Yet we would want that the text produced is dynamically connected to other preexisting and browsable text.

In ALFRESCO our generator (Carenini *et al.* 1993) intervenes during a dialogue where the user is interested in obtaining some information. The user is able both to make precise requests through language and browse around through a preexisting hypertextual network. At a certain point the user may want to receive some detailed information that is best conveyed by the system by generating a piece of text. This piece of text is produced by taking into account what seemed to be of interest for the user (in the previous portion of the interaction) and linked to the preexisting text. If a piece of generic text existed that was performing the same function, it is substituted by the newly generated text; the buttons in the new text link it in a user-oriented way to the rest of the hypertextual network and the rest of the network has links pointing to it (in ALFRESCO the hypertextual network is concerned with what some art critics say about masterpieces and painters, and includes links to fresco images).

Interest for a given topic is assumed to be either a consequence of the activation of that topic in context (e.g. a specific request by the user) or of the anticipated exposition of the user to an art work (remember that the system includes a videodisc from which images of frescoes are retrieved). The interest model, consisting in an activation/inhibition network whose nodes are associated with ordered sets of individual concepts, develops and becomes more focused in the course of the interaction between the user and the system.

The strategic generator chooses in particular what other instances (frescoes, tables etc.) to mention in the text, given its user's interest model. After the tactical generation part (Pianesi 1993) the whole text is enriched with the buttons that link it to the particular images and the particular pieces of hypertext that seem to be relevant for the user, altering so the preexisting hypertextual network.

The generator starts from an internal, a-linguistic representation, but the result is a text that permits access to other preexisting hypertext and images in a personalized way. Underlying this is the belief that the role of hypertext in a natural language centered interactive system is to allow the user to explore the surroundings of the focus of his attention and to provide a noncommitting modality of interaction, characterized by a fast turnaround that may possibly result in some other stimulus for further requests.

There has been other recent work on combining text generation and hypertexts. Reiter and colleagues (Reiter *et al.* 1992) have addressed the problem of new hypertext dynamically generated as the user performs further requests by clicking the available buttons in the current text. The fact that, as the user moves further, new specific text is generated presupposes that all the relevant knowledge is coded in an internal format and can be expressed linguistically on request. Beside this aspect the browsing modality is not really the goal for Reiter and colleagues. For instance the user is not supposed to move around the network with a bird's eye view just to have an idea about what information is available for certain areas. Instead hypertext buttons are a way for guiding and limiting the local follow up requests that the user may wish to express (see also Moore and Swartout 1990): they help tune the model the user has of the system with the system's actual capabilities. Work by Nagao and colleagues (Kurohashi 1992) addresses the automatic construction of an hypertext out of an encyclopedic text, providing links of various types and the resulting environment.

The creation of dynamic links, the role of user modelling in this process, the relation between generated text and preexisting text, the mutual contribution of exploration and goal-oriented behaviour are all themes that will be the object of further research. Very interesting is the fact that some of the complexities of language change in this context. Certainly an information access dialogue with the system becomes very different. For understanding this we need new models (Slack and Conati, to appear) and expansion of proposals for discourse modelling such as Grosz and Sidner's (1986) to include the explorative dimension.

6. LANGUAGE AND METALANGUAGE

One of the most difficult things in NLP is dealing with complex pragmatics. Among the many complex aspects, metalinguistic expressions like "let us go back to my previous question . . ." and reference of all kinds (e.g. through pronouns, through definite noun phrases such as "the lady that directs John's office" etc.) can be seen in a new light, if we take into account the medium, in particular the display. Of course the situation is different from our familiar human-human communication. The most obvious observation is that it is easy to maintain a history of what was said. Sentences in the dialogue can be kept on the screen and parts of speech are there in front of us, not somewhere in our mind, possibly transformed.

Discourse understanding involves segmentation into discourse units, not determined only by contiguity. Different theories emphasize different aspects. What is always considered central for understanding is building a structuring of the discourse and determining a coherence among contributions, both within a segment and globally among a segment and the other ones that make a complete discourse.

I think it is interesting to consider the possibility of communicating to the user the structure and the coherence keys that the system is inferring in the course of the ongoing dialogue in a direct way with a fast turnaround, low cognitive load and higher degree of interactivity.

We are currently experimenting with a prototype that has the following goals:

a) To give feedback to the user on the coherence relation found between the current input sentence and the ongoing discourse. The hypothesis is that feedback of this sort expressed in a very direct way may often be enough to reassure the user of the correct interpretation by the system (as opposed to disruptive and boring paraphrases by the system).
b) To give a possibility to the user to redirect a misinterpreted analysis by imposing coreferences through direct pointing to parts of speech in the discourse. The possible options for references must be emphasized by the system through discourse processing, yielding a limited and immediate search space to the user.
c) To change the interpretive context by imposing a certain insertion position in the discourse structure, again through direct manipulation.

The key concept is the introduction of graphical aspects for this purpose. Coloured or graphically differentiated links that denote different relations and key parts of speech in the cohesion relation are bound to the links. The graphical structure indexes sentences and other modality events (represented with icons) that have occurred in the dialogue so far, making available for pointing the parts of speech that the pragmatic processor considers admissible; the user can have intuitive feedback and the possibility of intervening directly.

In a certain sense this is an aid for a slightly handicapped system, one that needs some benign help on the pragmatic side when it has done wrong, and one that "knows" the user wants to be reassured it is doing the right thing without limiting the naturalness of the dialogue. On the other side in explorative dialogs it becomes another instrument for limiting disorientation, this time operating at a linguistic metalevel.

What has been briefly described here has been implemented in an experimental prototype (Zancanaro *et al.* 1993), integrated in both the overall systems mentioned in Section 4. It will be interesting to study other pragmatic aspects with this display-exploiting approach; intuitively it seems to provide the fast turnaround for readjusting pragmatic interpretation that would be otherwise very difficult for state of the art NLP systems and up to a point for humans too.

7. NEW SCENARIOS

The future may open up some new scenarios. I shall put forward some personal ideas.

So far we have begun exploring the relation between a linguistic modality and other modalities such as gestures, graphics etc. Hypertext integration is different because complementation is found there in another aspect concerned with language, albeit one with a very superficial processing and not involving machine understanding. I believe that very important in the future will be the design of the integration among different "full-fledged" linguistic modalities within the same system. I have not talked much about speech input so far. Speech technology is progressing and will certainly have a key role in the appeal of language communication with computers. Yet probably in the near future the capacity of speech will not match the (however limited) capabilities of language understanding in NLP systems. Then the problem arises of possibly having both spoken and written linguistic input within the same system. What should be the role of each modality? One possibility is that the spoken channel is used for clear particular tasks, such as metalinguistic utterances, in the vein of what has been described earlier. Another possibility is that spoken language is the basic device and written language intervenes just to clarify or edit when the speech recognizer fails, perhaps just on missing fragments. Other possibilities are conceivable in particular applications.

One very interesting aspect is the appearance of pen-based systems: they are characterized not only by the use of the pen for writing but also by the adoption of the same tool (as opposed to a mouse) to cause actions by clicking, or to draw. The consequences of this on language are still to be explored; handwriting recognition has about the same quantity of problems as speech recognition and it will be quite some time before pen-based system will be at the level of recognizing sentences with sizeable vocabularies and flexibility. Exciting is the perspective of having speech and pen-based (handwriting, drawing and pointing) input used creatively, for instance with an underlying hypermedial environment, as sketched above.

With respect to generation, the combination of synthetised language and written parts is promising and has been experienced in human-human communication: aren't we unable to speak without transparencies?

What will be the possible consequences of what has been discussed so far in this paper? They may be pervasive, for individual information, for communicating with other humans, even for interacting with objects. Let us briefly hint at some possible scenarios.

7.1. *Personal Information Spaces*

The systems we are accustomed to will qualitatively change to become an amplification of the human mind, more than simply an alternative to sequential books, as is the case with hypertexts. We shall get accustomed to integration of different functionalities centered on natural language: language and hypermedia connected as said before, but possibly other tools, such as linguistic spreadsheets: "what if I go to play tennis tomorrow morning?" may result in a set of consequences (depending on the underlying scheduling and reasoning program) described by a generator. In retrieving information the dimension would be more private, more linked to personal experience, than in interacting with another human being (such as an assistant), e.g. "when have I read this?". Technological progress in content-based image retrieval will be an important complement to written information retrieval. The possibility of putting together multimedia answers and combining retrieved images dynamically, for example integrated by descriptions, are mind blowing.

7.2. *Computer-Mediated Human-Human Communication*

The global village perspective opens problems of filtering and routing messages: the cost of copying and sending messages is practically nil and we are submerged with uninteresting unspecific messages. I guess we are beginning to understand, working with e-mail, that this is a dangerous technology if not complemented with something that deals with the contents of the message (see Lay *et al.* 1988). But apart from this we also know the potential of working together on the same text at a distance. Exciting knowledge-based systems have been developed for computer supported cooperative work even for people working in the same meeting room (see Stefik *et al.* 1987). A different view is that of the hypertext research community. Nelson's Xanadu (1981) for example is intended to provide online libraries to which people can add their own links and annotations on other people's work as well as on their own papers (see also Barrett 1989).

I think that a combination of both views will have an impact not just on cooperative work but on information exchanges of any kind. Say that a certain amount of the sent message can be put in an internal format. When the message reaches its destination it can be reconstructed, taking into account the model of the receiver that the destination computer has. We know that the message is better understood if linked to previous knowledge on the part of the receiver, best if linked to "subjectively criticized" knowledge; of course also this is usually in linguistic format, but may be complemented with images and graphics. The reconstructed message will incorporate the new contents (the part new for the receiver) and perhaps just recall some of the previous knowledge providing dynamic links to preexisting multimedial material, and, beside, different levels of elaboration of the material.

So the message at the beginning can be written, perhaps with a high level editor to maximize its "digestibility" by the system: in any case the originator knows that it will take a new form before being read.

Though this may sound projected in the far future, it is not so far away considering some restricted domain and restricted text *genre*. But let us think big for a moment: what have been the big steps in the history of human-human linguistic communication between persons distant in space and time? There has not been much change since humans used to engrave on tablets (we are celebrating 5000 years since the Sumers introduced writing). Gutenberg's invention permitted making text available to more persons across space and time; more modern devices still keep text or oral messages in the same form as they were generated at the origin. A radical change can be envisioned now, instead; one that amplifies and materializes the creative process of reading.

7.3. *Communicating with Objects*

With the free-falling prices of chips and electronic devices we shall have interfaces between humans and objects without even knowing there are computers in between. The first step is in electronic appliances of course. But also static objects will possibly react to human presence or will possibly provide information on events. At Xerox PARC a whole environment of communicating intelligent sensors "that know you" has been experimented with (Weiser 1991). Eventually it will be possible to talk to them and have them report to us. For this, probably the role of speech is essential, you do not want to have keyboards attached to most objects, but a small tablet may be ok and as output it may provide complementary graphic information. How we shall talk to objects remains to be seen. But to mention just one thing, learning will never be the same if objects interact with you symbolically. Maybe the beginning of the story of Pinocchio will have to be rewritten: for our grandchildren it will not be strange that a log talks.

Again some limited application may be less far away than what it would seem at first, though I must admit that the potential impact of this particular area must be better understood. In the end *it is* strange if we end up talking to objects, isn't it?

CONCLUSIONS

I have emphasized the aspects specific for my argumentation and may have left the impression that we do not need much basic research in NLP. I think exactly the opposite, for the ambitious purpose outlined here. Natural language processing as in the good ol' days is still a combination of formalism and creativity, interdisciplinary approaches and specific theories and techniques. But something new and important is happening, something that aims beyond what people have been used to. I would call all this visible interactive communication. It is quite different from the type of hypermedia that are now being developed. There, basically, the interface space is finite, even if one dimension may be added. Here the infinite creativity of human language is potentially preserved as the fundamental communication instrument. Long range developments depend on efforts in various areas hinted at in this paper, but also in other AI areas such as knowledge representation, planning, learning etc. I guess it can be important for all AI to take seriously this concrete chance to possibly help shape the evolution of communication and human potential. As Niels Bohr once put it: it is difficult to make predictions, especially about the future. But let us assume that the observer of NLP that I mentioned at the beginning would come back again after a dozen more years, older and probably wiser. I bet she will answer positively to the question asked in the title.

ACKNOWLEDGEMENTS

I would like to thank Jon Slack, Carlo Strapparava and Achille Varzi for useful discussions and the referees and Paul Mc Kevitt for helpful notes.

NOTE

* This is a revised version of an invited talk that was delivered at the *10th European Conference on Artificial Intelligence* in Vienna, and published in the Proceedings (B. Neuman, ed.), John Wiley & Sons, 1992, pp. 853–862.

REFERENCES

Allgayer, J., Harbusch, K., Kobsa, A., Reddig, C., Reithinger, N. & Schmauks, D. (1989). XTRA: A Natural-Language Access System to Expert Systems. *Intl. J. on Man-Machine Studies* **31**: 161–195.

Appelt, D. E. (1985). *Planning English Sentences*. Cambridge University Press.

Arens, Y., Miller, L., Shapiro, S. C. & Sondheimer, N. K. (1988). Automatic Construction of User Interface Displays. In Proceedings of *The Seventh AAAI Conference*. St. Paul, Minnesota.

Arens, Y. & Hovy, E. (1990). How to Describe What? Towards a Theory of Modality Utilization. In Proceedings of *The Twelfth Cognitive Science Conference*. Cambridge, MA.

Barrett, E. (1989). Textual Intervention, Collaboration, and the Online Environment. In Barrett, E. (ed.) *The Society of Text*. MIT Press.

Bush, V. (1945). As We May Think. *Atlantic Monthly* **7**: 101–108.

Carenini, G., Pianesi, F., Ponzi, M. & Stock, O. (1993). Natural Language Generation and Hypertext Access. *Applied Artificial Intelligence* **7**: 135–164.

Cohen, P. R., Dalrymple, M., Moran, D. B., Pereira, F. C. N., Sullivan, J. W., Gargan Jr, R. A., Schlossberg, J. L. & Tyler, S. W. (1989). Synergetic Use of Direct Manipulation and Natural Language. In Proceedings of *The CHI'89*, 227–233. Austin, Texas.

Conklin, J. (1987). Hypertext: An Introduction and Survey. *IEEE Computer* **20**(9).

Dahlbäck, N. & Jönsson, A. (1989). Empirical Studies of Discourse Representations for Natural Language Interfaces. In Proceedings of *The Fourth Conf. European Chapter of the ACL*, 291–307. Association for Computational Linguistics.

Dale, R. (1992). Visible Language: Multimodal Constraints in Information Presentation. In Dale, R., Hovy, E., Rösner, D. & Stock, O. (eds.) *Aspects of Automated Language Generation*, 281–283. Springer.

Feiner, S. & McKeown, K. (1990). Coordinating Text and Graphics in Explanation Generation. In Proceedings of *The AAAI-90*, 442–449. Boston, MA.

Franconi, E. (1990). The YAK Manual: Yet Another KRAPFEN. *IRST Manual 9003-01*. IRST. Trento, Italy.

Grosz, B. J. & Sidner, C. L. (1986). Attention, Intentions and the Structure of Discourse. *Computational Linguistics* **12**(3): 175–204.

Halasz, F. G. (1988). Reflections on NoteCards, Seven Issues for the Next Generation of Hypermedia Systems. *Communications of the ACM* **31**(7).

Hollan, J., Rich, E., Hill, W., Wroblenski, D., Wilker, W., Wittenburg, K. & Grudin, J. (1988). An Introduction to Hits: Human Interface Tool Suite. *MCC, Tech. Rep. ACA-HI-406-88*. Austin, Texas.

Hovy, E. (1988). *Generating Natural Language under Pragmatic Constraints*. Lawrence Erlbaum Associates.

Hovy, E., & Arens, Y. (1991). Automatic Generation of Formatted Text. In Proceedings of *The Ninth AAAI Conference*, 92–97. Anaheim, CA.

Kass, R. & Finin, T. (1988). Modeling the User in Natural Language Systems. *Computational Linguistics* **14**(3): 5–22.

Kobsa, A. & Wahlster, W. (eds.) (1989). *User Models in Dialog Systems*. Springer.

Kurohashi, S., Nagao, M., Sato, S. & Murakami, M. (1992). A Method of Automatic Hypertext Construction from an Encyclopedic Dictionary of a Specific Field. In Proceedings of *The Third Conference on Applied Natural Language Processing*, 239–240. Trento, Italy: Association for Computational Linguistics.

Lay, K. Y., Malone, T. W. & Yu, K. C. (1988). Object Lens: A "Spreadsheet" for Cooperative Work. *ACM Transaction on Office Information Systems* **6**: 332–353.

Lavelli, A., Magnini, B. & Strapparava, C. (1992). An Approach to Multilevel Semantics for Applied Systems. In Proceedings of *The Third Conference on Applied Natural Language Processing*, 17–24. Trento, Italy: Association for Computational Linguistics.

Lavelli, A. & Stock, O. (1990). When Something is Missing: Ellipsis, Coordination and the Chart. In Proceedings of *The Thirteenth International Conference on Computational Linguistics, COLING-90*, 184–189. Helsinki, Finland: Association for Computational Linguistics.

Lemke, A. & Fischer, G. A. (1990). Cooperative Problem Solving System for User Interface Design. In Proceedings of *The Eighth AAAI Conference*, 479–484. Boston, MA.

MacLaughlin, D. M. & Shaked, V. (1989). Natural Language Text Generation in Semi-Automated Forces. *BBN Report 7092*.

Mackinlay, J. D. (1986). *Automatic Design of Graphical Presentations*. Ph.D. dissertation, Stanford University.

Maybury, M. T. (1991). Planning Multimedia Explanations Using Communicative Acts. In Proceedings of *The Ninth AAAI Conference*, 61–66. Anaheim, CA.

Maybury, M. T. (ed.) (1993). *Intelligent Multimedia Interfaces*. AAAI Press/MIT Press: Menlo Park, CA/Cambridge, MA.

Moore, J. D. & Swartout, W. (1990). Pointing: A way toward explanation dialogue. In Proceedings of *The Eighth AAAI Conference*, 457–464. Boston, MA.

Nelson, T. H. (1981). *Literary Machines*. Swarthmore, PA 19801: Nelson, T., P.O. Box 128.

Oviatt, S. L. & Cohen, P. R. (1989). The Effects of Interaction on Spoken Discourse. In Proceedings of *The Twenty-Seventh Meeting of the ACL*, 126–134. Vancouver, Canada: Association for Computational Linguistics.

Oviatt, S. L. & Cohen, P. R. (1991). discourse Structure and Performances Efficiency in Interactive and Noninteractive Spoken Modalities. *Computer Speech and Language* **5**(4): 297–326.

Paris, C. L. (1987). Combining discourse Strategies to Generate Descriptions to Users Along a Naive/Expert Spectrum. In Proceedings of *The IJCAI-87*, 626–632. Milan, Italy.

Pianesi, F. (1993). Head Driven Bottom Up Generation and Government and Binding: A Unified Perspective. In Horacek, H. & Zock, M. (eds.) *New Concepts in Natural Language Generation*, 187–214. Printer: London.

Reiter, E., Mellish, C. & Levine, J. (1992). Automatic Generation of On-Line Documentation in the IDAS Project. In Proceedings of *The Third Conference on Applied natural Language Processing*, 64–71. Trento, Italy: Association for Computational Linguistics.

Samek-Lodovici, V. & Strapparava, C. (1990). Identifying Noun Phrase References, the Topic Module of the ALFRESCO System. In Proceedings of *The ECAI-90*, 573–578. Stockholm, Sweden.

Schmauks, D. (1987). Natural and Simulated Pointing. In Proceedings of *The Third Conference of the European Chapter of the ACL*, 179–183. Association for Computational Linguistics.

Slack, J. & Conati, C. (to appear). Modeling Interest: Exploration of an Information Space. To appear in *Acta Phsychologica on Cognitive Ergonomics*.

Stefik, M., Foster, G., Bobrow, D., Kahn, K., Lanning, S. & Suchman, L. (1987). Beyond the chalkboard: Using computers to support collaboration and problem solving in meetings. *Communication of the ACM* **30**(1): 32–47.

Stock, O. (1989). Parsing with Flexibility, Dynamic Strategies and Idioms in Mind. *Computational Linguistics* **15**(1): 1–18.

Stock, O. (1991). Natural Language and Exploration of an Information Space: the ALFRESCO

Interactive System. In Proceedings of *The IJCAI-91*, 972–978. Sydney, Australia: Morgan Kaufmann.

Strapparava, C. (1991). From Scopings to Interpretation: The Semantic Interpretation within the ALFRESCO System. In Ardizzone, Gaglio & Sorbello (eds.) *Trends in Artificial Intelligence, Proceedings of The Second Congress of the Italian Association for Artificial Intelligence*, 281–290. Springer-Verlag.

Stringa, L. (1990). An Integrated Approach to Artificial Intelligence. *IRST-Technical Report 9012-11*. IRST: Trento, Italy.

Suchman, L. A. (1987). *Plans and Situated Action*. Cambridge University Press.

Wahlster, W. (1988). User and Discourse Models for Multimodal Communication. In Sullivan, J. W. & Tyler, S. W. (eds.) *Architectures for Intelligent Interfaces: Elements and Prototypes*. Addison-Wesley.

Wahlster, W., André, E., Bandyopadhyay, S., Graf, W. & Rist, T. (1992). WIP: The Coordinated Generation of Multimodal Presentations from a Common Representation. In Slack, J., Ortony, A. & Stock, O. (eds.) *Communication from Artificial Intelligence Perspective; Theoretical and Applied Issues*, 121–143. Springer Verlag.

Weiser, M. (1991). The Computer for the 21st Century. *Scientific American* **265**(3): 66.

Zancanaro, M., Stock, O. & Strapparava, C. (1993). Dialogue Cohesion Sharing and Adjusting in an Enhanced Multimodal Environment. In Proceedings of *The IJCAI-93*, 1230–1236. Chambery, France: Morgan Kaufmann.

Artificial Intelligence Review **9**: 147–165, 1995.

Generating Coherent Presentations Employing Textual and Visual Material

ELISABETH ANDRÉ and THOMAS RIST

German Research Center for Artificial Intelligence (DFKI), Stuhlsatzenhausweg 3, D-66123 Saarbrücken. Email: {andre, rist}@dfki.uni-sb.de

Abstract. The objective of the work described in this paper is the development of an intelligent generation system which is able to combine textual and visual material. As coherent presentations cannot be generated by simply merging verbalization and visualization results into multimedia output, the processes for content determination, medium selection and content realization in different media have to be carefully coordinated. We first show that multimedia presentations and pure text follow similar structuring principles. Based on this insight, we sketch how techniques for planning text and discourse can be generalized to allow the structure and contents of multimedia communications to be planned as well. In particular, we explain how our approach handles the crucial task of process coordination.

Key words: multimedia generation, presentation planning, communicative acts, coherence.

1. INTRODUCTION

Multimedia systems which employ several media such as text, graphics, animation and sound for the presentation of information have become widely available during the last decade. A walk through any computer exhibition shows that almost all companies have enriched their product range with multimedia functionality concerning display, storage, processing and creation of multimedia documents. With regard to the presentation of information, this technology offers not only the choice between media, but also the chance to utilize a combination of several media in which the strength of one medium will overcome the weakness of another.

Automated presentation systems as components of user interfaces to next-generation expert systems, control panels and help systems aim at presentations which are tailored to individual users in particular situations. The fact that it is impossible to anticipate the needs and requirements of each potential user in an infinite number of presentation situations leads to the idea of an intelligent system that automatically generates presentations on the fly in a context-sensitive way. The benefits of using an automated presentation system as back-end to an application program are twofold. While the application developer will be released from the burden of presentation design, the user of an application can expect intelligible presentations satisfying his individual information needs and style preferences.

Recently, there has been increasing interest in the design of automated presentation systems which take advantage of multimedia technology to make presentations more effective (cf. Arens *et al.* 1993b; Badler *et al.* 1991b; Feiner and McKeown 1991; Marks and Reiter 1990; Maybury 1993; Roth *et al.* 1991; Stock and the ALFRESCO Project Team 1993; Wilson *et al.* 1992; Wahlster *et al.* 1993). The main working steps that such intelligent multimedia systems have to accomplish are:

- **Content selection and organization**
  In some cases, the application system more or less determines the contents, and the presentation system only has to eliminate irrelevant details and to organize the rest. For other applications, it is up to the presentation system to extract the information to be communicated from a knowledge base. When determining the contents of a presentation, the system should follow the maxims of Grice (1975) – which are of course not restricted to natural language. On the one hand, the system has to ensure that all relevant information will be encoded. On the other hand, the user should not be unnecessarily informed about facts he already knows. Content organization is not restricted to medium-specific clustering of information. The system also has to ensure structural compatibility between related presentation parts in different media.
- **Coordinated distribution of information on several media**
  Employing different media when presenting information does not automatically contribute to the success of communication – as the great number of more or less badly designed presentations shows. Examples include conventional paper-printed illustrated documents in which pictures may be superficial or even confuse readers (see also the experimental findings of text-picture researchers discussed in Levie (1987), Molitor *et al.* (1989), and computer-based multimedia presentations which, rather than facilitating comprehension, overload a user's perceptual capabilities). An optimal exploitation of different media requires a presentation system to decide carefully when to use one medium in place of another and how to integrate different media in a consistent and coherent manner. This also includes determining an appropriate degree of complementarity and redundancy of information presented in different media. A presentation that contains no redundant information at all tends to be incoherent. If, however, too much information is paraphrased in different media, the user may concentrate on one medium after a short time and probably overlook information.
- **Medium-specific content realization**
  To optimally exploit the available media, a presentation system must manage the medium-specific encoding of information. A straightforward approach is to rely on dedicated generation components, such as a text generator and a graphics generator, which incorporate design expertise and provide mechanisms for the automated selection, creation and combination of textual and graphical elements. However, such components cannot be used as uni-directional backend systems which only produce textual or pictorial output. Since

the results of the different generators should be tailored to each other, each generator has to know how other generators have encoded information. Therefore, each generator has to provide an explicit representation of its encodings.

- **Laying out the generation results**
  Presentation fragments provided by the generators have to be arranged in a multimedia output. A purely geometrical treatment of the layout task would, however, lead to unsatisfactory results. Rather, layout has to be considered as an important carrier of meaning. For example, two pictures that serve to contrast objects should be placed side by side. When using dynamic media, such as animation and speech, layout design also requires the temporal coordination of output units.

In the WIP project, we aimed at the development of a presentation system that automatically accomplishes the tasks described above. The resulting WIP prototype is able to synthesize presentations that combine textual and visual material, all of which has been generated by the system. A brief overview of WIP can be found under the DFKI site description in this volume. For more details on WIP's central components and the system architecture we refer to André *et al.* (1993), Wahlster *et al.* (1993). In this paper, we focus on the basic structuring principles of our approach to multimedia generation. Furthermore, we sketch how a plan-based approach can be used for the realization of a multimedia presentation system. Finally, we show how to coordinate the processes for content selection, organization and medium selection.

2. METHODOLOGICAL BASIS

Since a lot of progress has been made in natural language generation, we were optimistic about generalizing concepts developed for natural language generation in such a way that they become useful in the broader context of multimedia presentations. Although new questions arise, e.g. how to optimally divide the work between the available presentation media, many tasks in multimedia generation closely resemble problems occurring in natural language generation, in particular, the selection and the organization of the contents of the presentation.

2.1. *Multimedia Generation as a Goal-Directed Activity*

Our approach is based on the assumption that not only the generation of text, but also the generation of multimedia presentations can be considered as a sequence of acts that aims to achieve certain goals (cf. André and Rist 1990). We presume that there is at least one act that is central to the goal of the whole document. This act is referred to as the *main act* (MA). Acts supporting the main act are called *subsidiary acts* (SA).[1] Since main and subsidiary acts can, in turn, be composed of main and subsidiary acts, a hierarchical document structure results. While the root of the hierarchy generally corresponds to a complex communicative act such as describing a process, the leaves are elementary acts, i.e., speech acts (cf. Searle 1980) or pictorial acts (cf. Kjorup 1978).

In Fig. 1, an example of a document fragment[2] is shown with its intentional structure. The goal of this document fragment is to get the user to remove the cover of the water container of an espresso machine. This goal is seen in the words "Remove the cover." After reading the instruction, the user knows that he is required to remove the cover. However, the instruction on its own does not guarantee that he is willing to accomplish the request and also able to do so. These two goals are to be achieved by means of the picture and the verbal utterance "to fill the water container." We can also associate certain goals with the single picture parts. For example, the two arrows are to ensure that the user knows the trajectory of the object to be manipulated.

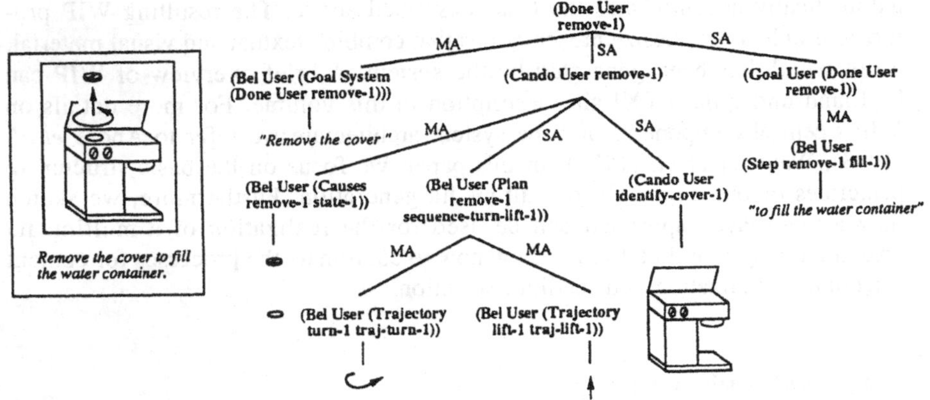

Fig. 1. Intentional structure of a document fragment.

2.2. *An Extended Notion of Coherence for Multimedia Presentations*

A number of text linguists have characterized coherence in terms of coherence relations that hold between the parts of the text (e.g. see Grimes 1975; Hobbs 1978). Perhaps the most elaborate set is presented in Rhetorical Structure Theory (RST, cf. Mann and Thompson 1987), a theory of text coherence. Examples of RST-relations are *Motivation, Elaboration, Enablement, Interpretation* and *Summary.* Psychologists and pedagogues have investigated the role a particular picture plays in relation to accompanying text passages. For example, Levin has found five primary functions (cf. Levin *et al.* 1987): *Decoration, Representation, Organization, Interpretation* and *Transformation.* Hunter and colleagues distinguish between: *Embellish, Reinforce, Elaborate, Summarize* and *Compare* (cf. Hunter *et al.* 1987).

An attempt at a transfer to the relations proposed by Hobbs to pictures and text-picture combinations has been made in Bandyopadhyay (1990). Many psychological and pedagogical studies focus on the various functions of pictures in illustrated documents (cf. Willows and Houghton 1987; Houghton and Willows

1987). Unfortunately, these studies only consider whole pictures, i.e., they do not address the question of how a picture is organized. To get an informative description of the whole document structure, one has to consider relations between picture parts or between picture parts and text passages too. For example, a portion of a picture can serve as background for the rest of the picture or a text passage can elaborate on a particular section of a picture.

Figure 2 shows the rhetorical structure of the document fragment. The document is composed of a request, a motivating part and a part that enables the user to carry out the action. Rhetorical predicates can also be associated with single picture parts. For example, the depiction of the espresso machine serves as a background for the rest of the picture.

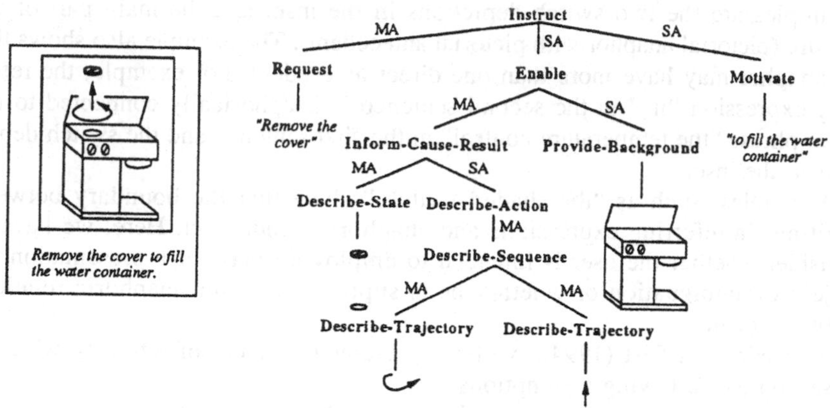

Fig. 2. Rhetorical structure of a document fragment.

2.3. *Cohesive Links between Text and Graphics*

Effective means to establish cohesive links between textual and visual material are referring expressions involving both media. In a multimedia discourse, the following types occur:

Multimedia referring expressions refer to world objects via a combination of at least two media. Each medium conveys some discriminating attributes which in sum allow for a proper identification of the intended object. Examples are natural language expressions that are accompanied by pointing gestures and text-picture combinations where the picture provides information about the appearance of an object while the text restricts the visual search space as in "the switch on the frontside".

Crossmedia referring expressions do not refer to world objects, but to document parts in other presentation media (cf. Wahlster *et al.* 1991). Examples of crossmedia referring expressions are "the upper left corner of the picture" or "Fig. x". In most cases, crossmedia referring expressions are part of a complex multimedia referring expression where they serve to direct the reader's attention to parts of a document that are needed to find the intended referent.

Anaphoric referring expressions refer to world objects in an abbreviated form (cf. Hirst 1981) presuming that they are already explicitly or implicitly introduced in the discourse. The presentation part to which an anaphoric expression refers back is called the antecedent of the referring expression. In a multimedia discourse, we have not only to handle linguistic anaphora with linguistic antecedents, but also linguistic anaphora with pictorial antecedents, and pictorial anaphora with linguistic or pictorial antecedents. For example, the noun phrase "the temperature control" in the first sentence in Fig. 3 refers back to the corresponding switch depiction in the picture (linguistic anaphor with pictorial antecedent). The antecedent of the espresso machine depiction in the picture is the noun phrase "your machine" in the document title (pictorial anaphor with linguistic antecedent). Anaphoric relationships can also be established between picture parts. Examples are the two switch depictions in the inset and the main part of the picture (pictorial anaphor with pictorial antecedent). The example also shows that an anaphor may have more than one direct antecedent. For example, the referring expression "its" in the second sentence is anaphorically connected to the noun phrase "the temperature control" in the first sentence and the switch depiction in the inset.

Examples, such as "the shaded switch," show that the boundary between multimedia referring expressions and anaphora is indistinct. Here, we have to consider whether the user is intended to employ all parts of a presentation for object disambiguation or whether he is supposed to infer anaphoric relations between them.

In André and Rist (1994), we have presented a model of referring which is based on the following assumptions:

1. When a presenter refers to an object, the addressee is intended to activate a mental representation of this object which is already available or which has to be built up (see also Appelt and Kronfeld 1987). Mental representations can be activated not only by textual, but also by graphical or mixed descriptions.
2. Failure and success of referring acts can be explained by the user's ability to recognize certain links between these mental representations and the corresponding object descriptions.

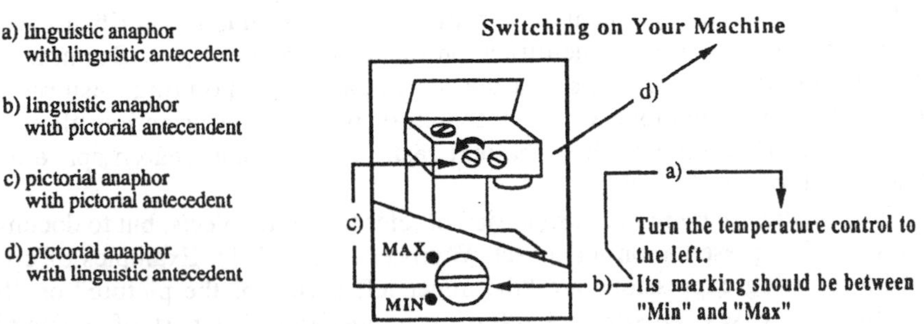

Fig. 3. Different types of anaphora occurring in a sample document.

In addition, the model takes into account that the user's and system's knowledge about the identity of objects doesn't necessarily coincide. For example, the system may believe that the user has different representations for one and the same object without knowing how they are related to each other. In order to describe the links a user has to infer in understanding a referring expression, we have introduced the following predicates:

- The predicate *(Coref repl rep2)* is used to express that two representations *repl* and *rep2* are representations of the same world object.
- The predicate *(Encodes means information context-space)* specifies the semantic relationship between a textual or graphical means and the information the means is to convey in a certain context space.
- The predicate *(EncodesSame pl p2 context-space)* expresses a cohesive relationship between two presentation parts *pl* and *p2*. It is satisfied if and only if *pl* and *p2* encode the same object.

To illustrate which kinds of coreferential links between referring expressions, world objects and elements of the presentation the user has to infer, let's again have a look at the document fragment shown in Fig. 3. We assume that the user is requested to turn the temperature control. Furthermore, we presume that the user knows of the existence of the on/off switch and the temperature control, has visual access to the two switches, but is not able to tell them apart. Let *rl_u* be a representation for the temperature control the user activates when looking at the picture and *r2_u* be a representation for the temperature control which results from the user's previous knowledge about espresso machines. In the diagrams below, we use the abbreviations *ES, C* and *E* for the *EncodesSame, Coref* and *Encodes* respectively.

To understand the document fragment shown in Fig. 3, the user must be able to infer the anaphoric link between the noun phrase "the temperature control" and the left switch in the main part of the picture. Furthermore, he has to recognize the Encodes-Links between "the temperature control" and *r2_u* and the left switch depiction in the main part of the picture and *rl_u*. From this knowledge, he is expected to infer the Encodes-Link between "the temperature control" and *rl_u* and the Coref-Link between *rl_u* and *r2_u* (cf. Fig. 4a). To understand the second sentence, the user has to infer two anaphoric relationships: the EncodesSame-relationship between the pronoun "its" and the noun phrase "the temperature control" and the EncodesSame-relationship between "its" and the switch depiction in the inset. From these relationships, the Encodes-relationships between "its" and *rl_u* (cf. Fig. 4b) and the switch in the inset and *rl_u* (cf. Fig. 4c) result. Finally, the Encodes-relationships between the two switch depictions and *rl_u* lead to the EncodesSame-relationship between the switch depictions (cf. Fig. 4d).

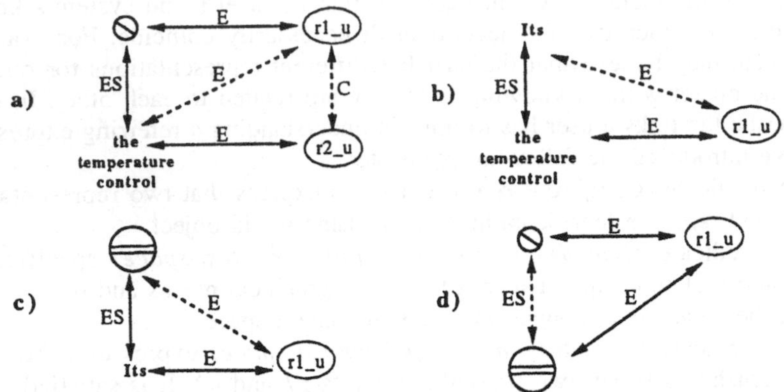

Fig. 4. Referring diagrams for the document fragment shown in Fig. 3.

3. BUILDING A MULTIMEDIA PRESENTATION SYSTEM

3.1. *Planning the Contents and the Structure of Presentations*

As argued in the preceding section, text-picture combinations are similar to text in their structuring principles. In particular, a presentation is characterized by its intentional structure that is reflected by the presenter's intentions and by its rhetorical structure that is reflected by various coherence relations.

Therefore, it seems reasonable to use text planning approaches not only for the organization of the textual parts of a multimedia presentation, but also for structuring the overall presentation. An essential advantage of a uniform structuring approach is that not only relationships within a single medium, but also relationships between parts in different media can be explicitly represented.

To represent presentation knowledge, we have defined presentation strategies which refer to both text and picture production. Each presentation strategy is represented by a header, an effect, a set of applicability conditions and a specification of main and subsidiary acts. Whereas the header of a strategy is a complex communicative act (e.g. to enable an action), its effect refers to an intentional goal (e.g. the user knows a particular object). To represent intentional goals, we use the same notation as in Hovy's RST planner (cf. Hovy 1988). The expression *(Goal P x)* stands for: The presenter *P* has *x* as a goal. *(Bel P x)* should be read as: *P* believes that *x* is satisfied. *(BMB P U x)* is an abbreviation for the infinite conjunction: *(Bel P x)* & *(Bel P (Bel U x))* & *(Bel P (Bel U (Bel P x)))*, etc. The applicability conditions specify when a strategy may be used and constrain the variables to be instantiated. The main and subsidiary acts form the kernel of the strategies. Our representation formalism is similar to that proposed in Moore and Paris (1989). However, we introduce an additional slot for the medium. In doing so, we are able to define medium-independent presentation strategies as well as strategies that apply only for specific medium combinations. Examples of presentation strategies are shown below. Strategy

S1 can be used to introduce an object by showing a picture of it. In this strategy, two kinds of act occur: the elementary act S(surface)-Depict and two complex communicative acts (Label and Provide-Background). The first subsidiary act serves to inform the user about the name of the object, the second is to enable its identification in the picture.

(S1) **Header:** (Introduce System User ?object Graphics)
Effect: (BMB System User (Isa ?object ?concept))
Applicability Conditions:
(Bel System (Isa ?object ?concept))
Main Acts:
(S-Depict System User ?object ?pic-obj ?picture)
Subsidiary Acts:
(Label System User ?object ?medium)
(Provide-Background System User ?object ?pic-obj ?picture Graphics)

To accomplish the second task, strategy S2 may be applied. The main act of this strategy is again an elementary act (S-Depict). Instead of specifying the subsidiary act, only the goal to be achieved is indicated. Whereas the strategy prescribes graphics for the main act, it leaves the medium open for the subsidiary act.

(S2) **Header:** (Provide-Background System User ?x ?px ?picture Graphics)
Effect: (BMB System User (Encodes ?px ?x ?picture))
Applicability Conditions:
(And (Bel System (Encodes ?px ?x ?picture))
(Bel System (Perceptually-Accessible-p U ?x))
(Bel System (Part-of ?x ?z)))
Main Acts:
(S-Depict System User ?z ?pz ?picture)
Subsidiary Acts:
(Achieve System (BMB System User (Encodes ?pz ?z ?picture)) ?medium)

To automatically build up presentations, the strategies are considered operators of a planning system. Starting from a communicative goal, the system searches for presentation strategies whose effect subsumes this goal. If such a presentation strategy is found, the expressions in the body are treated as new subgoals. The result of the presentation planning process is a refinement style plan in the form of a directed acyclic graph (DAG). The leaves of this DAG are elementary speech acts or pictorial acts that are forwarded to the medium-specific generators. Note that the medium-specific generators receive not only requests for producing output, but also requests for evaluating their generation results. For example, the subsidiary act of strategy S2 is forwarded to the graphics generator which has to analyze the picture *?picture* to find out whether the object *?z* is identifiable. A further strategy is only applied if the evaluation leads to a negative result. This point underscores the tight connection between image generation and image understanding.

Since there may be several strategies for achieving a certain goal, criteria for ranking the effectiveness, the side-effects and costs of executing presentation strategies are needed. To prioritize presentation strategies, we use selection rules. For example, the selection rule below suggests the use of graphics rather than text when presenting spatial information.

IF (isa ?current-attribute-value SPATIAL-CONCEPT)
THEN (TryBefore *graphics-strategies* *text-strategies*)

Extended studies of relevant psychological literature (e.g., see Willows and Houghton 1987; Houghton and Willows 1987) and our own analyses of various illustrated documents form the basis of our selection rules and presentation strategies. For the generation of instructions, we currently distinguish between 7 information types (concrete, abstract, spatial, covariant, temporal, quantification, negation) with several subtypes and 10 communicative functions (attract-attention, compare, elaborate, enable, elucidate, label, motivate, evidence, background, summarize). To find out which medium or media combination conveys them best, we have analyzed various documents. For example, it is very difficult or even impossible to graphically depict quantifiers (such as *some* or *a few*) whereas graphics are in general the preferred medium for conveying spatial information. Furthermore, we consider criteria such as user characteristics or resource limitations when selecting presentation media. However, the identification of design criteria is an ongoing research area. As more sophisticated models of a user's understanding processes become available, our presentation strategies and selection rules can be refined accordingly.

The plan-based approach is also used for the generation of referring expressions. As in strategy (S3), acts for activating representations may occur in presentation strategies as part of a superordinate speech act.

(S3) **Header:** (Request System User ?action Text)
Effect: (BMB System User (Goal System (Done User ?action)))
Applicability Conditions:
(And (Goal System (Done User ?action))
(Bel System (Complex-Operating-Action ?action))
(Bel System (Agent ?agent ?action))
(Bel System (Object ?object ?action)))
Main Acts:
(S-Request System User (?action-spec (Agent ?agent-spec) (Object ?object-spec)))
Subsidiary Acts:
(Activate System User (Action ?action) ?action-spec Text)
(Activate System User (Agent ?agent) ?agent-spec Text)
(Activate System User (Object ?object) ?object-spec Text)

Strategy (S3) can be used to request the user to perform an action. In this strategy, two kinds of act occur: an elementary speech act (S(urface)-Request) and three activation acts for specifying the action and the semantic case roles associated with the action (Activate). The strategy prescribes text for the subsidiary acts because the resulting referring expressions (*?action-spec, ?agent-spec* and *?object-spec*) are obligatory case roles of an S-Request speech act which will be conveyed by text. For optional case roles any medium can be taken. To activate representations, strategy (S4) may be applied, which simultaneously enriches the user's knowledge about the identity of objects.

(S4) **Header:** (Activate System User (?case-role ?rep-1) ?spec Text)
Effect: (BMB System User (Coref ?rep-1 ?rep-2))
Applicability Conditions:
(And (BMB System User (Encodes ?pic-obj ?rep-1 ?context))
(Bel System (Coref ?rep-1 ?rep-2))
(Bel System (Bel User (Isa ?rep-2 Thing))))
Main Acts:
(Provide-Unique-Description System User ?rep-2 ?spec Text)
Subsidiary Acts:
(Achieve System (BMB System User (EncodesSame ?spec ?pic-obj ?context)) ?medium)

The strategy only applies if there already exists a picture, if the system knows how the two representations *?rep-1* and *?rep-2* are related to each other and if the system's model of the user's beliefs contains *?rep-2*. If the strategy is applied, the system (a) provides a unique description for *?rep-2* (main act) and (b) ensures that the user recognizes that this description and the corresponding image specify the same object (subsidiary act). For (a), we use a discrimination algorithm similar to the algorithm presented in Reiter and Dale (1992). However, we have investigated additional possibilities for distinguishing objects from their alternatives. We are able to refer not only to features of an object in a scene, but also to features of the graphical model, their interpretation, and to the position of picture objects within the picture (see also Wazinski 1992). A detailed description of our discrimination algorithm can be found in Schneiderlöchner (1994). Task (b) can be accomplished by correlating the visual with the textual focus, by redundantly encoding object attributes, or by explicitly informing the user about a Coref-relationship. Such a Coref-relationship can be established by strategies for the generation of crossmedia referring expressions (as in "The left switch in the figure is the temperature control") or by strategies for annotating objects in a figure. (S5) is an example of such a strategy. It only applies if the system believes that there is a coreferential relationship between *?rep-1* and *?rep-2* and if it is mutually believed that there is a textual element which encodes *?rep-1* and a pictorial element which encodes *?rep-2*.

(S5) **Header:** (Establish-Coreferential-Link System User ?rep-1 ?rep-2 Graphics)
Effect: (BMB System User (Coref ?rep-1 ?rep-2))
Applicability Conditions:
(And (BMB System User (Encodes ?spec-1 ?rep-1 ?text-passage))
(BMB System User (Text-Obj ?spec-1))
(BMB System User (Encodes ?spec-2 ?rep-2 ?picture))
(BMB System User (Pic-Obj ?spec-2)))

Main Acts:
(S-Annotate System User ?spec-1 ?spec-2 ?picture)

3.2. *Process Coordination*

While most people agree on the nature of the decision processes for content selection, content organization and medium selection, architecture models for the processes remain an issue for discussion.

In SAGE (Roth *et al.* 1991), relevant information is selected first and then organized by the text and graphics generators. After that, the generated structures are transformed into text and graphics. A disadvantage of this method is that text and graphics are built up independently of each other.

In COMET (Feiner and McKeown 1991), a tree-like structure that reflects the organization of the presentation to be generated is built up first. This tree is extended by the medium-specific generators in a monotone manner. The system does not allow for revisions caused by medium selection.

Arens and colleagues (Arens *et al.* 1993a) propose a strict separation of planning and medium selection processes. During the planning process, their system fully specifies the discourse structure, which is determined by the communicative goals of the presenter and the content to be communicated. After that, special rules are applied to select an appropriate medium combination. After medium selection, the discourse structure is traversed from bottom to top to transform the discourse structure into a presentation-oriented structure. A problem with this approach is that the presentation structure obviously has no influence on the discourse structure. The selection of a medium is influenced by the discourse structure, but the contents are determined independently of the medium.

In AIMI (Maybury 1993), content selection and content organization are done in parallel. Although AIMI performs medium selection during content selection, dependencies between content selection and medium selection can be handled only to a limited extent. For example, AIMI's operators contain complex communicative acts, such as *Identify (S, H, entity)* which may be realized by either text or graphics. However, since AIMI does not associate medium constraints with such acts, it is not able to express that in a certain context this act should be accomplished by a particular medium.

Our work is distinguished from the work described above in that we use an integrated approach for content selection, content organization and medium selection. The advantage of such an approach is that it facilitates the coordination of the different decision processes. As described in the preceding section, the header of our strategies contains an additional slot for the medium for which constraints can be defined and propagated during the planning process. Depending on whether the main acts of a strategy are to be realized in text, graphics, or both media, the values *Text, Graphics* or *Mixed* are assigned.

The medium remains unspecified until medium decisions are made for the main acts of a strategy. Assume the system decides to compare two objects by describing the different values of a common attribute. At this time, the only restriction is that both descriptions should be realized in the same medium. Once the system has decided on the medium for the attribute value of the first object, the result of this decision is propagated to the part of the DAG that refers to the description of the second object (cf. Fig. 5).

Since the presentation planner has no direct access to knowledge concerning medium-specific realization, it cannot consider this information when building up a candidate document structure. Consequently, it may happen that the results provided by the generators deviate to a certain extent from the initial document plan. Such deviations are reflected in the DAG by output sharing, structure sharing and structure adding (see also André and Rist 1993). Output sharing occurs when parts of the generated output are reused for different purposes. Structure sharing is similar to output sharing. It occurs when not only parts of the output, but also a more complex part of the DAG is shared. Whereas structure sharing leads to simplifications of the initial document plan, structure adding results in a more complex plan. For example, it occurs if the graphics generator is expected to integrate information in a single picture, but is only able to convey the information by generating several pictures.

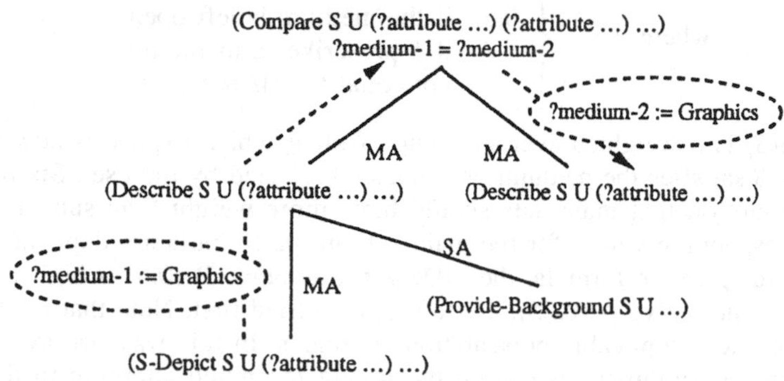

Fig. 5. Propagating medium information.

By means of the following system runs, we illustrate how our system handles the dependencies between content selection, content organization and medium selection. In all system runs, we suppose the system is requested to present a domain plan for setting a modem for reception of data, i.e. the goal *(Instruct System User set-for-reception-1 ?Medium)* has to be accomplished. To show how medium selection influences content selection and content organization and vice versa, we vary the generation parameter 'medium preferences' in each system run.

System run 1: preferred medium graphics

In the first system run, we assume that the user prefers graphics to text. When looking for strategies that match the presentation goal, the system finds two possibilities: Alternative A is to verbally request the user to set a certain code switch to a certain position and to enable him to carry out that action using a medium not yet specified. Alternative B is to describe the action to be carried out and the result to be achieved. Whereas the first alternative prescribes text for the main act, the second alternative leaves the medium for all acts open. The presentation planner now has to select the strategy which best corresponds to the user's preferences. To prioritize the strategies, we suggest the following heuristic:

Let *PM* be the preferred medium, *S* a strategy, a_i with $1 \leq i \leq n$ main acts of *S*, a_i with $n+1 \leq i \leq n+m$ subsidiary acts of *S*. To each act a_i, we assign a value v_i which depends on the medium the strategy prescribes for a_i. For example, if graphics is preferred to text, as in our case, graphical acts get the value 1 whereas 0 is assigned to textual acts. Acts for which the medium is unknown at definition time get the value 0.5 since the system still has a chance to instantiate them with the preferred medium at runtime. The medium-specific degree of suitability, *MDS(S)*, is defined as follows:

$$MDS(S) := \frac{2\sum_{i=1}^{n} v_i + \sum_{i=n+1}^{n+m} v_i}{2n + m}$$

$$\text{where } v_i = \begin{cases} 1 & \text{if } S \text{ prescribes } PM \text{ for } a_i \\ 0.5 & \text{if the medium is left open} \\ 0 & \text{if } S \text{ prescribes a medium} \\ & \text{not equal to } PM \text{ for } a_i \end{cases}$$

MDS(S) is a weighted average value of all v_i which expresses how well the strategy *S* satisfies the medium preferences indicated by the user. Starting from the assumption that main acts should have more weight than subsidiary acts, the corresponding values for the main acts in the formula are duplicated.

According to the formula, the MDS for alternative B (0.5) is higher than the MDS for alternative A (0.25). Therefore, B is tried first. Note that the heuristic only considers applicable presentation strategies. In this way, we avoid inadequate media combinations caused by paying too much attention to the user's preferences.

After some expansions, Describe-Orientation and Describe-Trajectory are posted as new subgoals. At this time, the presentation planner instantiates the media. Due to the medium preferences, the presentation planner chooses graphics for both subgoals. The same goes for the Describe-Result goal. Note that medium choices are postponed as long as possible to avoid a situation in which decisions have to be retracted because they are not realizable. Therefore, the medium variable corresponding to the instructing act was not instantiated with graphics immediately after applying strategy B. Figure 6 shows the presentation structure that has been built up so far and the values of the medium slots at the time when the corresponding strategy was applied.

Note that the presentation planner has created three background substructures. When processing these substructures, the graphics generator discovers that it is possible to convey the information requested in a single picture. Consequently, the document structure can be simplified by structure sharing as shown in Fig. 7. This figure also shows the settings of the medium slots after the medium propagation process.

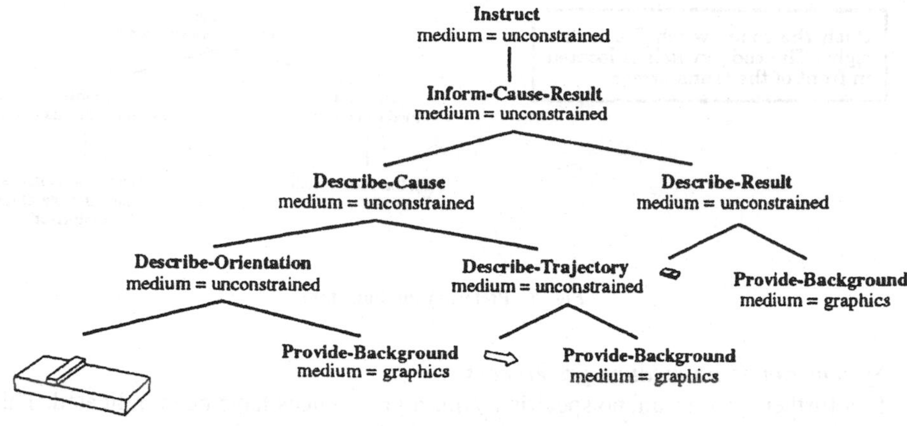

Fig. 6. Preferred medium graphics.

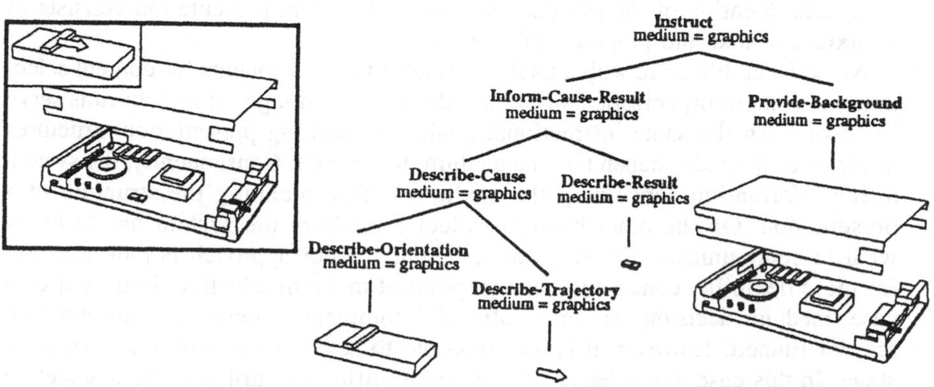

Fig. 7. Presentation structure after factoring out the background subtrees.

System run 2: preferred medium text

In a second system run, we assume that text is the preferred medium. Now, alternative A gets the value 0.83 whereas 0.5 is assigned to alternative B. As a consequence, the system chooses alternative A and verbally requests the user to push the code switch S-4 to the right. As mentioned above, this alternative leaves open which medium should be chosen for the Enable-Act. When looking for strategies to accomplish this act, the system finds two possibilities. The first is to verbally describe the position of all objects involved; the second prescribes graphics for the same task. Since the MDS for the first strategy is higher than the MDS for the second, the presentation planner chooses the first possibility and verbally informs the user where the code switch is located. The presentation structure of this case is shown in Fig. 8.

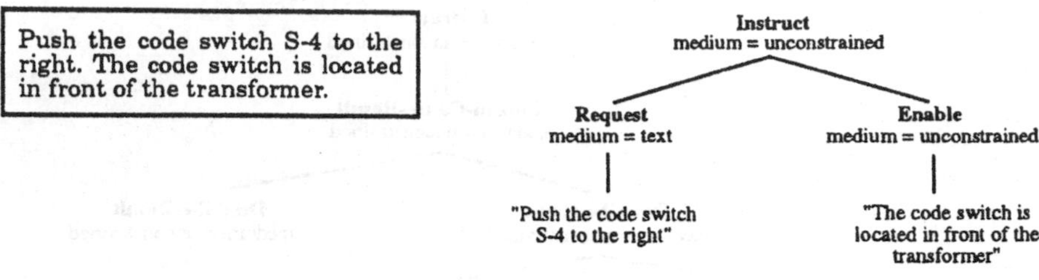

Fig. 8. Preferred medium text.

System run 3: no medium preferences

In a further system run, no specific medium preferences have been indicated. This time, the presentation planner applies possibility A, which is the first strategy that matches the presentation goal. As in the previous system run, the request is conveyed by text. However, since there are no medium preferences, the system follows the selection rule presented in Section 3.1 and uses graphics to describe the spatial location of the switch. As a result, the final presentation consists of a mixture of text and graphics (cf. Fig. 9).

No serial architecture with a total ordering of the components for content selection and content organization would be adequate. Although all system runs serve to accomplish the same instructional goal, the resulting presentation structures differ since they also depend on the medium to be used. Consequently, the system needs information concerning the medium before planning the structure of a presentation. On the other hand, to select a medium the system has to know what to communicate. An essential advantage of our approach is that it allows for more flexibility concerning the timepoint of medium selection. In the extreme case, medium decisions are taken after the complete contents of a presentation are determined. However, it is also possible to select a medium at a very early stage. In this case, the selected medium may influence further content selection

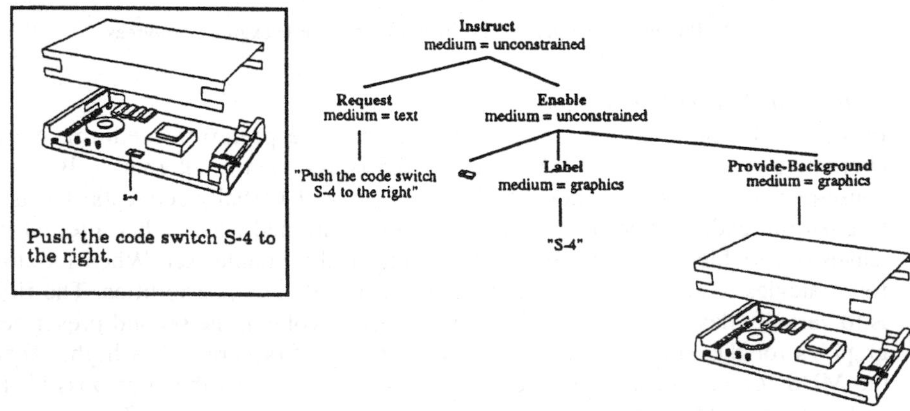

Fig. 9. No medium preferences.

and content organization processes. Despite this flexibility, it may happen that a presentation must be reorganized as in the first example.

4. CONCLUSION

Starting from the insight that multimedia presentations follow similar structuring principles as pure text, we have extended work on text-planning to the broader context of multimedia presentations. We sketched a plan-based approach for the automated synthesis of multimedia presentations. The operators of this planning approach are presentation strategies which refer to both text and picture production. A distinguishing feature of our work is that we use a highly integrated approach for content selection, organization and media selection. A uniform planning formalism facilitates the simultaneous coordination of the central subtasks a multimedia presentation system has to accomplish.

Our approach has been utilized for the implementation of the multimedia presentation system WIP. Depending on the value combination of generation parameters, WIP conveys the same information either with text, graphics, or coherent text-picture combinations.

The design of intelligent multimedia presentation systems is a multidisciplinary endeavor. In particular, this area benefits from research in computer vision and natural language processing. In fact, our work on the design of a multimedia presentation system started with a study of illustrated documents in order to find out how to structure and render a text-picture combination in such a way that an addressee's joint image- and text-understanding processes will eventually lead to the behavior intended by the presenter. As a methodological basis we fell back on well-known concepts from the area of natural language processing like speech acts, rhetorical relations and referring expressions and showed that they take on an extended meaning in the context of multimedia communication.

ACKNOWLEDGEMENTS

The work presented here has been supported by the German Ministry of Research and Technology (BMFT) under grant ITW8901 8. We would like to thank Paul Mc Kevitt and an anonymous reviewer for their helpful comments.

NOTES

[1] This distinction between main and subsidiary acts essentially corresponds to the distinction between *global* and *subsidiary speech acts* in Searle (1980), *main speech acts* and *subordinate speech acts* in van Dijk (1980), *dominierenden Handlungen* and *subsidiären Handlungen* in Brandt *et al.* (1983) and between *nucleus* and *satellites* in RST (Mann and Thompson 1987).

[2] The example is a slightly modified and translated version of instructions for the Philips espresso machine HD 5649.

REFERENCES

André, E. & Rist, T. (1990). Towards a Plan-Based Synthesis of Illustrated Documents. In Proceedings of *The Ninth ECAI*, 25–30. Stockholm. Also as DFKI Research Report RR-90-11.

André, E. & Rist, T. (1993). The Design of Illustrated Documents as a Planning Task. In Maybury, M. (ed.) *Intelligent Multimedia Interfaces*, 94–116. AAAI Press. Also as DFKI Research Report RR-92-45.

André, E. & Rist, T. (1994). Referring to World Objects with Text and Pictures. In Proceedings of *The Fifteenth COLING*, Kyoto, Japan (to appear).

André, E., Finkler, W., Graf, W., Rist, T., Schauder, A. & Wahlster, W. (1993). WIP: The Automatic Synthesis of Multimodal Presentations. In Maybury, M. (ed.) *Intelligent Multimedia Interfaces*, 75–93. AAAI Press. Also as DFKI Research Report RR-92-46.

Appelt, D. & Kronfeld, A. (1987). A Computational Model of Referring. In Proceedings of *The Tenth IJCAI*, 640–647. Milan, Italy.

Arens, Y., Hovy, E. & van Mulken, S. (1993a). Structure and Rules in Automated Multimedia Presentation Planning. In Proceedings of *The Thirteenth IJCAI*, volume 2, 1253–1259. Chambéry, France.

Arens, Y., Hovy, E. & Vossers, M. (1993b). Describing the Presentational Knowledge Underlying Multimedia Instruction Manuals. In Maybury, M. (ed.) *Intelligent Multimedia Interfaces*, 280–306. AAAI Press.

Badler, N., Barsky, B. Zeltzer, D. (eds.) (1991a). *Making Them Move: Mechanics, control, and Animation of Articulated Figures*. Morgan Kaufmann: San Mateo, California.

Badler, N., Webber, B., Kalita, J. & Esakov, J. (1991b). *Animation from Instructions. In Badler* et al, 51–93.

Bandyopadhyay, S. (1990). *Towards an Understanding of Coherence in Multimodal Discourse*. Technical Memo TM-90-01, Deutsches Forschungszentrum für Künstliche Intelligenz (DFKI), Saarbrücken, Germany.

Brandt, M., Koch, W., Motsch, W. & Rosengren, I. (1983). Der Einfluß der kommunikativen Strategie auf die Textstruktur – dargestellt am Beispiel des Geschäftsbriefes. In Rosengren, I. (ed.) *Sprache und Pragmatik Lunder Symposium 1982*, 105–135. Almquist & Wiksell: Stockholm.

Costabile, M. F., Catarci, T. & Levialdi, S. (eds.) (1992). *Advanced Visual Interfaces (Proceedings of AVI '92, Rome, Italy)*. World Scientific Press: Singapore.

Feiner, S. K. & McKeown, K. R. (1991). Automating the Generation of Coordinated Multimedia Explanations. *IEEE Computer* **24**(10): 33–41.

Grice, H. P. (1975). Logic and Conversation. In Cole, P. & Morgan, J. L. (eds.) *Syntax and Semantics: Speech Acts* **3**: 41–58. Academic Press: New York.

Grimes, J. E. (1975). *The Thread of Discourse*. Mouton: The Hague, Paris.

Hirst, G. (1981). *Anaphora in Natural Language Understanding*. Springer: Berlin, Heidelberg.

Hobbs, J. (1978). *Why is a Discourse Coherent?* Technical Report 176, SRI International: Menlo Park, CA.

Houghton, H. A. & Willows, D. M. (1987). *The Psychology of Illustration, Instructional Issues*, volume 2. Springer: New York, Berlin, Heidelberg, London, Paris, Tokyo.

Hovy, E. H. (1988). Planning Coherent Multisentential Text. In Proceedings of *The Twenty-Sixth ACL*, 163–169.

Hunter, B., Crismore, A. & Pearson, P. D. (1987). Visual Displays in Basal Readers and Social Studies Textbooks. In Willows, D. M. & Houghton, H. A. (eds.) *The Psychology of Illustration, Basic Research*, volume 2, 116–135. Springer: New York, Berlin, Heidelberg.

Kjorup, S. (1978). Pictorial Speech Acts. *Erkenntnis* **12**: 55–71.

Levie, W. H. (1987). Research on Pictures: A Guide to the Literature. In Willows, D. M. & Houghton, H. A. (eds.) *The Psychology of Illustration, Basic Research*, volume 1, 1–50. Springer: New York, Berlin, Heidelberg.

Levin, J. R., Anglin, G. J. & Carney, R. N. (1987). On Empirically Validating Functions of Pictures in Prose. In Willows, D. M. & Houghton, H. A. (eds.) *The Psychology of Illustration, Basic Research* **1**: 51–85. Springer: New York, Berlin, Heidelberg.

Mann, W. C. & Thompson, S. A. (1987). *Rhetorical Structure Theory: A Theory of Text Organization.* Report ISI/RS-87-190. Univ. of Southern California, Marina del Rey, CA.
Marks, J. & Reiter, E. (1990). Avoiding Unwanted Conversational Implicatures in Text and Graphics. In Proceedings of AAAI-90, volume 1, 450–456. Boston, MA.
Maybury, M. (ed.) (1993). *Intelligent Multimedia Interfaces.* AAAI Press.
Molitor, S., Ballstaedt, S.-P. & Mandl, H. (1989). Problems in Knowledge Acquisition from text and Pictures. In Mandl, H. & Levin, J. R. (eds.) *Knowledge Acquisition from text and Pictures,* 3–35. North Holland: Amsterdam, New York, Oxford, Tokyo.
Moore, J. D. & Paris, C. L. (1989). Planning Text for Advisory Dialogues. In Proceedings of *The Twenty-Seventh ACL,* 203–211. Vancouver.
Reiter, E. & Dale, R. (1992). A Fast Algorithm for the Generation of Referring Expressions. In Proceedings of *The Fourteenth COLING,* volume 1, 232–238. Nantes, France.
Roth, S. F., Mattis, J. & Mesnard, X. (1991). Graphics and Natural Language as Components of Automatic Explanation. In Sullivan, J. W. & Tyler, S. W. (eds.) *Intelligent User Interfaces,* 207–239. ACM Press: New York, NY.
Schneiderlöchner, F. (1994). *Generierung von Referenzausdrücken in einem multimodalen Diskurs.* Master's thesis, Fachbereich Informatik, Universität des Saarlandes, Saarbrücken, Germany.
Searle, J. R. (1980). *Speech Acts: An Essay in the Philosophy of Language.* Cambridge University Press: Cambridge, England.
Stock, O. & the ALFRESCO Project Team (1993). ALFRESCO: Enjoying the Combination of Natural Language Processing and Hypermedia for Information Exploration. In Maybury, M. (ed.) *Intelligent Multimedia Interfaces,* 197–224. AAAI Press.
van Dijk, T. A. (1980). *Textwissenschaft.* dtv: München.
Wahlster, W., André, E., Graf, W. & Rist, T. (1991). Designing Illustrated Texts: How Language Production is Influenced by Graphics Generation. In Proceedings of *The Fifth EACL,* 8–14. Berlin, Germany.
Wahlster, W., André, E., Finkler, W. Profitlich, H.-J. & Rist, T. (1993). Plan-Based Integration of Natural Language and Graphics Generation. *AI Journal* **63**: 387–427. Also as DFKI Research Report RR-93-02.
Wazinski, P. (1992). Generating Spatial Descriptions for Cross-Modal References. In Proceedings of *The Third Conference on Applied Natural Language Processing,* 56–63. Trento, Italy.
Willows, D. M. & Houghton, H. A. (1987). *The Psychology of Illustration, Basic Research,* volume 1. Springer: New York, Berlin, Heidelberg, London, Paris, Tokyo.
Wilson, M., Sedlock, D., Binot, J.-L. & Falzon, P. (1992). An Architecture For Multimodal Dialogue. In Proceedings of *The Second Vencona Workshop for Multimodal Dialogue.* Vencona, Italy.

Artificial Intelligence Review **9**: 167–188, 1995.

The Design of a Model-Based Multimedia Interaction Manager

YIGAL ARENS and EDUARD HOVY

Information Sciences Institute, of the University of Southern California, 4676 Admiralty Way, Marina del Rey, CA 90292-6995, U.S.A.; e-mail: {arens,hovy}@isi.edu

Abstract. We describe here the conceptual design of *Cicero*, an application-independent human-computer interaction manager that performs run-time media coordination and allocation, so as to adapt dynamically to the presentation context; knows what it is presenting, so as to maintain coherent extended human-machine dialogues; and is plug-in compatible with host information resources such as "briefing associate" workstations, expert systems, databases, etc., as well as with multiple media such as natural language, graphics, etc. The system design calls for two linked reactive planners that coordinate the actions of the system's media and information sources. To enable presentational flexibility, the capabilities of each medium and the nature of the contents of each information source are semantically modeled as Virtual Devices – abstract descriptions of device I/O capabilities – and abstract information types respectively in a single uniform knowledge representation framework. These models facilitate extensibility by supporting the specification of new interaction behaviors and the inclusion of new media and information sources.

Key words: human-computer interaction management, presentation planning, information integration, discourse structure, information-to-medium allocation, Virtual Devices.

1. INTRODUCTION: THE MOTIVATION FOR *CICERO*

As computer systems grow more complicated, system builders and users are faced with an increasing proliferation of media and information resources. A key problem now confronting system builders is to determine in what form to display given information and how to apportion it among available media for optimal communicative effectiveness. Usually, these decisions are made by the system designer during system construction. However, interfaces that dynamically "design" themselves at run-time are in a much better position to respond to ever-changing and hard-to-foresee display demands than interfaces whose design is fixed when the system is built, and this is a key feature of *Cicero*.

1.1. *The Problem: A Proliferation*

Computer users today face an increasingly grave problem: information overload. Current interface hardware and software are capable of providing high quality images, business and other graphics, video, text, sounds, and voice in increasingly many forms and varieties. At the same time, high speed processing and networking are making available an enormous amount of computational power and data that users of computer systems may need to harness, interact with, feed information to and view results from. To work effectively, computer users must make full use of the many available interface modalities to support tasks such as command and control, transportation planning, and health care provision. However, without well-coordinated, nonredundant, and intelligently supportive displays, users may easily be swamped by the immense amounts of information provided.

System builders attempting to address this problem face a related dilemma. They have at their disposal a bewildering choice of input and output media, each with its own behaviors and capabilities. To develop the best possible system, they have to mix and match media to application data types, anticipating in their interface design all the possible configurations of information that may have to be input or displayed. But interface development is already a major component of the cost of software systems: studies have shown that even standard interface technology often comprises over 50% of a system's code. Without fundamental change in how interfaces are designed, incorporating multimedia capabilities will likely increase interface complexity and cost to an extent that would make them prohibitively expensive in any but the most common environments and situations. A way *must* be found to lower the complexity, and hence the cost, of multimedia interfaces.

There is only one long-term answer to this problem of media and information proliferation: an intelligent human-computer Interaction Manager that mediates between application system and information on the one hand and media and the user on the other. Such an Interaction Manager must be able to dynamically plan, present, and integrate information input and output, automatically coming up with the optimum use of media, using principles of good interface design and knowledge of information characteristics and media capabilities. Such an interaction manager removes the burden of low-level interface design from the system builder and supports the user's ongoing interaction. And, if it is properly designed, the interaction manager also allows easy extension to incorporate new media, facilitates easy porting to new application domains, and is tailorable to individual user preferences and capabilities.

1.2. *The Solution: An Interaction Manager as Mediator*

In this paper we outline the structure of *Cicero*, one possible approach to solving the central elements of this problem. Although *Cicero* is not an existing system, portions of it have been studied, designed, and tested as prototypes by the authors and various collaborators. *Cicero* is an Interaction Manager, a tailorable runtime information allocation and integration planner. Given a collection of information that needs to be displayed to the user, the Interaction Manager will automatically construct a coherent and coordinated presentation using a combination of available media. Given the need for input, the Interaction Manager's task is to put up the appropriate media substrates (e.g., maps, text input windows, etc.) and integrate the various actions of the user into a coherent whole. For both input and output, the Interaction Manager will liaise between the domain application system (whether it be an expert system, a database, etc.) and the media supported by the workstation environment.

Cicero is not just another human-computer interface. Rather, it is designed to serve as an interface capability platform onto which different applications and different media can be grafted without altering the basic operation of the system. To achieve this general-purpose ability, the Integration Manager performs its job using a collection of declarative models that embody all knowledge needed to manage interface communication. In particular, it must have access to both generic and specific knowledge about the characteristics of information to be displayed or input, the characteristics of available media, the communicative context, the presenter's (whether human or machine) communicative goals, and the perceiver's goals, interests, abilities and preferences.

The situation is envisioned as follows. On the one hand *Cicero* has the data that needs to be presented (or a description of the type of data that must be input by the user), and on the other a collection of media that may be used, possibly in some combination, for this purpose. Instead of having the match between data and media coded into the interface – the situation one typically finds today – *Cicero* makes the match dynamically. Considering properties of the data, the communicative goals involved, the present interaction in the context of the ongoing dialogue, etc., it obtains properties required from the display. It then proceeds to select media with features that satisfy the display desiderata and to create the content of the display itself.

Figure 1 contains an overall view of *Cicero*'s architecture and major modules. The general architecture of the proposed architecture is described in Section 2. and the central components in Section 3. The general system structure is described in Section 3.1, the semantic models in Section 3.2, the output presentation planners in Section 3.3, and the input information integrator and discourse manager in Section 3.4.

The authors have done substantial theoretical and experimental work on this problem at USC/ISI over the past six years. *Cicero* is based upon work on presentation planning (Arens and Hovy 1990, Arens *et al.* 1993a, b, Hovy and Arens 1990, 1991), the SIMS integrated data and information access system (Arens *et al.* 1993c), the II Integrated Interfaces display system (Arens *et al.* 1988), the Penman natural language and text planning systems (Penman 1988, Hovy 1988), the Loom knowledge representation system (MacGregor 1988), and experience in semantic modeling in numerous projects and domains.

2. ARCHITECTURE

2.1. *The* Cicero *Approach*

When constructing complex software environments, system builders usually have to link together pre-built software modules, each with its own I/O, data requirements, and view of the world. Too often modules provide no support for the

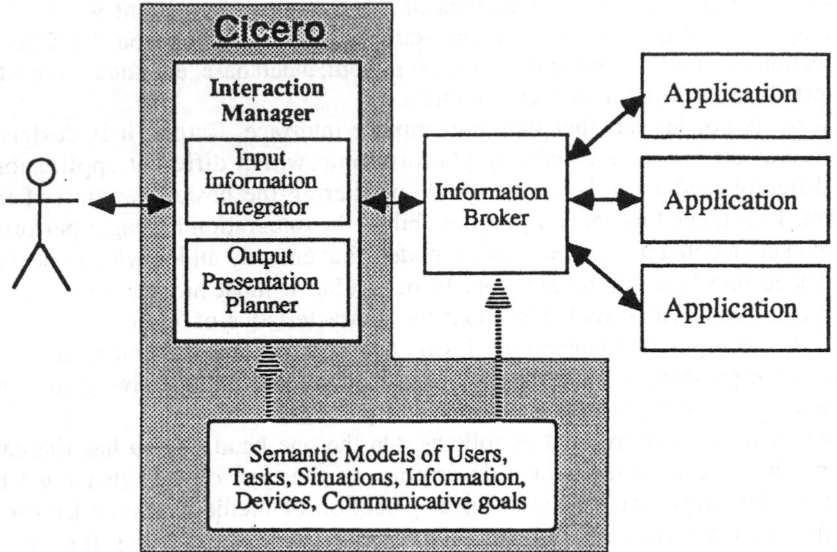

Fig. 1. Overall view of *Cicero* architecture and major modules.

linking, making interfacing between the systems daunting and time-consuming: data known to one system must be retyped to another; the output of one system almost matches the input to the next, but must be filtered or edited. This problem is especially pronounced when the system builder wants to attach pre-built interface media to the main application system.

This problem exists because, as modules are built or brought into an environment, they introduce functionalities that are not always perfectly defined in terms of shared abstractions between the various developers. While it is possible in principle to build extremely well-integrated custom systems under a single abstraction of the users and their tasks, such systems are built at great expense and the shared abstraction breaks down as soon as a user with similar interests but a different perspective needs to access the data or functionality of the system. We cannot avoid the fact that systems come with boundaries. If we artfully design them, some users can live entirely within those boundaries. However, sooner or later someone who does not fit the mold of intended users will come along and the integration of components will break down.

In *Cicero*, we overcome this problem by using an architecture that embodies a single high-level generic framework in which the information relevant to the various modules and data resources can be homogenized and integrated effectively in a single set of abstractions. Such a homogeneous framework not only enables a uniform interface between all modules, it allows new modules to be added with minimum overhead and become immediately useful to the system and the interface. Thus we are not interested in building yet another human-computer interface. What we strive for is a generic interaction platform that can be tailored as needed to be used over and over again in new environments. This platform includes two types of components: powerful interaction modules and an architecture that supports them.

In early recognition of the need for a single framework to embed multiple components to form a functioning system, the ABE system was developed some time ago. ABE (Erman *et al.* 1987) was a gallant attempt that fell short because it did not fully take into account the semantics of the intermodule and user-system communication, just the syntax. Since it contained no common underlying ontological (model-based) definitions of domain knowledge and processing plans and methods, individual modules had no way of using common knowledge effectively or of making their results known in general – they had to agree with each other module that used their output on the meaning of each term employed in the output, an expensive design. For the system to be extensible, multi-purpose, and able to support a powerful interface, the architecture must capture the functional rationale of each module in a semantic goal/plan language that is interpretable by all other pertinent modules, including the interaction manager.

The *Cicero* architecture embodies, at its core, one overall semantic network that organizes a set of semantic models, each of which captures the abstractions characterizing the nature and functionality of a particular module. For each type of module – a database, the application system, a User Model, a medium such as a natural language generator, etc. – a taxonomy of high-level concepts that define its *generic* nature, operation, and capabilities must be created. Tools are to be provided for characterizing the nature of any specific database or medium driver in terms of these generic models. Using these abstractions, the operation of *Cicero*'s central interaction modules – the two linked presentation planners (Section 3.3) and the information integrator (Section 3.4) – is defined the presentation plans and heuristic constraint matching rules.

The set of generic models, organized under *Cicero*'s high-level taxonomy, must be represented in a powerful knowledge representation system. In our prototypes we have chosen Loom (MacGregor 1988) for this purpose. The models themselves are discussed in Section 3.2. Whatever specific details of any model may be, once its capabilities are defined in terms of the appropriate generic abstractions, it can be used effectively in *Cicero*'s management of the human-computer interaction.

For example, assume the user wants to input a location in the world. Assume he or she has the choice in the current dialogue of pointing on a map displayed on a touch-sensitive screen or typing in the coordinates. Unless the map displayed is of very fine scale, the generic map medium model characteristics of the current map display will include the value *low* for the feature *granularity*. Coordinates, on the other hand, are defined in the natural language medium model as having the value *high* for *granularity*. The input coordinator module will accept either input provided by the user, and annotate it with the values obtained from the medium model he or she used (in this case, the appropriate *granularity*). This information may then influence how subsequent dialogue is managed in the next interaction (in the case of *low granularity*, the interaction manager may spawn a subgoal to request more specific details of the *location*). Generic values will be defined in each semantic model and used in the information integrator, the presentation planner, etc. Particular combinations of the generic values, as they describe each particular module in the current incarnation of *Cicero*, will be specified by the system builder at the time of adding the module to *Cicero*, using the specification tools provided.

2.2. *Benefits of the Architecture*

Building *Cicero* around this model-based architecture provides two important immediate benefits: extensibility and portability. The semantic models support extensibility as follows. Once a generic model of a type of module – say, a database – has been built, the other modules of the system can base their decisions on the descriptions contained in the model. For example, a typical presentation planner plan stipulates that when information carries the value *high* for the feature *urgency*, it should be presented on a medium whose model contains the characteristic *high* for the feature *noticeability* (such as a speech synthesizer or a flashing icon). Whenever a new medium is added to the system, once its specific characteristics have been defined in terms of the appropriate generic model, all the system's other modules will immediately be able to make use of it.

The characteristics of various media must be represented in a class of models which we called *Virtual Devices* in a recent study (ISAT 1991). A Virtual Device is a model of a particular I/O functionality that may be realized by numerous different combinations of hardware and/or software. For example, the 2-dimensional pointing device (a Virtual Device) may be realized by the following concrete devices: the mouse, the touchscreen, and the light pen. Of course, not all concrete devices may conform identically to the specifications of the Virtual Device; in which case their differences can be noted in terms of the (standardized) terms of the Virtual Device. Also, Virtual Devices may be underspecified, in which case concrete devices will display significant differences (during their design and use), possibly causing a revision of the Virtual Device specification toward greater precision.

Note that the existence of these common underlying definitional models does not mean that their use is mandatory for each module internally. Module designers remain free to use their own internal working knowledge and structures, as long as they produce results that are well-defined with respect to the shared underlying model. The powerful inferential capabilities that the knowledge representation system offers will be used to enforce the syntactic and semantic well-formedness of the module definitions and serve as a consistency check on the operation of each module.

With respect to portability, the same modeling philosophy applies. Once generic models are built of tasks, information types, and communicative goals and dialogue structures, a new application domain can be handled by defining its data types in terms of the generic information model. A new application can be handled by defining its particular task structure in terms of *Cicero*'s task model and by defining the kinds of interactional paradigms required in terms of *Cicero*'s dialogue model.

3. COMPONENTS OF THE INTERACTION MANAGER

An interaction manager that (a) dynamically plans and coordinates the operation of the media and information resources at hand, (b) understands enough about the domain and the discourse to maintain an extended dialogue, and (c) supports plug-in compatibility, necessarily involves numerous components. This section describes the core aspects of the *Cicero* system.

3.1. *Overview*

As explained in Section 2, the architecture of *Cicero* makes the details of software and hardware modules transparent to the system builder by representing in a set of underlying generic models all aspects of each module and task, and marking which aspects are salient and which are not for each particular module. In our prototype systems we have chosen the knowledge representation language Loom for representing the common underlying models. These models contain definitions of the types of module functionality, including the types of domain knowledge and data, the types of communication among modules and between the module and the user, and the display capabilities of the media modules. Such a set of central models enables the definition of the application domain and the available information resources of the underlying information system in terms of the user's conceptualizations, facilitating effective user interaction. Our previous work as identified the need for five distinct models, all taxonomized under a single high-level set of semantic terms:

- media characteristics and capabilities;
- information characteristics;
- application tasks and interlocutor goals;
- communicative goals and discourse structure;
- user's capabilities and preferences.

Employing these models are the system's two central processing modules:

- two linked Presentation Planners, which handle output;
- the Information Integrator, which handles input.

These two modules share access to the:

- Discourse Manager, whose function it is to maintain the discourse structure and to ensure coherent interaction with the user.

Peripheral to the run-time interaction management, but central to the addition of new modules or information to the system, are a set of acquisition tools, including:

- user model acquisition tool;
- media modeling tool;
- task structure and domain information modeling tool.

A more detailed picture of the architecture of *Cicero* is given in Figure 2 (the Information Broker of Figure 1 is used only when more than one application is present; otherwise, the single application links directly to *Cicero* through the task and information models). Full arrows indicate information flow and shaded arrows, data dependencies. The remainder of Section 3 describes these components in more detail.

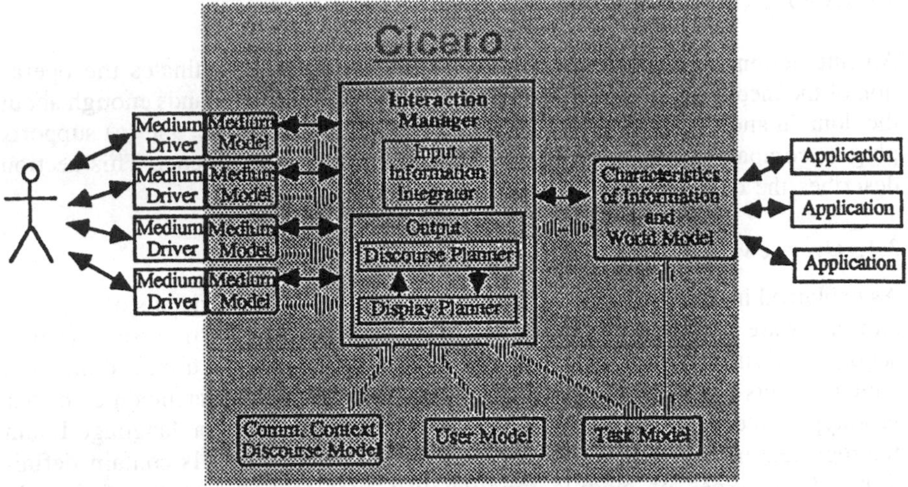

Fig. 2. Architecture and modules of *Cicero*.

3.2. *Models*

This section briefly describes the five types of models required to achieve effective dynamic human-computer interface management. The details of these models derive from a significant amount of study and experimentation by the authors and others. References are provided below as appropriate.

3.2.1. *Model of Media Characteristics*

To ensure generality and to facilitate the plug-in-compatibility of new media, semantic models of generic media types, capabilities, requirements, etc., must be built. These generic models, the Virtual Devices, will then support the specialized definition of any particular individual media driver as an independent agent. The two planners employ the generic models to reason about the display characteristics of each medium, judging potential applicability, suitability for display, etc.

A Virtual Device is a model of a particular I/O functionality that may be realized by numerous very different combinations of hardware and/or software. This model contains all relevant parameters defining the class of devices that perform the indicated function. Our preliminary studies indicate that each Virtual Device should contain, in addition to parameters for functionality, specifications and evaluation measures for (at least) the following:

- Hardware: limits of resolution; latency; device tolerances; etc.
- Software: data accuracy; data rate; etc.
- Human (cognitive): short-term memory requirements; communication protocol (language, icons, special terminology); etc.
- Human (physical): muscle groups and actions required; associated fatigue factors; etc.

- Usage: techniques of use (traditional menu vs. pie-chart menu, etc.); performance characteristics; etc.

Any actual device – that is, a concrete instantiation of the Virtual Device – should be measured using the standards and metrics specified in the Virtual Device parameter slots.

The resulting Virtual Device can be seen as an abstract model of a class of devices that conform to its specifications, or as an ideal for such concrete instances to strive towards. Since specialized subgroups of Virtual Devices will be formed fairly rapidly, it will be possible to create a taxonomy of Virtual Devices, an organization of increasingly specialized specifications for media that provide an arbitrarily specific but still standardized language with which to describe and compare different media. Associated taxonomies, of functions, techniques of use, human and task characteristics, etc., can also be formed. These Virtual Devices form the models used by Intelligent Agents and interface construction tools, somewhat along the lines described in (Szekely *et al.* 1993).

In (Arens *et al.* 1993a) we develop an extensive set of terms that describe some of the media characteristics most important in presentation planning and coordination. Characteristics will be defined in Virtual Devices using the following terms:

- **medium:** a single mechanism by which to express information.
- **exhibit:** a complex exhibit is a collection, or composition, of several simple exhibits. A simple exhibit is what is produced by one invocation of one medium.
- **substrate:** the background to a simple exhibit that establishes the physical or temporal location, and often the semantic context, in which new information is to be interpreted.
- **information carrier:** that part of the simple exhibit which, to the consumer, communicates the principal piece of information requested or relevant in the current communicative context.
- **carried item:** the piece of information represented by the carrier; the "denotation" of the carrier.
- **channel:** an independent dimension of variation of a particular information carrier in a particular substrate.
- **internal semantic system:** some information carriers exhibit an internal structure that can be assigned a "real-world" denotation, enabling them subsequently to be used as substrates against which other carriers can acquire information by virtue of being interpreted within the substrate.

In addition to the internal semantics listed above, media differ in a number of other ways which can be exploited by a presenter to communicate effectively and efficiently. These characteristics include:

- **carrier dimension:** the number of dimensions required to exhibit the information.
- **internal semantic dimension:** the number of dimensions in the internal semantic system of the carrier or substrate.
- **temporal endurance:** whether the exhibit varies during the presentation.

- **granularity:** whether arbitrarily small variations along any dimension of presentation having meaning.
- **medium type:** the type of medium necessary for presenting the created exhibit.
- **default detectability:** how intrusive to the consumer the exhibit will be.
- **baggage:** a gross measure of the amount of extra information a consumer must process in order to become familiar enough with the substrate to correctly interpret a carrier.

3.2.2. *Model of Characteristics of Information to be Displayed or Input*
We list here a few items from the vocabulary of presentation-related characteristics of information as required for semantic models that support *Cicero*'s presentation planning and information integration, as identified in (Arens *et al.* 1993a, Burger and Marshall 1993). Broadly speaking, three subcases must be considered when choosing a presentation for an item of information: intrinsic properties of the specific item; properties associated with the class to which the item belongs; and properties of the collection of items that will eventually be presented, and of which the current item is a member.

- **dimensionality:** how items of information can be decomposed into simpler items.
- **transience:** whether the information expresses some currently changing state or not.
- **urgency:** how urgently the information must be communicated.
- **order:** a property of a collection of items all displayed together as a group.
- **density:** whether an arbitrarily small change of the carrier on the substrate carries meaningful information or not.
- **naming function:** the role information plays relative to other information present.
- **volume:** the amount of information to be presented.

3.2.3. *Model of Application Task and Interlocutors' Goals*
Particularly in the field of natural language research, there has been much work identifying and classifying the possible goals of a producer of an utterance – work which can quite easily be applied to multimedia presentations in general.

Automated text generators, when possessing a rich grammar and lexicon, typically require several producer-related aspects to specify their parameters fully. For example, the PAULINE generator (Hovy 1988) produced numerous variations from the same underlying representation depending on its input parameters, which included the following presenter-oriented features:

Producer's goals with respect to perceiver: These goals all address some aspect of the perceiver's mental knowledge or state, and include:

- **affect perceiver's knowledge:** takes such values as *teach, inform, and confuse.*
- **alter perceiver's goals:** these goals cover warnings, orders, etc.
- **affect perceiver's opinions of topic:** values include *switch, reinforce.*
- **involve perceiver in the conversation:** *involve, repel.*
- **affect perceiver's emotional state** (not planned for *Cicero*): of the hundreds of possibilities we list simply *anger, cheer up, calm.*

Producer's goals with respect to the producer-perceiver relationship: These address both producer and perceiver, for example:

- **affect perceiver's emotion toward producer:** values include *respect, like, dislike.*
- **alter relative status:** formality of address forms in certain languages.
- **alter interpersonal distance:** values such as *intimate, close, distant.*

For our purposes, we have chosen to borrow and adapt a partial classification of a producer's communicative goals from existing work on Speech Acts. More details are provided in (Arens *et al.* 1993b).

3.2.4. *Model of Discourse and Communicative Context*

The discourse structure purposes and relations are taken from our work (Hovy 1988, Hovy *et al.* 1992) operationalizing and extending the relations of Rhetorical Structure Theory (Mann and Thompson 1988), which holds that textual discourses are coherent only if adjacent segments are related according to the constraints imposed by a small set of relations such as *Purpose* (signaled in text by "in order to" or "so that"), *Sequence* (signaled by "then", "next", etc.), *Solutionhood* (no English cue phrase), and so on. We provided a taxonomy of approximately 130 relations in (Hovy *et al.* 1992). In the work planned here, however, the relations will be used to indicate communicative constraints among portions of the discourse, as well as necessarily linguistic realizations (if any) of such constraints.

3.2.5. *Model of User's Goals, Interests, Abilities and Preferences*

Our work has only begun to address this issue. Existing research provides considerable material with a bearing on the topic, including especially the work in Cognitive Psychology on issues of human perception which influence the appropriateness of media choices for presentation of certain types of data. A survey and discussion of these results is presented in (Vossers 1991). The User Modeling community describes the kinds of user models appropriate for computational language generation and parsing. The PAULINE text generator (Hovy 1988) contains several categories of characteristics of the perceiver, including:

- **presentation display preferences:** settings for presentation planner rule weights
- **knowledge of the topic:** *expert, student, novice*
- **language ability:** *high, low*
- **interest in the topic:** *high, low*
- **opinions of the topic:** *good, neutral, bad.*

3.3. *Output: Presentation Planning and Design*

3.3.1. *Two Linked Reactive Planners Required*

As illustrated in (Hovy and Arens 1993), the planning of multimedia displays requires two distinct reactive planners whose actions are interleaved: one to plan the underlying discourse structure (that is, to order and interrelate the information to be presented) and the other to allocate the media (that is, to delimit the portions to be displayed by each individual medium). The former process has been the topic of several studies in the area of automated text planning, in which the traditional methods of constructing tree-like plans in deliberative, top-down, planning mode have been applied with varying amounts of success (see the discussions of COMET and WIP in Section 4). The latter process remains less amenable to the top-down planning approach, which is why we propose a reactive planner.

Given the conceptual similarity of the task to that of automated text generation, one might consider generalizing a text planner that already performs the tasks of information selection and organization to include a process that allocates the information to specific media for presentation. We demonstrated the possibility of doing this for the natural language medium alone in (Hovy and Arens 1991). Unfortunately, as the selection of media becomes larger and the information to be displayed more flexible, a more sophisticated approach is needed. The combinatorial possibilities inherent in such a diverse rule set of plan library make the appealing straightforward top-down planning approach of text planning infeasible. We found it necessary, in prototype systems, to represent and reason with the underlying structure of the communication as a distinct entity in its own right. The different communicative functions that different portions of the information presented play – they may provide core information, or simply support, elaborate upon, or contrast with other portions, etc. – must be known to the presentation planner if it is to understand the perceiver's responses adequately and is to respond to them coherently. The logical structure of the communication we call the *Discourse Structure*. While a top-down planning system has been shown in text planning work to be capable of constructing a discourse structure of the required type, down to the level of specificity at which the information-to-medium allocation rules can operate, the production of coherent, pleasing, and effective presentations may require significant reorganizations of the discourse structure, as described in the example below. Therefore a second, distinct, planning process is needed; it constructs out of the initial discourse structure a separate, generally not isomorphic, *Presentation Structure*. As we have shown, the medium allocation planner has a more bottom-up nature. The sophisticated presentation planning system WIP (Wahlster *et al.* 1991), for example, contains both a top-down and a bottom-up phase, although it does not create a distinct presentation structure. In our formulation, the discourse structure simply provides the basic organization of the information to be presented. It is neutral with respect to the media and layout of the eventual presentation. As described in Section 3.2.4, the Discourse and Presentation structures employ relations form operationalized Rhetorical Structure Theory to ensure coherence of the discourse.

By applying its media allocation rules, the presentation planner transforms the discourse structure into a presentation structure. Once the presentation structure is complete, each presentation segment is sent to the appropriate medium generator, whose results are then composed by the layout specialist and presented on the screen.

However, even this mixed top-down and bottom-up planning paradigm is not adequate for the task. Consider first the operation of the bottom-up media allocation planner: at some point, its rules may call for it to arrange material from two separate portions of the discourse structure to be presented in a single display (for an example see (Arens *et al.* 1993b)). In order to signal to the perceiver what is going on, however, the display must include a message, possibly a line of text, explaining that due to the basic similarity of the material two separate sets of information are shown in the same display. This may happen, for example, when the display planner recognizes that it needs to display two tables to summarize separate subsets of information requested by the user. It may then create a new window to place those tables in, but it has to add an explanatory caption that will identify the window and its contents. Whose function is it to plan what to say as the explanation and where to link it in the discourse structure? Surely not the media allocation planner's, for it has no control over what content is to appear. In this circumstance, the media allocation planner properly must activate the content planner with the goal to plan an appropriate explanatory message. As a result, the content planner will have to alter the discourse structure by inserting the new message. The additional content may very well require changes to previously existing portions of the discourse structure – even portions for which a presentation structure has already successfully been created.

Next, consider the operation of the content planner. At some point, its rules may call for optional additional material that expands some already established idea. Whether or not to include this material may very well depend on how able the display medium chosen to display the original idea is to include additional material (we have all at some point "stuck a bit more in because it will fit so nicely"). But whose task is it to determine which medium to use? Certainly not the content planner's. Therefore, in this circumstance, the content planner properly must activate the media allocation planner with the goal to find an appropriate medium. As a result, both discourse and presentation structures will be altered.

It is clear that neither planner can proceed in simple deliberative fashion: each planner's core structure is changing as a result of the operation of the other planner. What is required are two reactive planners similar to the planner embodied in the PENGI system (Agre and Chapman 1987), that contain numerous rules that fire when they match the context and produce result in the next incremental step of behavior, without overmuch concern for long-range planning.

3.3.2. Cicero's *Presentation Planners*

It is difficult to imagine a multimedia presentation planning system creating a realistically flexible type of presentation without engaging in the kind of dialogue described above. As long as a modularization of expertise exists – that is to say, as long as distinct modules have access to functionally distinct sets of rules or collections of data – the modules are going to have to be able to plan partially, ask each other for information, and replan or continue planning further steps.

The optimal modularization of the presentation planning process is a deep question that, we believe, can be fully answered only when sufficiently sophisticated working systems are built. Based on our experiments with prototype systems, *Cicero* should contain two linked reactive planners that perform run-time discourse construction and medium allocation planning, as outlined and tested in (Arens *et al.* 1993b, Hovy and Arens 1993), as follows:

1. Content planning process (Planner 1)
Operators construct the Discourse Structure from data elements and their inter-relationships. Planning decisions are based upon:
- presenter's communicative goal(s),
- characteristics of data available for presentation,
- perceiver's knowledge, goals, interests, etc.

2. Media display planning process (Planner 2)
Operators construct the Presentation Structure out of information in the Discourse Structure. Planning decisions are based upon:
- information currently displayed: data elements (from Discourse Structure),
- displayed configurations of data elements as larger identifiable units (from Presentation Structure),
- characteristics of media currently employed (on screen, etc.),
- characteristics of other media available at hand.

To illustrate the working of the Presentation Planners and Information Integrator – the central processing modules of *Cicero* – we include a worked example from the domain of Swiss cheese sales as described in (Arens *et al.* 1993b). For the years 1988 and 1989, the database contains the following (numbers represent Kilotons of cheese sold in the region and year):

Ident	Region	1988	1989
A.	East Europe	4.3	5.6
B.	Switzerland	13.1	14.0
C.	Outside Europe	5.3	5.5
D.	West Europe	15.7	17.2

Addressing the Information Integrator, the user types in (or menus) the following request, which is integrated into the Discourse Structure (see Section 3.3.1) as a presentation goal (phrased here in English):

display the top three sales regions in 1988 and 1989

Immediately after receiving the new communication goal, the Information Integrator activates Planner 1. Accessing the semantic model describing the domain information, Planner 1 posts a query to the application system (in this simple example, a database) to retrieve the appropriate information for each year. Receiving this information, Planner 1 builds the discourse structure in Figure 3 (the relations *Join* and *TemporalSequence* are interclausal relations from Rhetorical Structure Theory).

Its task completed (for now), Planner 1 hands off the discourse structure to

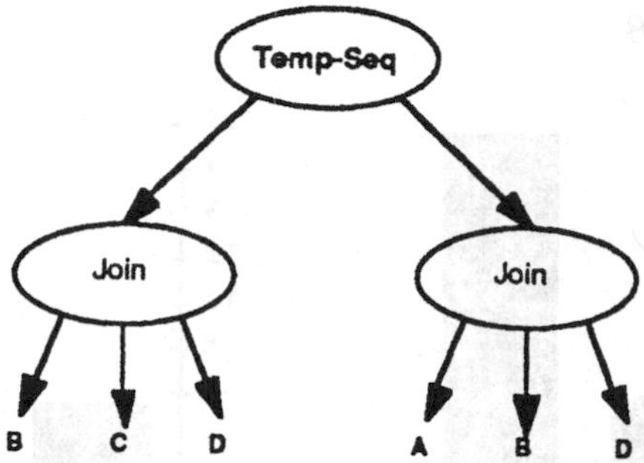

Fig. 3. Discourse structure built by Planner 1.

the media allocation planner (Planner 2). This planner traverses the structure bottom-up and left-to-right in order to create the presentation structure defined earlier. It uses rules such as

```
;;; Display data under Elaboration or Contrast relations
;;; using same medium if information is of same type,
;;; merging leaf nodes from both subtrees.  Apply separately
;;; to each leaf node.

R2: IF AND (OR (relation == ELABORATION)
               (relation == CONTRAST))
          (type (contents (leaf1)) == type (contents (leaf2)))
          (medium (leaf1) == medium (leaf2))
    THEN (create presentation-node
              loc: current-relation-node
              contents: (leaf1 leaf2)
              medium: medium (leaf1))
```

to merge together presentation segments (if possible) and to assign appropriate presentation media. Individually, the two segments of the discourse structure would give rise to the two bar charts shown in Figure 4.

Upon attempting to merge the two presentation segments for years 1988 and 189, Planner 2 is blocked; the relevant merging rule finds insufficient data (visually expressed in Figure 5). This rule is indexed by numerical data of this form linked by the relation TemporalSequence.

What to do? Either Planner 2 has to give up and produce two separate bar charts, or – if Planner 1 is reactive – it can simply pass the discourse structure back to Planner 1 with a characterization of the problem: Insufficient information; request for field A for 1988 and field C for 1989.

Planner 1 obligingly retrieves and adds the information requested to the discourse structure, which now resembles Figure 3 with an extra leaf node for each year. But from the retrieval Planner 1 has learned something of potential interest: there are no other possibilities; the four fields A, B, C, and D together fully cover the range of sales regions for each year. Whether or not this information could be relevant for the presentation is not within the expertise of Planner

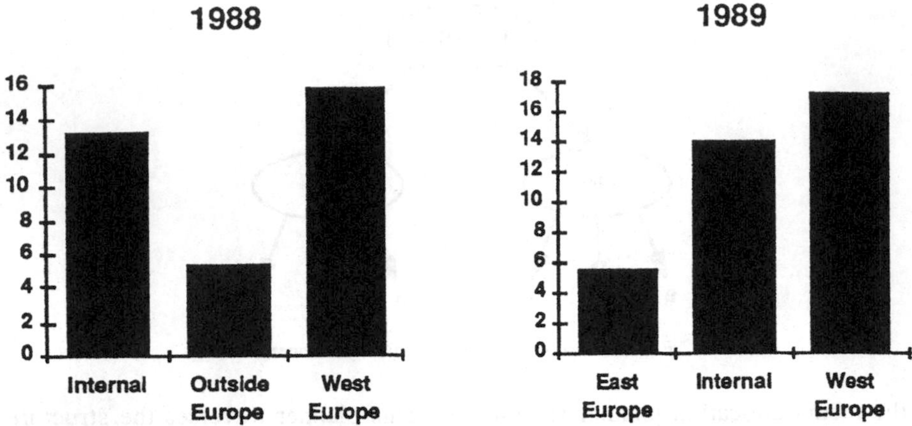

Fig. 4. Bar charts if generated individually from discourse structure.

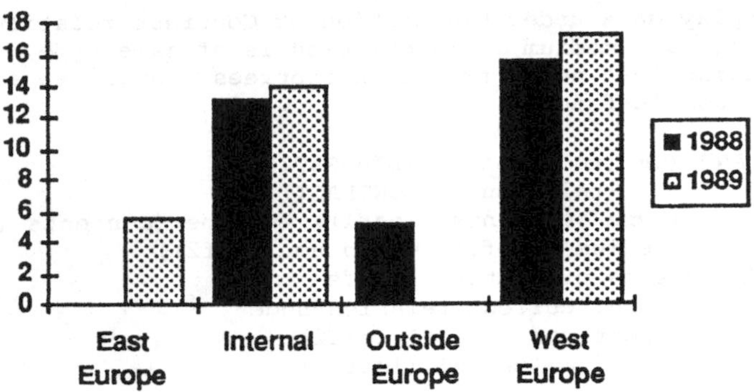

Fig. 5. Bar charts if generated individually from discourse structure.

1 (nor should it be). Therefore either it can ignore this information or – if Planner 2 is reactive – it can inquire whether this information of possible use to Planner 2. (Simply adding this information to the discourse structure at this point is not appropriate because that would indicate that this information *must* be expressed.)

By matching against its rule collection, Planner 2 determines that, indeed, the full coverage of the range of sales regions – in fact, the full coverage of *any* range – is potentially very useful, because several rules use this information to initiate the construction of pie charts. Planner 2 therefore signals the desirability of this information to Planner 1.

Accordingly, Planner 1 adds the coverage information to the discourse structure and Planner 2 takes over. After determining that, for each year individually, both bar chart and pie chart are possible media, the planner seeks to merge the two presentation segments. Finding all the relevant information present, the bar chart merging rule succeeds, and the final presentation resembles Figure 5 with all columns properly filled.

Another presentation alternative remains: although the two pie charts cannot be merged, they can be produced side by side, as illustrated in Figure 6.

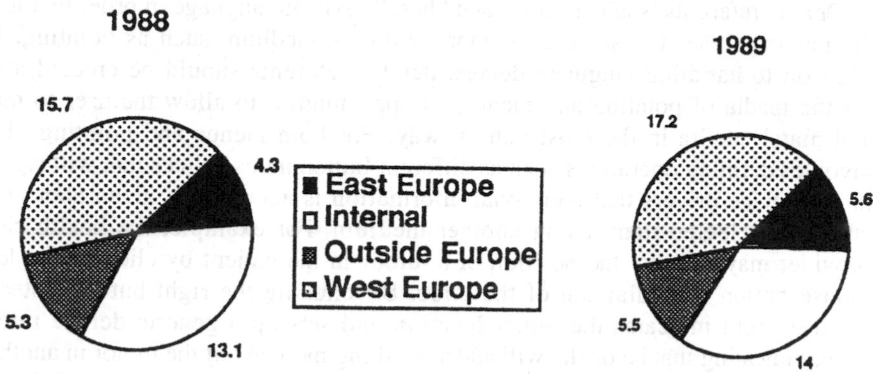

Fig. 6. Alternative final presentation, with complete data.

3.4. *Input: Information Integration*

Just as for its output facilities, *Cicero*'s input facilities consist of modules that operate on and with the set of generic and specific semantic models. Three types of module are required to handle input: the input media themselves (with associated models); the information integrator module; and the input half of the discourse manager.

3.4.1. *Input Media*

Interaction Managers generally have to handle input from the following types of media:

- menus,
- restricted natural language type-in,
- speech,
- a 2-dimensional pointing device such as a touchscreen or mouse.

Saying that *Cicero* "handles" such media means that generic Virtual Device models must be created for them. Once the Virtual Devices are defined, specific media drivers must be developed and the appropriate specific device models for them must be created and linked to the Virtual Device models. Software transducers must be written to convert the output from each device driver to the standard homogeneous knowledge representation format, as outlined in Section 2.

3.4.2. *Information Integrator*

The core problem facing multimedia input in an interaction manager such as *Cicero* is the problem of integrating information from different media. For example, when a health care provider touches a specific field of a displayed table and types in the command "*change this to 23.4 mg*", the system must interpret the touched field as a particular data cell and then integrate the logical address of the cell with the deictic referent "this", in order to produce the user's complete disambiguated command.

Deictic referents (such as "this" and "here") exist in language in order to allow the language user to use another, more suitable, medium, such as pointing. In addition to handling language deixes, deictic referents should be created also for the media of pointing and menus, as opportunities to allow the user to mix and match media in the most natural way. For both menus and pointing, this involves defining operations such as different button mouse clicks that will signal to the device drivers that additional information is about to be given about the currently selected item, using another medium. For example, the health care provider may indicate the position of a tumor in the patient by clicking the left mouse button on a diagram of the torso. By clicking the right button instead, the user both indicates the tumor location and sets up a generic deictic reference, indicating that he or she will add something more about the tumor in another medium, such as typing. On encountering such a deictic referent, *Cicero*'s information integrator must inspect the semantic types of all the most recent inputs from all media, and employ a set of generic and/or domain-specific concept matching heuristics to infer how to resolve the deixis. If, to continue the example, the health care provider also typed in "*below the pancreas*" after performing the right button click, *Cicero*'s information integrator must then link up the locational information of the pointing gesture (defined by its nature to be of type *location* in the generic information model) with the English phrase (which is also interpreted as a *location*, since this is the definition of the preposition "below"), to create an enhanced output representation containing both pieces of information.

As shown in research on the CUBRICON system (Neal *et al.* 1990), deictic reference falls into three classes:

- the deictic gesture/word accurately indicates the intended object;
- the gesture/word indicates more objects than were intended, but includes the intended object;
- the gesture/word misses the intended object altogether.

According to Neal *et al.*, the first type is generally problem-free. The second type can generally be disambiguated by domain-independent heuristics (such as the rule used in the example above, that deictically signaled information of the same conceptual type belongs together). Creating such domain-independent heuristics to effect information integration is not difficult, since the intended referent is among the set indicated. Unfortunately, such heuristics are often of no use when the intended object is missing altogether. In this case, the integrator has to fall back to discourse knowledge.

As described in Section 3.3, one of the two linked planners creates the Discourse Structure, a tree-like structure that represents the organization and contents of the interaction at the current time. Every time the system is provided more material to present, the discourse structure is extended, using appropriate semantic and rhetorical relations, to link the new material coherently to previous displays. When the medium is text, these relations give rise to such conjunctive cue words and phrases as "in order to", "because", "then", and "unless".

The Discourse Structure has another function as well: it supports the disambiguation of unmatched deictic referents. By providing the context of the current user input – all the previous interactions, structured into a tree so as to show their interrelationships – the discourse structure contains a record of every possible referent so far encountered in the dialogue, ordered by importance and recency. The information integrator will search this structure in ever-widening contexts until it finds one or more referents that satisfy its heuristics, or until it reaches a threshold distance after which *Cicero* should simply signal that the referent is not understood.

In order to maintain the up-to-date status of the Discourse Structure, every user input must be added to the appropriate leaf of the Structure once it has been fully interpreted. This updating will be performed by the Input Manager of the discourse management module. Although the automated parsing of discourse is a very difficult unsolved problem in general (see, for example (Cohen *et al.* 1990)), the domains typically addressed are structured enough to support high-level structures called scripts (Schank and Abelson 1977), which provide possible attachment points and legal dialogue moves for the user's inputs. An analysis of typical user tasks in each domain must be performed to identify the appropriate scripts, which must then be coded into *Cicero*'s semantic model of the application tasks.

4. COMPARISON TO SIMILAR SYSTEMS

Cicero embodies a general and plug-in extensible solution to the problem of managing presentations by integrating and allocating information to a collection of available media. This involves explicitly representing the capabilities and characteristics of available media, the information to be presented, users' communicative abilities, needs and preferences, and the system's communicative goals.

An extensive survey (see Vossers 1992) of relevant literature in a variety of fields, including book design and graphic illustration, psychology, and cognitive science conducted at USC/ISI underscores how hard it is to describe rules that govern good presentations, but establishes that people do follow rules when choosing media to create communications. Useful results exist which can be formalized and incorporated into a computational system. We describe a powerful notation for representing the rules and numerous example rules in (Arens *et al.* 1992, Vossers 1992). This work builds upon our previous experience in the Navy Briefing Workstation II (Arens *et al.* 1988, Arens *et al.* 1991), and upon other recent work in multimedia interfaces that provides promising steps toward a more formal and computational theory. (Mackinlay 1986a) described the automatic generation of a variety of tables and charts; (Feiner 1991, Wahlster *et al.* 1991, Neal *et al.* 1990, Burger and Marshall 1991) and several others illustrate various aspects of the processing and knowledge required to automate more general multimedia computer presentation design.

Work on automatic presentation is evolving along two distinct lines: systems dealing only with graphics (APT (Mackinley 1986b), BOX, SAGE), and systems dealing with a combination of natural language and line drawings (II, COMET (Feiner and McKeown 1990), WIP (Wahlster *et al.* 1991). Systems of the first type concentration entirely (or primarily) on one medium of presentation, and hence do not develop generic models of media capabilities. As discussed in (ISAT 1991), however, generic models (called there Virtual Devices) are necessary to ensure the plug-in compatibility of new media. On the other hand, though systems of the second type employ more than one medium for presentation, they currently pay little attention to the generality of their method of selecting an appropriate medium; neither the static rules of II, nor the limited backtracking in the presentation structure of COMET, nor the library of medium-specific text/presentation plans of WIP are general enough to support portability of the systems to a new domain or presentation environment without a great deal of redesign and new development. Our approach of creating semantic models for all the relevant aspects of the multimedia dialogue greatly eases the system's portability to new domains and the inclusion of new media with a minimum of additional effort, since nothing in the presentation designer or media or information agents need be altered; all that must be updated resides in declarative models.

With regard to user interface management systems such as UIDE (Foley *et al.* 1991), HUMANOID (Luo *et al.* 1993, Szekely *et al.* 1993), and MIKE (Olsen 1986), *Cicero* complements them. These types of systems focus on assisting the system designer to construct an appropriate interface at design time (addressing such tasks as manually selecting and specifying which media to use for what information, how to lay out the screen, how to configure the media, etc.). *Cicero*'s presentation manager concentrates on only some of these tasks, but performs them automatically at run-time (once the appropriate models and intelligent agents are defined), providing much greater adaptability to the presentation circumstances.

The Integrated Interfaces system II provided an early practical demonstration of the feasibility of an integrated multimedia interface with dynamic presentations. It developed an interface that provided for multiple integrated modalities of communication, was sensitive to the properties of the data being displayed, and was modifiable to suit user preferences. A demonstration system in the domain of naval situation briefings was built and generated considerable enthusiasm among naval officers who currently perform a similar task manually. The work on II forms, in part, a basis for the design of *Cicero*.

5. CONCLUSION

As computer systems grow more complicated, system builders and users are faced with an increasing proliferation of media and information resources. A key problem now confronting system builders is to determine in what form to display given information and how to apportion it among available media for optimal communicative effectiveness. Usually, these decisions are made by the system designer during system construction. However, interfaces that dynamically "design" themselves at run-time are in a much better position to respond to ever-changing and hard-to-foresee display demands than interfaces whose design is fixed when the system is built. To support the reasoning required for such a capability, an Interaction Manager needs generic and specific models of at least five kinds of information: characteristics of the media at hand, characteristics of the information to be presented, the nature and preferences of the perceiver, the system's own communicative goals, and a model of the application task. To make maximally effective use of this knowledge, the system includes two linked reactive planners for presentation planning as well as a powerful information integrator to handle input. *Cicero* is one example of the architecture required to support this kind of reasoning.

REFERENCES

Agre, P. E. & Chapman, D. (1987). Pengi: An Implementation of a Theory of Activity. *Proceedings of The 6th AAAI*, 196–201. Seattle, WA.

Arens, Y. & Hovy, E. (1990). How to Describe What? Towards a Theory of Modality Utilization. *Proceedings of the 12th Annual Conference of the Cognitive Science Society*, 487–494. Cambridge, MA.

Arens, Y., Miller, L., Shapiro, S. C. & Sondheimer, N. K. (1988). Automatic Construction of User-Interface Displays. *Proceedings of The 7th AAAI Conference*, 808–813. St. Paul, MN.

Arens, Y., Miller, L., & Sondheimer, N. K. (1991). Presentation Design Using an Integrated Knowledge Base. In Sullivan, Joseph, W. and Tyler, Sherman W. (eds.) *Intelligent User Interfaces*, 241–258. Addison-Wesley: Reading.

Arens, Y., Hovy, E. H. & Trimble, J. (1992). An Automatic Presentation Builder. Unpublished ms, USC Information Sciences Institute.

Arens, Y., Hovy, E. H. & Vossers, M. (1993). On the Knowledge Underlying Multimedia Presentations. In Mark Maybury (ed.) *Intelligent Multimedia Interfaces*, 280–306. AAAI Press.

Arens, Y., Hovy, E. H. & Van Mulken, S. (1993). Structure and Rules in Automated Multimedia Presentation Planning. *Proceedings of IJCAI-93*, 231–235. Chambéry, France.

Arens, Y., Chee, C. Y., Hsu, C-N. & Knoblock, C. A. (1993). Retrieving and Integrating Data from Multiple Information Sources. *International Journal of Intelligent and Cooperative Information Systems* **2**(2): 127–158.

Burger, J. & Marshall, R. (1991). AIMI: An Intelligent Multimedia Interface. *Proceedings of The 9th AAAI Conference*, 23–28. Anaheim, CA.

Erman, L. D., Lark, J. S. & Hayes-Roth, F. (1987). ABE: An Environment for Engineering Intelligent Systems. Technical Report TTR-ISE-87-106, Teknowledge Inc., Palo Alto, CA.

Feiner, S. & McKeown, K. R. (1990). Coordinating Text and Graphics in Explanation Generation. *Proceedings of The 8th AAAI*, 442–449.

Feiner, S. (1991). An Architecture for Knowledge-Based Graphical Interfaces. ACM/SIGCHI Workshop on *Architectures for Intelligent Interfaces: Elements and Prototypes*. In Sullivan, Joseph W. & Tyler, Sherman W. (eds.) *Intelligent User Interfaces*, 259–279. Addison-Wesley: Reading.

Foley, J., Kim, W., Kovacevic, S. & Murray, K. (1991). UIDE – An Intelligent User Interface Design Environment. In Sullivan, J. & Tyler, S. (eds.) *Archietectures for Intelligent User Interfaces: Elements and Prototypes*, 339–384. Addison-Wesley: Reading.

Hovy, E. H. (1988). Planning Coherent Multisentential Text. *Proceedings of The 26th Annual Meeting of the Association for Computational Linguistics*, 163–169. Buffalo, N.Y.

Hovy, E. H. & Arens, Y. (1990). When is a Picture Worth a Thousand Words? – Allocation of Modalities in Multimedia Communication. Presented at the *AAAI Symposium on Human-Computer Interaction*, Stanford University.

Hovy, E. H. & Arens, Y. (1991). Automatic Generation of Formatted Text. *Proceedings of The 10th AAAI*, 92–97. Anaheim, CA.

Hovy, E. H. & Arens, Y. (1993). The Planning Paradigm Required for Automated Multimedia Presentation Planning. In *Human-Computer Collaboration: Reconciling Theory, Synthesizing Practice*. Papers from the 1993 Fall Symposium Series, AAAI Technical Report FS-93-05.

Hovy, E. H., Lavid, J., Maier, E., Mittal, V. & Paris, C. L. (1992). Employing Knowledge Resources in a New Text Planning Architecture. In Dale, R., Hovy, E., Rösner, D. & Stock, O. (eds.) *Aspects of Automated Natural Language Generation*, 57–72. Heidelberg: Springer Verlag Lecture Notes in AI number 587.

Intelligent User Interfaces. Arens Y., Feiner, S., Foley, J., Hovy, E., John, B., Neches, R., Pausch, R., Schorr, H. & Swartout, W. (1991). USC/ISI Research Report No. ISI/RR-91-288, September 30, 1991.

Luo, P., Szekely, P. & Neches, R. (1993). Management of Interface Design in Humanoid. *Proceedings of INTERCHI'93*, 107–114. Amsterdam, The Netherlands.

MacGregor, R. (1988). A Deductive Pattern Matcher. *Proceedings of AAAI-88*, 403–408. St. Paul, MN.

Mackinlay, J. (1986). *Automatic Design of Graphical Presentations*. Ph.D. dissertation, Stanford University.

Mackinlay, J. (1986). Automating the Design of Graphical Presentation of Relational Information. *ACM Transactions on Graphics Special Issue on User Interface Software Part I*. **5**(2): 110–141.

Mann, W. C. & Thompson, S. A. (1988). Rhetorical Structure Theory: Toward a Functional Theory of Text Organization. *Text* **8**(3): 243–281.

Neal, J. G., Shapiro, S. C., Thielman, J. R., Lammens, J. M., Funke, D. J., Byoun, J. S., Paul, R., Dobes, Z., Glanowski, S. & Summers, M. S. (1990). Intelligent Multi-Media Integrated Interface Project. SUNY Buffalo and RADC Technical Report TR-90-128.

Neches, R., Foley, J., Szekely, P., Sukaviriya, P., Luo, P., Kovacevic, S. & Hudson, S. (1993). Knowledgeable Development Environments Using Shared Design Models. *Proceedings of the International Workshop on Intelligent User Interfaces*, 183–190. Orlando, FL.

Olsen, D. (1986). MIKE: The Menu Interaction Kontrol Environment. *ACM Transactions on Graphics*. **17**(3): 43–50.

The Penman Project. (1988). *The Penman Primer, User Guide, and Reference Manual*. Unpublished USC/ISI documentation.

Schank, R. & Abelson, R. (1977). *Scripts, Plans, Goals and Understanding: An Inquiry into Human Knowledge Structures*. Hillsdale: Lawrence Erlbaum Associates.

Szekely, P., Luo, P. & Neches, R. (1993). Beyond Interface Builders: Model-Based Interface Design. *Proceedings of INTERCHI'93*, 383–390. Amsterdam, the Netherlands.

Vossers, M. (1991). *Automatic Generation of Formatted Text and Line Drawings*. Master's thesis, University of Nijmegen, The Netherlands.

Wahlster, W., André, E., Bandyopadhyay, S., Graf, W. & Rist, T. (1991). WIP: The Coordinated Generation of Multimodal Presentations from a Common Representation. In Ortony, A., Slack, J. & Stock, O. (eds.), *Computational Theories of Communication and their Applications*, 190–213. Springer Verlag, Berlin.

Artificial Intelligence Review **9**: 189–203, 1995.

Discourse Structures in Iconic Communication

COLIN BEARDON

Rediffusion Simulation Research Centre, Faculty of Art, Design & Humanities, University of Brighton, Grand Parade, Brighton BN2 2JY, England; e-mail: ceb7@vms.brighton.ac.uk

Abstract. The success of the WIMP interface, the convergence towards multimedia platforms and the growing use of the Internet combine to place new demands on the systems we use to communicate with one another. Proposals for iconic languages are not new but the computer offers the ability to incorporate interactivity and animation into iconic writing and reading systems. One approach to developing computer-based iconic communication systems derives from the visual arts (i.e. graphic design, illustration, film animation, documentary video, etc.). An alternative approach is derived from computational linguistics in that the syntactic or semantic structure of language is retained while iconic images are used in place of words. Differences between the study of natural language and the design of an iconic language are discussed and the components of one particular system, IconText, are described. Of particular interest is the attempt to capture some pragmatic aspects of communication, both in terms of conveying the intentions of the author and concerning the sequential delivery of the message.

Key words: icons, iconic languages, conceptual dependency, discourse.

1. INTRODUCTION

The success of the WIMP interface has shown that manipulating images on a two-dimensional screen is vastly more popular than using a keyboard to enter one-dimensional symbolic text. Already the familiar screen-based icon with its associated text name is evolving into new forms and we have examples of 'picons' (or 'picture icons') which embed a full-colour image, 'micons' (or 'moving icons') which display an animation or video sequence, and 'earcons' (or 'auditory icons') which utilise sound (Gaver 1989). The convergence towards a digital form of representation for images, films, drawings, music, speech, soundtracks and texts, means that our computer screen is no longer a window into a world of symbol processing but has become a rich canvas full of potential signifiers. ASCII text is no longer the dominant form in which information is captured, represented and presented. Recent technological developments create the need for more appropriate forms of communication if we are to encompass the different media that are in circulation and to communicate via our computers with other authors and readers.

On top of this development we have the globalisation of communication which, at least for the educated elites in each country, is manifest in the sudden surge of interest in the Internet. The extension of "the net" will require provision of the technical means of communication, a pricing system to make it economically viable, and a simple, common language for communication across natural language barriers. Baecker and Small (1990) make some initial steps in this direction with their idea of animating icons. An attempt to address domain specific communication issues was made by Mealing and Yazdani (1992) particularly in their system to facilitate hotel booking without using natural language text. In a more recent system, MUSLI, proposed by Lennon and Maurer (1994), hypermedia techniques and dynamic abstract symbols are combined in order to attempt to provide significant enhancements to existing means of communication. These systems are seen as an attempt to break out of existing forms of communication and to see the computer, not as an intelligence with which we have to communicate, but as a medium to facilitate human-to-human communication by providing the means to create, disseminate, store, retrieve and display whatever we wish.

2. ICONIC COMMUNICATION

2.1. *Iconicity*

There is a potential problem with terminology so, for the purposes of this article, I shall use the word 'icon' to refer to any stylised graphical image. Small, stylised graphical images, in the form of heiroglyphs, were the basis of our modern form of writing and led to our alphabet. Earlier this century there were several attempts to develop universal languages based upon icons. Working in the 1920s and 1930s, Otto Neurath developed 'Isotype' (Neurath 1978) which was strongly influenced by ideas from logical positivism and, particularly, the picture theory of meaning (Wittgenstein 1961). Later, in the 1950s, Charles Bliss developed 'Blissymbolics' which is based upon linguistic concepts and comprises a visual lexicon and simple compositional rules (Bliss 1965). The Bliss system not only has icons for common nouns but has icons as markers, such as 'plural' and 'male', which allow for the construction of complex icons for pronouns.

These typically modernist attempts were both based upon a set of atomic icons with predefined meanings and a set of compositional rules or techniques for creating iconic descriptions of objects and events. It was naively assumed that each simple pictorial representation would have a stable and universal interpretation. Edmondson (1994) argues persuasively that this assumption is false. Partly because the images are stylised, there is always an element of conventionality involved in the interpretation of an icon and, in this sense, iconicity is a matter of degree rather than of kind. An icon, as compared to a symbol, is less arbitrary and more accessible, though given the range of techniques for visual signification even this is not a simple scale. An iconic representation may embody a metaphor, or use metonymy, hyperbole, personification or any of a number of visual rhetorical techniques (Marcus 1979, Barker and Manji 1989).

Nevertheless, sets of icons have been used successfully in locations such as international airports to convey their meaning to people regardless of the natural languages they can understand. It can be argued that well-designed icons successfully overcome our linguistic diversity and this is certainly one of the great hopes of people working in this field. However it is already realised that icons are less successful in overcoming cultural diversity. For example, not all cultures are made up of men who wear long trousers and women who wear knee-length skirts. The fact that these icons are successful at communicating across linguistic and cultural barriers depends upon the ability of those whose normal viewpoint is not represented in the image to either recognise the reference within a different culture or simply learn the sign as a symbol. A parallel may be drawn here to recent attempts to standardise icons used in computer applications (ISO/IEC 1992). What is hoped will emerge is a set of permissible icons that can be used to refer to certain defined objects, for example a printer. The approach is necessarily cautious but may eventually produce a large set of conventionalised signs which will have to be learnt by any new entrant into the field of interface design. For some users these signs may retain a high degree of iconicity, but for others they will be purely conventional.

2.2. *Computer-based Iconic Languages*

The way that icons are used within contemporary WIMP interfaces form a small language, not unlike the language games described by Wittgenstein (1953). The set of icons refer to objects within the computer world (e.g. disks, files, applications) and there is a set of operations upon these icons (e.g. click, click-and-drag) that also have meaning in the computer world (e.g. move, copy, eject, run). Useful things can be achieved by simply pointing and clicking at objects. Within such icon languages the icons are made to behave in a predictable manner (Gittens 1986). However, despite different hardware devices, such as the three-button mouse, the sophistication of such languages is extremely limited by the simplicity of the actions that are capable of being represented.

The particular form of iconic communication discussed here takes a different starting point. It attempts to utilise three aspects of contemporary computer systems to enhance such communication. These are the computer's ability to display acceptable quality images on the screen, to change those images rapidly enough to give a sense of real-time animation, and to allow user interaction through the use of devices such as the mouse or touch-sensitive screen.

Much of the work on iconic communication is informed by studies of predominantly visual forms of communication (Marcus 1979, Mealing 1992, Dormann, forthcoming). These tend to concentrate upon the pragmatic aspects of communication and hope that the syntactic and semantic levels will be, if not self-evident, at least clarified within the pragmatic context. A system that does not do this, but has an algebra for combining icons into complex meaning units, is *Minspeak*™ (Barrow and Baker 1982). In general, though, the syntactic and semantic interpretation of each image is left very much to the reader.

2.3. *Natural and Iconic Languages*

I argue that this need not be so and that we can apply knowledge from the study of natural languages to create iconic languages that generate meaning in a consistent way at all three levels without being over prescriptive. In computer-based iconic languages, the atomic constituents of the language are represented by stylised graphical images. Meaning is suggested by icons at the first level through these individual icons which can derive their meaning from three sources: the interpretation of their image; their entry in a pictorial dictionary which attempts to explain the conventional meaning of the image; and through additional meanings that can be provided by authors.

Icons are composed into structures that are analogous to linguistic structures but exploit animation, interactivity and the two-dimensionality of the screen. These structures are not based upon the syntactic structure of language as that is notoriously misleading but rather upon attempts to capture directly the semantic structure. Woods (1978) described such formalisms as meaning representation languages (or MRLs) whose aim is to represent completely and unambiguously the meaning of any statement that can be made in natural language. If these MRLs really are clearer ways of expressing what we mean, then why not use them directly in iconic languages? Probably the most pictorial MRL is Conceptual Dependency (CD) (Schank 1973) and this was chosen as the basis of our initial work. The intention was never to implement CD as such but rather to develop a usable iconic language based upon the principles of CD.

A prototype general purpose graphical language, CD-Icon, based upon Conceptual Dependency was developed in HyperCard (Beardon 1992, 1993). The system allows for iconic messages to be both written and read and some testing has taken place. The results indicate that readers' interpretations of messages are accurate but they are not always complete (i.e. they do not always discover everything that is contained in the message). While these results were generally encouraging, they indicated some major limitations in an approach too closely based on CD:

- visual icons work well for the representation of physical things but are less successful in representing abstract concepts (Kay 1990);
- conceptual dependency relies heavily upon closed sets (e.g. the set of primitive actions) which seems unnecessarily restrictive; and
- complex messages can only be constructed by using physical relations such as space, time and causality.

3. ICONTEXT

The remainder of this paper describes the principles behind an iconic language called "IconText", which is is based around five types of window used to describe concepts, objects, events, relations and the context of the message.

3.1. *Concepts*

The first type of window enables us to select predefined icons which reflect concepts that we use to refer to things in the world. In natural language they would be represented by words such as "man", "car" or "black". We group them in a scrapbook, as in Figure 1, which can be browsed.

Fig. 1. Twelve icons in a scrapbook (representing *black, white, house, city, woman, man, telephone, dog, tree, book, car, aeroplane*).

If the intention of any icon is not clear then it can be interrogated by pointing at it, in which case an entry in an animated picture dictionary is shown giving an explanation of the normal reference of the icon. Authors will also be able to augment the explanation of any icon and generate new icons. Such changes will be transmitted as part of the message. When authors come to construct an iconic utterance they choose appropriate icons from the scrapbook and paste them into other windows. Icons have no properties and are not typed, so any icon can appear anywhere in any window.

There are some icons in the dictionary that are not intended to refer to physical things. These include the question mark (inserted into any window to indicate the focus of a question), icons that refer to types of event (e.g. change_location, change_state) and icons that refer to types of relation (e.g. ownership, equality, causality).

3.2. *Objects*

Icons can be placed within an object window to form a structure that refers to an object (e.g. "the black car"). An object is represented by a window that shows an icon for the head term and icons for its modifiers. The phrase "the black car" will contain an icon for "car" in the top left corner and the icon for black elsewhere within its frame (Figure 2).

The phrase "John's black car" introduces a new object (John) and a relation-

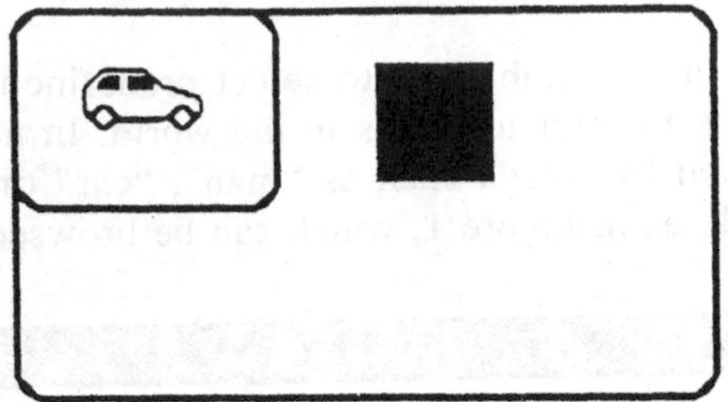

Fig. 2. Object window for 'the black car'.

ship (ownership) between the two objects. We create an object window for a male person with the name-label "John" (proper names are one of the few places where text is allowed) and add an ownership icon to the window for the car (see Figure 3). The details of this ownership relationship will be represented in a relation window (described in Section 3.4.).

The abstract symbol in Figure 3 was initially developed to indicate property ownership but we have found it possible to use it in context to express related concepts such as parenthood, nationality and physical inclusion. The hypothesis is that we are able to use a limited set of relational icons to generate a large number of interpretations in different contexts without there being serious problems of ambiguity.

An author is thus able to create a static window that serves as a descriptive phrase to refer to a particular object in the world. In other windows in which a reference to this object appears we may wish to refer to it by means of a single icon. The default is that the icon for the head concept will be used elsewhere in the system to refer to the object and thus it functions as an abbreviation whose full reference can be discovered by interrogation. This is similar to using the phrase "the car" in English once "John's black car" has been identified.

IconText also provides a facility akin to naming whereby the author can nominate an icon (which may be created especially for the purpose) specifi-

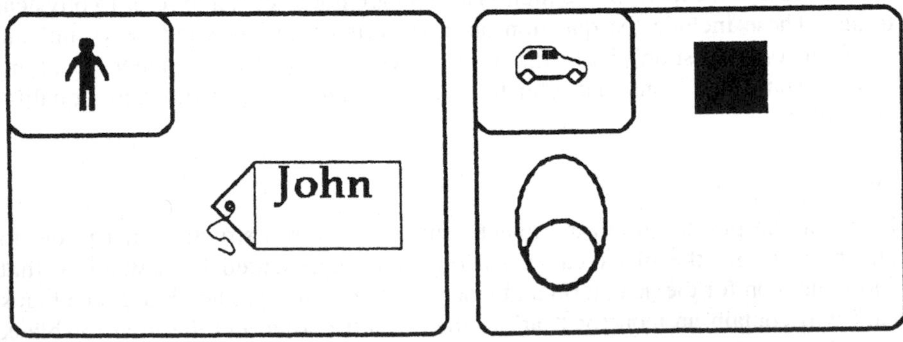

Fig. 3. Two object windows: (left) a man named John; (right) a black car with an owner.

cally to refer to an object. Figure 4 shows a possible icon which might be used as a name that is linked interactively to John's object window. It is of course possible that an author may choose a surprising name for an object, say using an aeroplane icon to name John (this may seem perverse but I once knew a boy whose nickname was derived from the name of an aircraft). The language will indeed allow this, just as English does, for it is not our intention to be restrictive about how people might use the language. There is a building close to where I live called "The Green Man" and it seems odd to create a language in which it is impossible to name it.

Fig. 4. A possible naming icon for John.

3.3. *Events*

Objects can be involved in events (e.g. "John went to London") and these are represented by an event window. Different event types have different windows, which means different visual representations and different slots, each with a definite position in two-dimensional space. Object icons can fill these slots but not all slots have to be filled (see Figure 5).

We can get an impression of the meaning of this event window from its static

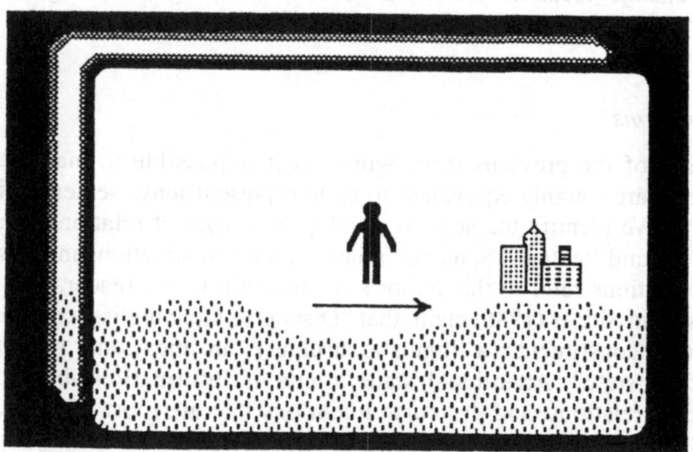

Fig. 5. An event window which superficially says that a man went to a city. Icons can be interrogated to find out which man and which city. The stacked window can be revealed to show how the event was carried out (e.g. by car).

representation – Figure 5 is about a man going to a city, but we do not know which man, which city or where the man came from. We can interrogate the objects to discover that the person is John and the city is London. We can also exploit animation to help us convey the meaning of the event: in this case the icon for John starts on the left and moves rightwards across the screen ending next to the icon for London.

Where there is an instrument, as in "John drove his black car to London", we adopt Schank's approach which restricts the instrument slot to events (i.e. John went to London has an instrument slot that is filled by John's car going to London). We do not show the instrument event as an explicit icon but place it on a stack of events immediately behind the current event. The deeper one goes into the stack, the more detail is provided about the action.

Tenses, moods, etc. are not shown in this window, but in a relation window (see Section 3.4). As was the case with objects, each event has a single icon which can be used to refer to it in other windows and the user has the power to choose a new icon to name the event if s/he wishes.

In CD all the verbs of natural language are represented by a set of 14 primitive actions with restrictions on what can fill their associated slots. While retaining this approach there is no compulsion to have a rigid set of primitives. In general there will be two types of window – one in which one or more icons change their location, and one in which an entity changes its properties or relations. These two basic events can be played out against a variety of backgrounds. Background graphics can describe a physical environment in which a move takes place or can describe a metaphor within which we can operate as if it were a physical space. An example would be Schank's division of memory into discrete areas such as "conscious processor" and "long term memory" and within which conceptualisations have locations (Schank 1973, p. 219). Different versions of the 'change_location' event can involve changing the background graphic, changing the location of a slot, or changing the trajectory of a slot during the animation.

3.4. *Relations*

By means of the previous three windows it is possible to make iconic statements that are roughly equivalent to simple present tense sentences in a natural language. We identify the need to develop two types of relations, which we call 'semantic' and 'textual'. Semantic relations refer to situations in the world while textual relations refer to the author's relationship to the reader.

Grosz and Sidner (1986) claim that "Discourse structure is a composite of three interacting constituents: a linguistic structure, an intentional structure, and an attentional state". Attentional state "contains information about the objects, properties, relations, and discourse intentions that are most salient at any given point." Because of the way we use interactivity, we do not rely upon context to clarify reference and so do not need to maintain an attentional state. Their distinction between what an author actually says and their intentions is significant but, for the purposes of an authoring system, it is unrealistic to expect authors to separately indicate their intentions. If we are to use intentional structure then we must find ways of integrating it into the authoring process, as is done by Tonfoni (1994).

Maier and Hovy (1991) have developed three identifiable metafunctions of language based upon systemic linguistics – ideational, interpersonal, and textual. Their textual function is very similar to Grosz and Sidner's attentional state and, again because of our use of interactivity, we do not need to pursue it for our purposes. They describe ideational meaning as, "the representation of experience of the world that lies about us and inside us" and add "It is meaning in the sense of 'content'." This type of meaning is what we expect to be conveyed in our 'semantic' relations and there are several examples related to the physical world (e.g. *spatial and temporal* relations, *causality*). We also include various social relations such as *ownership*, and cognitive relations such as *instance* as examples of semantic relations.

Relation windows provide a way of specifying these different kinds of relation between objects, events and relationships. The basic structure of such relationships is that the two related entities are shown on the left and right, while the relationship is shown in the middle. Where the relationship is of the form of attribute and value, then the attribute type is shown at the top and the value is shown at the bottom. Figure 6 indicates that a 'physical_transfer_event' (on the left) and a 'move_event' (on the right) are connected by a relation whose type is 'time' (top) and whose value is 'equal' (bottom). It is therefore equivalent to saying that the physical transfer takes place at the same time as the move.

In contrast to ideational meaning, interpersonal meaning is described by Maier and Hovy as "writer-and-reader oriented". This is information that an author can provide concerning the discourse structure of the message. Tonfoni (1994) suggests a set of iconic symbols for expressing such structure. In IconText such information is not just declarative but is used in the creation of the animation from the static message structure that the author has created. After the authoring process is complete we have a hypertext version of a message which we wish to present serially as an animation.

One example of how this works concerns the author's assumption as to what

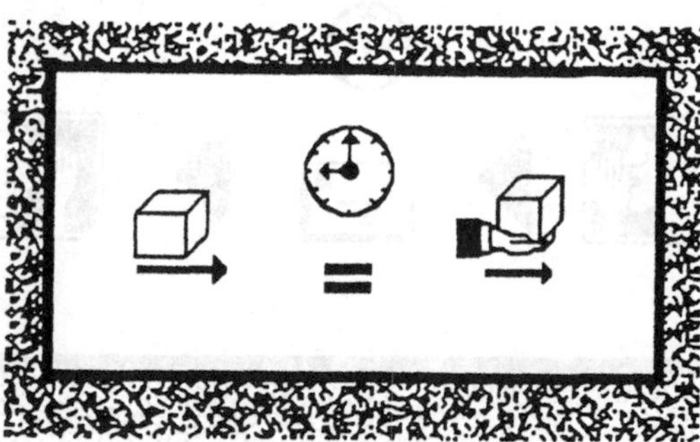

Fig. 6. A relation window indicating that a PTRANS took place at the same time as a MOVE.

the reader already knows (i.e. the given/new distinction in linguistics). We allow the 'given' part of the discourse to be identified by the author. During the animation these parts of the message will generally be presented first in order to orient the reader.

A second example is the focus of the message. We define a relational operator, for which we use the magnifying glass as an icon, that relates the message in the envelope (see Section 3.5.) to that part of the message that the author decides is the main focus (see Figure 12). The focus will often, but not always, indicate the starting point of the animation. For example, a declarative message that is expressed by the English sentence, "Mary drove to Manchester in her black car" will be presented in three consecutive stages: (1) an animation involving only Mary going to Manchester, (2) an animation explaining the instrument case involving a car going to Manchester, and (3) an explanation that the car was owned by Mary and was black in colour. If we transform this sentence into a question such as might be expressed by, "What colour car did Mary drive to Manchester?" then we need do more than replace the icon for 'black' by the question-mark icon: we also need to shift the starting point of the animation from the first event to the question mark (as well as taking into account what we assume the reader already knows).

3.5. *Envelope*

The envelope window appears first and always looks the same (Figure 7). It has standard slots representing the author, the reader, the message and the time of writing. These are linked to appropriate windows which may be completed. In the case of author and reader they are linked to object windows which, typically, give the name and address of the person but may also show a naming icon. The time may be linked to a window which represents the specified time. We do not yet have a sophisticated representation for time, which may require a specific notation or even a separate window, as in Ludlow (1992). The message

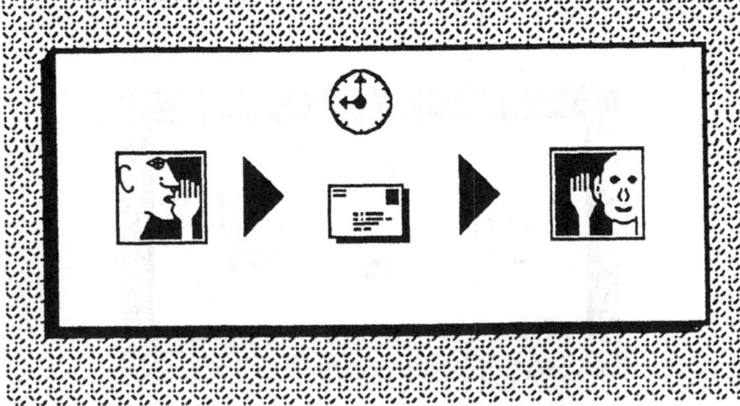

Fig. 7. The envelope window identifying 'me', 'you' and the time of writing.

icon is linked by the focussing icon to the relationship or event that is most central to the message. The four icons in this window are fixed and are available for use in all subsequent windows: they correspond to the English concepts, "me", "you", "this message" and "now".

4. AN EXAMPLE

As an example, we will show the static structures that represent the sentence, "Jim has the book because I took it to his house." The first stage is to define the four objects: myself, Jim, the book and the house. These are shown in Figure 8, in which both myself and Jim are given naming icons while the book and the house will be referred to simply by the icons for book and house respectively. A link is established between the author icon in the envelope and the object window for myself.

The second stage involves describing the event "I took the book to the house", which is an event of type MOVE, as shown in Figure 9. (MOVE is a change of location in which the agent and the object move together.) The icon by which this event will be recognised is shown to the left. This is the default icon for events of type MOVE.

Finally, temporal, causal and ownership relationships are built between entities as shown by the network in Figure 10. For purposes of explanation and comparison we include Figure 11 which shows the same diagram with words in place of the iconic symbols.

It is also necessary to indicate the intended discourse structure of the message. In this case it is to tell the reader that Jim now has the book, and the fact that

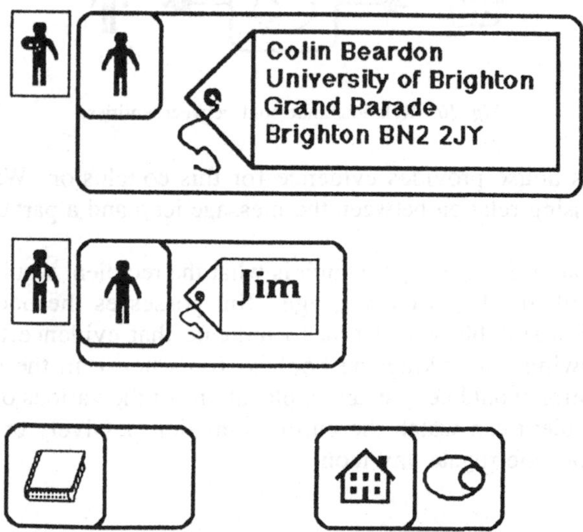

Fig. 8. Four objects: myself, Jim, the book and the house.

Fig. 9. An event: I take the book to the house (showing the default icon for a MOVE).

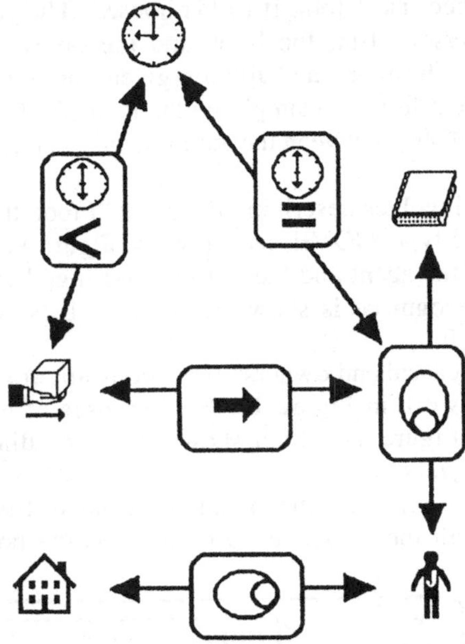

Fig. 10. Relations that hold between entities.

I took it to his house provides evidence for this conclusion. We declare this, using the focussing relation between the message icon and a part of the message (Figure 12).

An animation of this message, which is what the recipient would first receive, commences with the focussed message "Jim possesses the book now". It is followed, with a suitable visual link to indicate that evidence follows, by an animation showing "me taking the book to Jim's house in the past". Worked into this animation would be relevant explanations of the various objects encountered. The recipient can watch the entire animation passively or can intervene at any point and interrogate any icon.

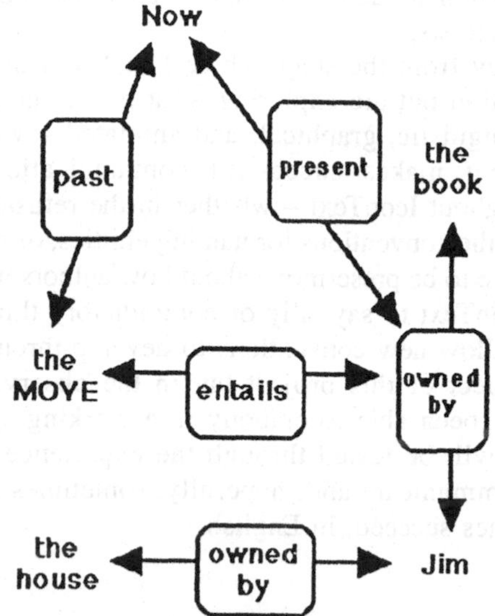

Fig. 11. Relations that hold between entitles as words.

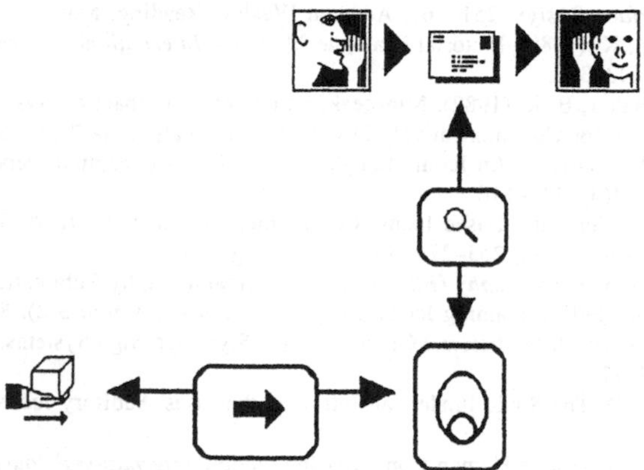

Fig. 12. Discourse relation identifying the focus of the message.

5. CONCLUSION

IconText is a system that will allow for the authoring of complex messages for communication to one or mor readers. It utilises icons in place of words, and uses the full two dimensionality of the screen, animation and interaction in order to allow a message to be read in two distinct ways – as a static hypertextual message that can be explored at leisure, or as an animation that will reveal the message as a sequence over time. Both the hypertextual structure and the narrative structure of the animation are derived from features of natural languages described by computational linguists.

We are a long way from the stage where IconText can be used for general purpose communication but are exploring what is common to various types of communication – linguistic, graphical, and animated – with a view to understanding better what makes successful communication in a multimedia environment. Throughout IconText – whether in the refusal to classify icons in terms of types, or in the conventions for naming entities, or in the ability to create new icons – we refuse to be prescriptive about how authors may use the language. Authors can use IconText to say silly or contradictory things, just as they can in English and we allow new conventions to develop through use.

A significant aspect of this project lay in the observations about natural language that it has been able to embody in a working system. The value of those observations will be tested through the experience of people using the system to try to communicate and, hopefully, sometimes succeeding – just as we try, and sometimes succeed, in English.

REFERENCES

Baecker, R. & Small, I. (1990). Animation at the Interface. In Laurel, B. (ed.) *The Art of Human-Computer Interface Design*, 251–267. Addison-Wesley: Reading, Mass.

Barker, P. & Manji, K. (1989). Pictorial Dialogue Methods. *International Journal of Man-Machine Studies* **31**(3): 323–348.

Barrow, H. G. & Baker, B. R. (1982). Minspeak, a Semantic Compaction System that Makes Self-Expression Easier for Communicatively Disabled Individuals. *Byte* **7**(9): 186–202.

Beardon, C. (1992). CD-Icon: An Iconic Language Based on Conceptual Dependency. *Intelligent Tutoring Media* **3**(4): 111–116.

Beardon, C. (1993). Computer-Based Iconic Communication. In Ryan, K. & Sutcliffe, R. (eds) *AI and Cognitive Science '92*, 263–276. Springer-Verlag: London.

Bliss, C. K. (1965). *Semantography (Blissymbolics)*. Semantography Publications: Sydney.

Dormann, C. (1994). Self-Explaining Icons. *Intelligent Tutoring Media* **5**(2): 81–85.

Edmondson, W. (1994). Abstraction and Organisation in Signs and Sign Systems. *Intelligent Tutoring Media* **5**(2): 63–72.

Gaver, W. W. (1989). The Sonic Finder: an Interface that uses Auditory Icons. *Human-Computer Interaction* **4**: 67–94.

Gittens, D. (1986). Icon-Based Human-Computer Interaction. *International Journal of Man-Machine Studies* **24**: 519–543.

Grosz, B. J. & Sidner, C. L. (1986). Attention, Intentions, and the Structure of Discourse. *Computational Linguistics* **12**(3): 175–204.

ISO/IEC (1992). *Information Technology – Text and Office Systems – Graphical Symbols Used on Screens: Interactive Icons*. Report No JTC1/SC 18. ANSI: U.S.A.

Kay, A. (1990). User Interface: A Personal View. In Laurel, B. (ed.) *The Art of Human-Computer Interface Design*, 191–207. Addison-Wesley: Reading, Mass.

Ludlow, N. D. (1992). *Pictorial Representation of Text: Converting Text to Pictures*. Ph.D. thesis, Dept. of Artificial Intelligence, University of Edinburgh.

Marcus, A. (1979). Visual Rhetoric in Pictographic-Ideographic. *Proceedings of The Second Congress of the International Association for Semiotic Studies*, 1501–1508. Vienna: Mouton publishers, New York.

Mealing, S. & Yazdani, M. (1992). A Computer-Based Iconic Language. *Intelligent Tutoring Media* **1**(3): 133–136.

Mealing, S. (1992). Talking Pictures. *Intelligent Tutoring Media* **2**(2): 63–69.
Maier, E. & Hovy, E. H. (1991) *Organizing Discourse Structure Relations Using Metafunctions*. Paper presented to the European Natural Language Generation Workshop: GMD-IPSI, Darmstadt.
Neurath, O. (1978). *International Picture Language*. University of Reading: Reading.
Schank, R. C. (1973). Identification of Conceptualisations Underlying Natural Language. In Schank, R. & Colby, M. (eds) *Computer Models of Thought and Language*, 187–247. W. H. Freeman: San Francisco.
Tonfoni, G. (1994). *Writing as a Visual Art*. Intellect Books: Oxford.
Wittgenstein, L. (1953). *Philosophical Investigations*. Blackwell: Oxford.
Wittgenstein, L. (1961). *Tractatus Logico-Philosophicus*, trans. Pears, D. F. & McGuiness, B. F. Routledge & Kegan Paul: London.
Woods, W. (1978). Semantics and Quantification in Natural Language Question Answering. In Yovits, M. (ed.) *Advances in Computers* **17**: 2–64. Academic Press: New York.

Artificial Intelligence Review **9**: 205–213, 1995.

Communicating Through Pictures

MASOUD YAZDANI and STUART MEALING

Department of Computer Science, Exeter University;
E-mail: masoud@dcs.exeter.ac.uk

Abstract. In this article we present design consideration for a visual language which may allow users with different linguistic backgrounds to communicate freely. This cross language communication uses icons which are graphically clear, semantically unambiguous, adaptable and, above all, simple.

Key words: icon, conceptual dependency, cross language communication, grammar, spelling, language.

INTRODUCTION

How could two people who do not know each other's language communicate with each other? Koji Kobayashi, chairman of the Japan's *Nippon Electric Co.* (NEC) foresees "a situation that would make it possible for any person in the world to communicate with any other person at any place and any time".

Kobayashi (1986) aims to exploit future developments in machine translation, speech synthesis and recognition. An English speaker may pick up the telephone and speak with a Japanese person in English. It would be the task of the telecommunication system to recognise the sounds and translate them into Japanese and later translate the reply into English. This proposal still is far from becoming a real possibility.

As an intermediate solution, Yazdani (1987) proposed an environment which could assist users of electronic mail systems to compose and understand messages in major European languages.

Email systems are currently passive, they do not provide tools needed for those who would like to use them as a multilingual facility. The proposed system was intended to be active and provide support (including a spelling checker and a grammar checker, etc.) to the user. It may, through a suite of linguistic systems, monitor the text being created, and offer help and specific remedial advice in language use.

This proposal was taken on board by the project for the European Open Learning Service (EPOS). The EPOS Project envisages the possibility of a network of students all over Europe, able to contact each other via a telecommunications network and having access to a range of educational products and databases. The aim is for the system to provide support for communication between course-ware designers, tutors, students and others, working in a team in different locations using computers which themselves may be spread over a large geographical area.

Originally, we saw our undertaking at the University of Exeter as the feasibility study of a multi-lingual interface to EPOS, the idea being that a student about to send a message to a tutor (or another student) who does not speak his language should be able to use the program to preprocess the note before sending it.

In order to do this task we began by building (Jones 1990) a suite of linguistic systems for Spanish, French and English (to be extended to other European languages) which could monitor the text being created. The system would detect spelling and grammatical errors, offer specific remedial advice as well as offering more general help with the grammar and spelling of the language.

In this project we intend to encourage users to communicate with speakers of other languages electronically. The growth of the use of various Email systems indicates that our service would be attractive to many potential users. The difference here is that we shall support the user with various linguistic tools which allow the user to communicate with others on the network who may not know his/her language.

The user composes a message through a special educational wordprocessor which assists him/her to compose messages in a foreign language. The writing tools would

a) detect spelling and grammatical errors,
b) offer specific remedial advice,
c) offer more general help with the grammar and spelling of the language.

The wordprocessor would also incorporate help facilities. The advice will be provided using the knowledge of both the mother tongue and the target language.

The correspondent also requires tools to understand the message. Online dictionaries and grammar analysers which could be used as translation aids already exist and as the user will be in charge of the process the task would not be as complex as machine translation. Our system would not be capable of dealing automatically with the semantics of the messages and the receiver of the message would need to ask for clarification (from the pen pal) if the meaning of any message was not clear.

In 1991 we were asked if we could use the remaining time on the project to investigate the possibility of producing a multi-lingual demonstration package ("Welcome Pack") which could describe EPOS to the users as they saw the system for the first time. As a result we produced a prototype system to show the concept of an iconic presentation.

AN ICONIC LANGUAGE

Mealing and Yazdani (1991) present design consideration for a visual language. Our criteria for icons are that they should be:

- Graphically clear;
- Semantically unambiguous;

- Without linguistic bias (culture, race?);
- Adaptable (open to modification to express shades of meaning);
- Simple (perhaps created within a 32 x 32 matrix).

We have tried to work in a simple computational environment in order that the ideas may have a wider application. However, we anticipate that a number of additional design aids may be used at a later date, including:

- Colour;
- Movement (micons);
- Background (picons);
- 3-Dimensional (CAD style space of 3D icons).

This iconic communication system uses icons which represent units of meaning greater than single concepts. In return the icons can explain themselves if needed in order to clarify the meaning and provide the context.

An icon should be able to explain its meaning:

1) in terms of more fundamental icons;
2) trace its development from photographic reference;
3) maybe even through natural language.

Such "self explaining icons" use simple animations to help the user understand the meaning of the message clearly and thus avoid the problem of ambiguity associated with static icons. Our work can be seen as an attempt to add computer animation to the work of the Isotype (Neurath 1978) movement.

Isotype has attempted to avoid ambiguity and complexity of natural language. The Isotype rules for creating new icons can be incorporated into our language and extended. New icons therefore may be produced by:

- Superimposition;
- Conjunction;
- concatenation;
- Transformation;
- Inheritance;
- Duplication;
- etc.

More recently Mealing (1992) presents a prototype hotel booking system developed in HyperCard™ which uses icons to allow a potential guest and hotel manager to communicate. The system is an initial attempt to create an interactive, iconic dialogue using hotel booking as the theme. The prototype system would allow a user to compose his complete booking requirement iconically and send the message to the hotel manager to reply to (again iconically). The design of the system has been divided into two independent stages of composition and comprehension.

HOTEL BOOKING

Hotel booking offers us the opportunity to apply iconic language in a simple dialogue – between a potential guest and a hotel manager. We have assumed no interaction between hotel and customer during the compilation of the message and its reply. A typical scenario could find a stranger in a foreign city operating a touch screen in the window of a tourist office, or a traveller contacting a foreign town's accommodation bureau through his home computer terminal.

The compilation of the booking message is accomplished in stages and at each stage the current domain is cued by a picture resident in the background. In sequence these are: a 'typical' hotel front (Figure 1), a 'typical' hotel reception area (Figure 2), and a 'typical' hotel bedroom (Figure 3), each new screen holding the background picture for a second before the information is faded in over it. Therefore, when dealing with the required room type(s) the background picture on screen would be of a room. Sub-domains might later require a typical bathroom, dining area etc. and in the future such images could even be live video.

The first screen (Figure 1) shows a hotel overlaid by an appropriate caption, and *clicking* anywhere on the image starts the booking sequence.[1] The screen then invites input of destination, cued by a map, and selection of hotel type, by selecting from cyclable 'star' ratings. Movement to the next screen is initiated by *Clicking* on the 'tick' icon, a convention observed throughout the package.

The second screen (Figure 2) shows a hotel reception area and invites selection of the dates and times of arrival and departure. The number of nights that have thus been booked is indicated by black bars which appear (and disappear) as each night is added (or removed), but whilst this added display is useful its meaning is not immediately clear in its present form. The 'tick' icon moves the user to the next screen.

The third screen (Figure 3) shows a room overlaid with icons permitting the selection of room type(s). Four icons each 'unlock' further related icons to enable

Fig. 1.

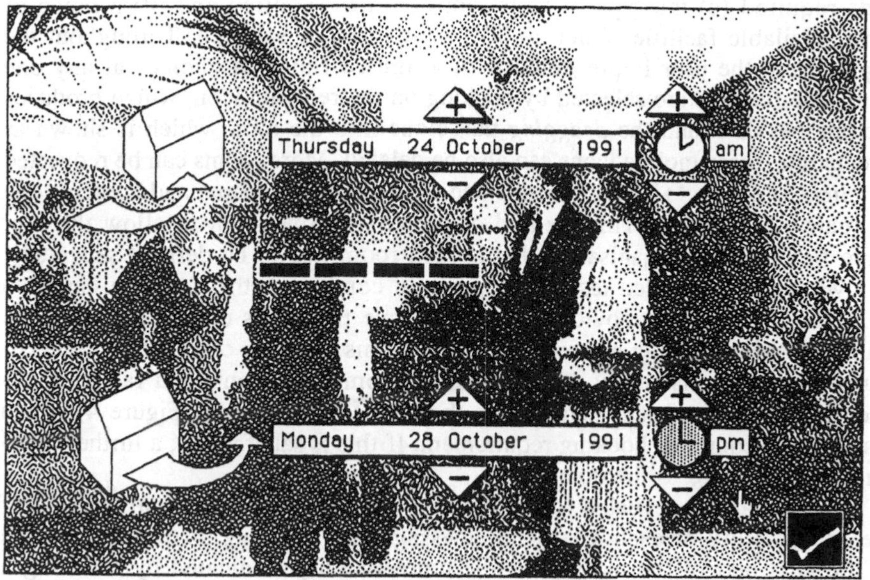

Fig. 2.

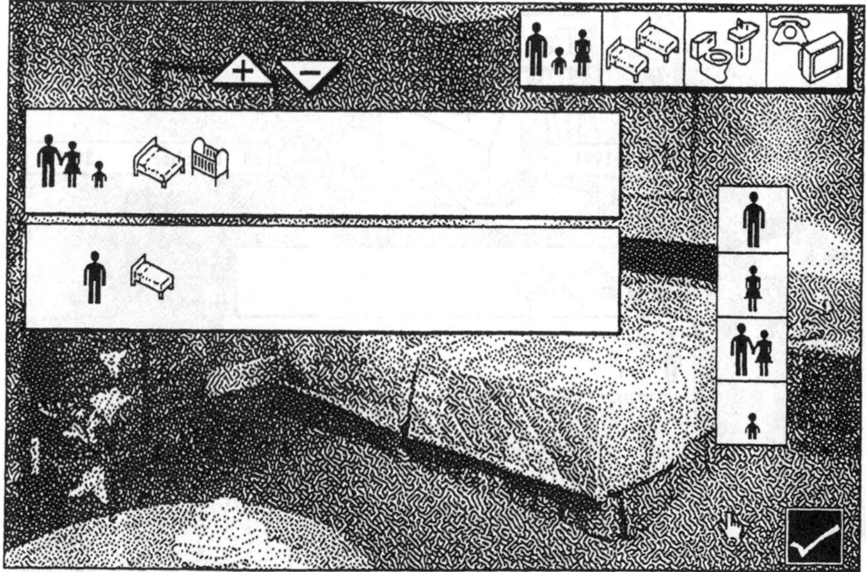

Fig. 3.

(a) the number and type of occupant to be shown (b) the number and type of beds required (c) the type of bathroom facilities required and (d) a range of other available facilities (such as TV) which can be selected. Throughout the application, the user is presented with a limited range of choices at any one time. The features are selected by clicking on the relevant icon, which produces a clone beside it and the *dragging* that clone into the room which is shown as a rectangle, these mobile icons can also be deleted. More rooms can be requested by *clicking* on the '+' and '–' icons and the rooms' occupants and contents can be rearranged to suit. This method of presentation was felt to allow the user more flexibility in organisation that if each room had to be defined separately, and whilst no controlled tests have yet been conducted, the interface has been found to be intuitively obvious. In order to cue the user's understanding of the principles of organising a room, the screen opens showing one room with occupants. When a satisfactory arrangement of rooms, occupants and facilities has been achieved, the 'tick' item moves the user to screen four (Figure 4) which displays the complete booking requirement. If this is satisfactory, a further 'tick' sends the message to the hotel.

The message is revealed to the hotel in stages (Figure 5). Confirmation of the acceptability of each part of the message (by selecting a 'tick') moves on to the next part of the message while unavailability (indicated by selecting a 'cross') brings up the range of available alternatives. In Figure 6 the choice of 'star' rating was unavailable and the alternatives are presented so that an alternative can be offered.

In Figure 7 it can be seen that the chosen bedding arrangement for the first

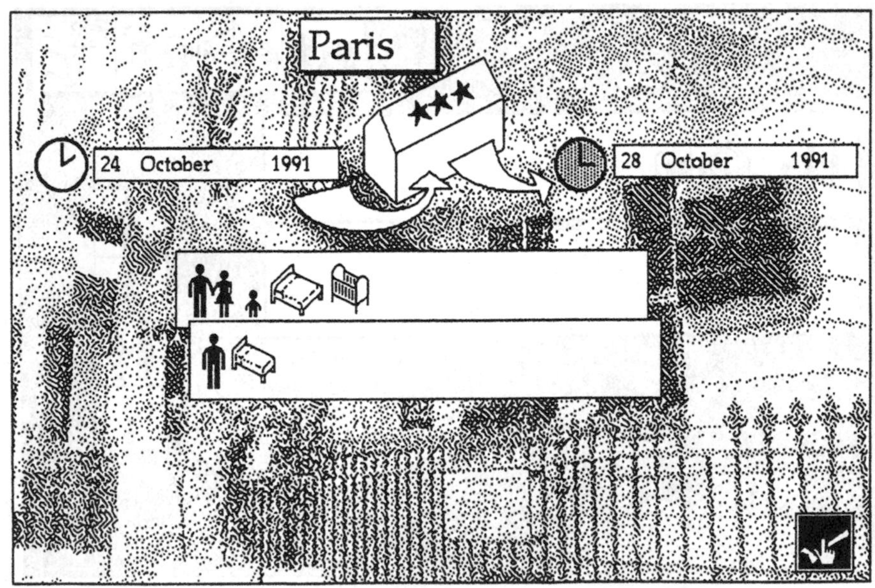

Fig. 4.

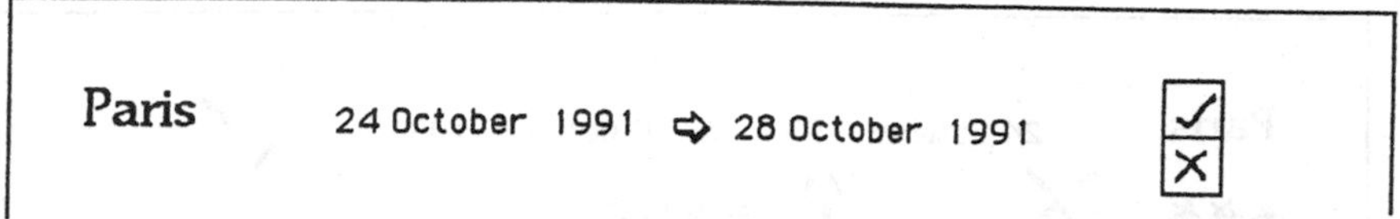

Fig. 5.

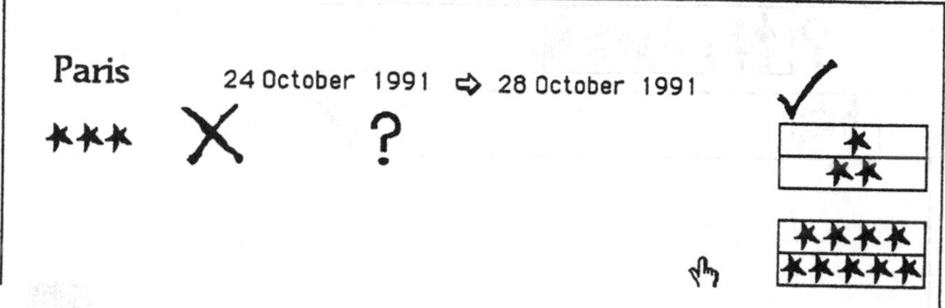

Fig. 6.

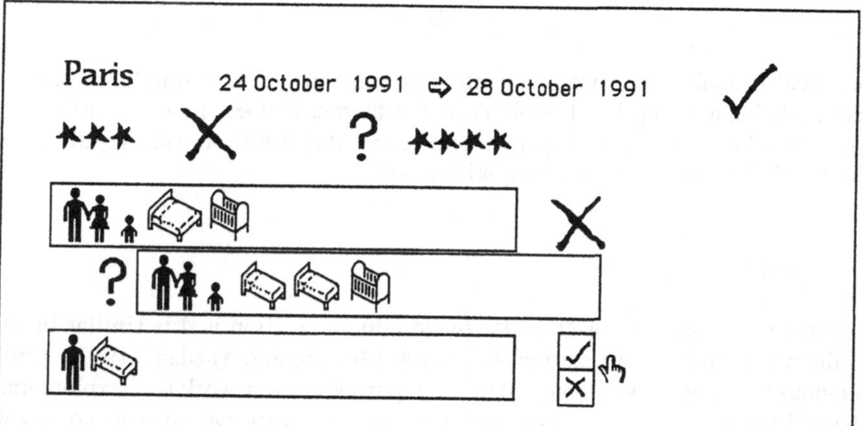

Fig. 7.

room is not available, and two singly beds are offered instead of the double bed requested. The large ticks and crosses indicate to the customer what is, and is not, available and the question mark precedes the alternative which is being offered ("Is this OK?"). The layout of the rooms and alternatives is intended to enhance their understandability. The cursor is about to select a 'tick' to indicate that the second room is available as requested.

The final message (Figure 8) is sent black to the customer who will then be able to accept or reject the alternatives offered, continue the dialogue, and confirm a booking. The application does not pretend to be comprehensive or the most

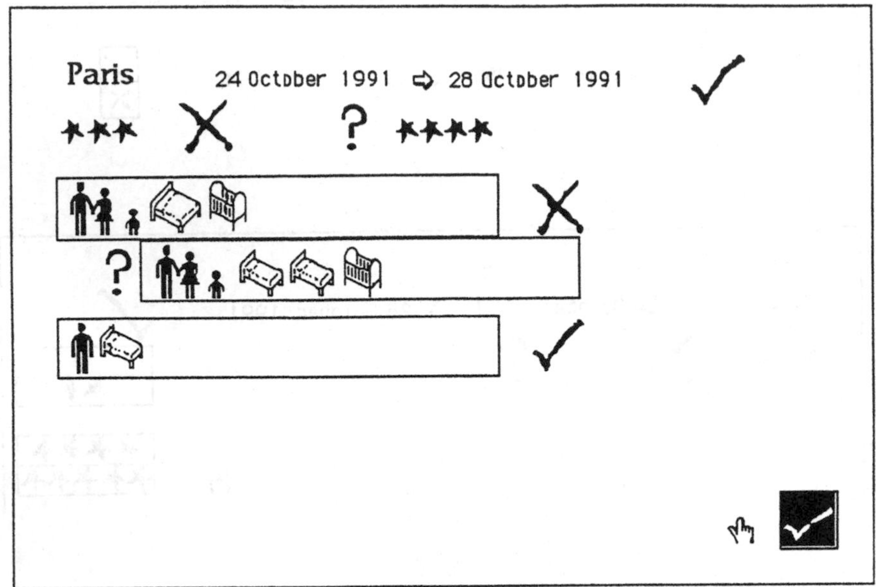

Fig. 8.

practical in real terms, but is an initial attempt to create a simple, interactive, iconic dialogue using hotel booking as the theme. It does, however offer much that could be used in a real system, and serves its purpose in starting to explore the possibility of communicating with icons.

CONCLUSION

Our work has the goal of cross language communication and is similar in sprit to the work reported in Beardon, Dormann, Mealing and Yazdani (1992). Unlike previous computer based icon systems, the purpose of our work is to explore unrestricted person to person communication. In this work we wish to go beyond the role of pictures as adjuncts to the written word but as replacement to it.

Beardon's (1992) work in particular is worthy of serious consideration as he has used Schank's (1975) Conceptual Dependency formalism, with the ultimate referential objects of the message being self-explaining icons. Messages are composed by selecting options from a small number of carefully designed screens which can be accessed recursively. The recipient receives and animated version of the message using actors which are represented by simple icons.

Beardon's system differs from ours in that there is a small element of syntactic structure which the user needs to learn. However, it shows that it is feasible to build a non-textual language for communication with few learned conventions. How much learning the user of an iconic language needs is a matter of debate between various groups in this expanding research community. What is unanimously agreed is that it is a worthwhile research topic to explore the various options in more detail.

NOTE

[1] This protoype is created in HyperCard™ and is operated with a standard mouse, but conversion to other input devices, such as a touch screen, is anticipated by the design.

REFERENCES

Beardon, C., Dormann, C., Mealing, S. & Yazdani, M. (1993). Talking with Pictures: Exploring the Possibilities of Iconic Communication. *Association for Learning Technology Journal* **1**(1): 26–39.

Beardon, C. (1992). CD-Icon: An Iconic Language Based on Conceptual Dependency. *Intelligent Tutoring Media* **3**(4): 111–116.

Jones, S. (1990). eL: A Multilingual Grammar Analysing System. Technical Report, Department of Computer Science. University of Exeter.

Kobayashi, K. (1986). *Computers and Communications*. MIT Press: Boston, MA.

Mealing, S. & Yazdani, M. (1990). A computer-Based Iconic Language. *Intelligent Tutoring Media* **1**(3): 133–136.

Neurath, O. (1978). *International Picture Language*. University of Reading.

Schank, R. (1975). *Conceptual Information Processing*. Amsterdam: North Holland.

Yazdani, M. (1987). Artificial Intelligence for Tutoring. In Whiting, J. & Bell, D. A. (eds.) *Tutoring and Monitoring Facilities for European Open Learning*, 239–248. Elsevier Science Publishers.

Yazdani, M & Goring, D. (1990). Iconic Communication, Technical Report, Department of Computer Science. University of Exeter.

Artificial Intelligence Review **9**: 215–235, 1995.

Language Visualisation: Applications and Theoretical Foundations of a Primitive-Based Approach

A. NARAYANAN, D. MANUEL, L. FORD, D. TALLIS and M. YAZDANI

Department of Computer Science, University of Exeter, Exeter EX4 4PT, U.K., e-mail: {ajit,dma,lindsey,dta,masoud}@dcs.exeter.ac.uk

Abstract. Language visualisation consists of using consistent and systematic mappings between language expressions and graphical forms, where the graphical forms constitute or convey the meaning of the expressions. Primitive-based applications are described for both natural and artificial language (story visualisation and program visualisation, respectively). On the basis of these and other applications some foundational concepts are identified in a bottom-up theory of visualisation. A universal visualisation system architecture is proposed, as is a basic visual object taxonomy for classifying any visualisation object. Also, preliminary steps are taken towards constructing a top-down theory.[1]

Key words: language visualisation, software visualisation, visualisation theory, language animation, primitive-based visualisation.

1. INTRODUCTION

The focus of this paper is on language visualisation, where 'language' encompasses both natural and artificial languages. The term 'language' is defined broadly as any system which systematically relates some physical signal (a symbol structure or expression, a sound, a gesture) to meaning. 'Visualisation' on the other hand can be defined as a consistently applied mapping between the incoming information that the visualisation is representing and the outgoing graphical form (Cox and Roman 1994). 'Language visualisation' is therefore the use of systematic and consistent mappings between language input and output graphical forms, where the graphical forms constitute or convey the meaning of the input language.

Software visualisation is an example of visualising artificial languages. For instance, a data structure such as an array can be visualised by representing its elements as rectangles, the sizes of which change over time as the values of the elements change (Figure 1). Instructions on data structures (e.g. conditionals, iteration, recursion) can be visualised by patterns of movement of the graphical objects corresponding to the data structures, where the patterns convey the meaning of the instruction. The motivation here is to identify ways in which

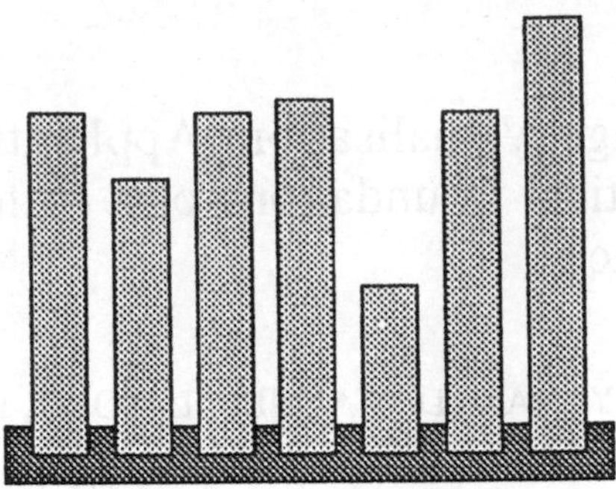

Fig. 1. A possible visualisation of an array. Each column represents one element of the array (here, seven elements), and the height represents the value of the element: the higher the column, the greater the value. Here, there is a direct mapping between data structure and the visual objects making the representation. The semantics of the data structure is portrayed visually, and the element with largest value (the seventh) is easily identified. If the visualisation is dynamic, the columns will change in height as the element values change.

the presentation of visual information and the consistency of the mapping can aid the process of understanding the behaviour of software for design, debugging, testing and educational purposes (Ford 1993a, c; Ford and Tallis 1993; Ford 1994; Manuel 1994).

Story visualisation is an example of visualising natural language, where the motivation is to produce images for disambiguating and aiding understanding of text.[2] For instance, a story of someone going to a restaurant can be visualised by representing individual expressions from the story in such a way that the relationships between agents, objects, recipients and props are clearly depicted (Narayanan *et al.* 1994). Also, the correct use of spatial propositions in English (Olivier and Tsujii 1994, Olivier *et al.* 1994) and other languages (Buschbeck-Wolf 1992; Reyero-Sans and Tsujii 1994) can be portrayed through visualisation. If the task is to facilitate language learning (Yazdani 1991; Yazdani and Mealing 1995), the context of sentences in the second language can be presented visually to the learner. If a system produces output in an unfamiliar language, e.g. Arabic (Narayanan and Hashem 1993, 1994), it can switch to visual representations of the text to aid understanding.

Visualisation of language can be static or dynamic. With static representations each expression of an artificial or natural language has its own visual representation independently of other expressions. Dynamic representations visually represent expressions depending on the representation of previous expressions, so that a sequence of visual representations is built up where the start configuration of a displayed representation follows from the end configuration of the previously displayed representation. Dynamic representations are in turn of two kinds. The first is goal-oriented, where only visual representations of individual expressions are presented, with each representation computed as a function of the previous representation together with any new information in the current expression, e.g. (Rajagopalan 1994; Ó Nualláin *et al.* 1994; Gapp and Maass 1994). The second is process-oriented, where the process of moving from one representation to the next, as well as any processes involved within a representation, are also visually displayed so that users can see all intermediate stages, but not necessarily at the same level of detail. For instance, special emphasis may be put on particular sequences in the visualisation because they are stressed in some way.

Designing a process-oriented visual representation system for language immediately raises the question of how detailed the process should be. At one extreme, there could be minimality, i.e. as few 'bridging' visualisations as possible, where bridging visualisations fill in gaps between what is explicitly expressed. At the other extreme, there is maximality, where there is smooth continuity across bridging representations *and* within a representation. For instance, visual maximality for the two expressions 'John entered the restaurant. He sat down' would fill in the gap between entering and sitting as well as what is involved in the process of 'entering' and 'sitting down'. Each of these actions would be continuously visualised. Such continuity leads to the idea of *language animation*, where language visualisation consists of designing and developing visual representations for individual, dynamic expressions as well as for the processes involved in moving from one expression to another (Narayanan *et al.* 1994).

2. PRIMITIVE-BASED VISUALISATION

It makes sense to adopt a primitive-based approach to dynamic visualisation, provided that the primitives are themselves dynamic, i.e. can represent changes of state or sequences of events. Extra procedures can be added for mapping from dynamic primitives in one expression/visualisation to those in subsequent expressions/visualisations. For example, consider the conceptual dependency (Schank 1972) primitive PTRANS, which is the primitive act of physically transferring an object from one location to another. Figure 2 contains 2-D and 3-D designs for PTRANS. Figure 3 provides designs for ATTEND (turning a sense organ in a certain direction), Figure 4 for MBUILD (constructing new information from old), and Figure 5 for ATRANS (the transfer of an abstract relationship such as 'possession'). Only the start and end points of the dynamic visual primitive are provided in these figures. In between there will be a sequence which provides continuity. The example 3-D visualisation (Figures 6–10) of 'going to a restaurant' introduces other visualisation primitives for MOVE (for moving a body part) and INGEST (for taking something inside one's body).

While conceptual dependency provides a neat primitive-based notation for the design of visualisation primitives (see (Beardon 1992, 1995) for the use of conceptual dependency primitives for the purpose of communicating by icons), alternative primitive-based language notations can also be used. The claim being made is that visualisation is facilitated if the source text to be visualised can be represented in a primitive-based form, where such primitives deal with actions, events and states, such as visualisation of parallel processes, e.g. (Turner and Cai 1992, Cai *et al.* 1994); connectionist networks, e.g. (Sharkey *et al.* 1994);

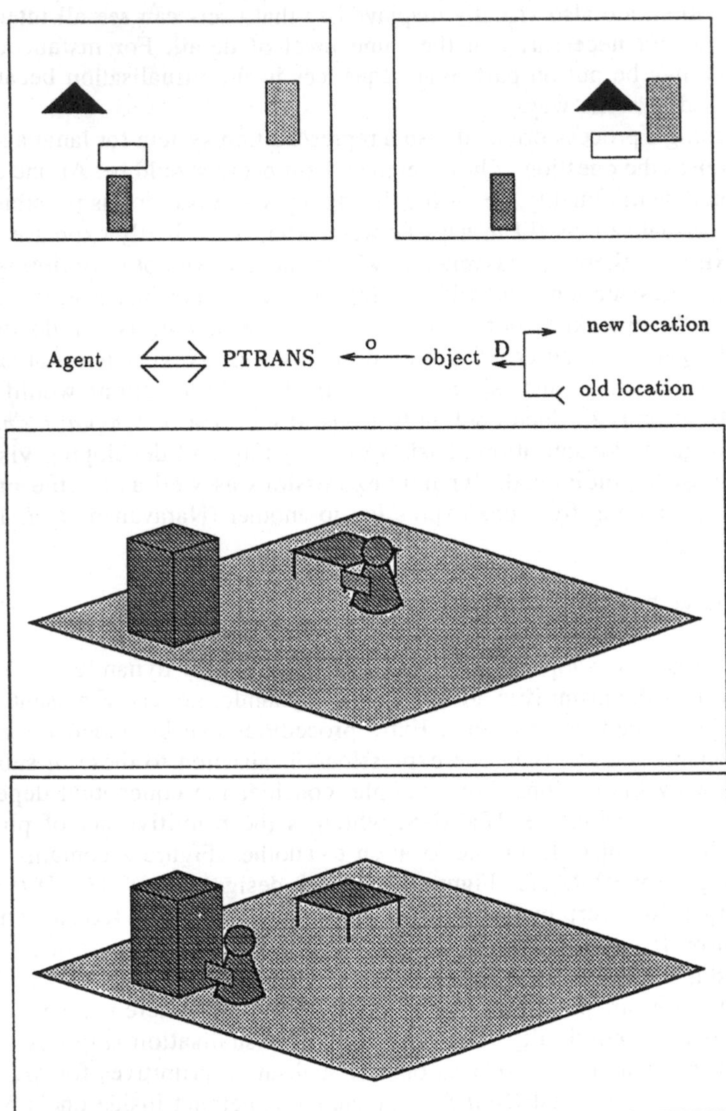

Fig. 2. 2-D and 3-D visualisations of the PTRANS primitive. In the 2-D design the agent (triangle) moves an object (white rectangle) from one location (filled rectangle at the bottom of the first box) to another (filled rectangle at the right of the second box). In the case of an agent PTRANSing himself/herself, there is no object, and the agent's movement from one location to another will be animated. What is shown here and in the other designs is just the start and end points of the animation. Bridging visualisations provide continuity of action. The nature and location of objects will depend on previous expressions and associated visualisations.

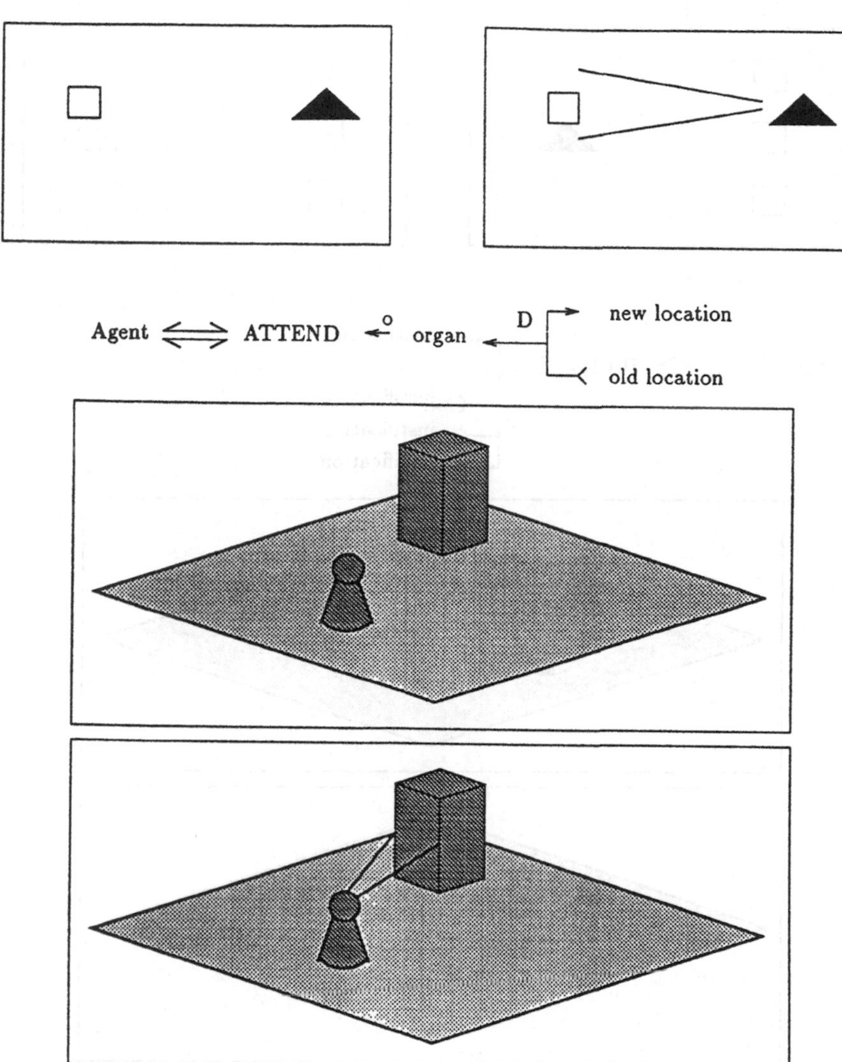

Fig. 3. 2-D and 3-D designs for the ATTEND primitive. Different ways of expressing attending with eyes, ears, and so on, can be designed.

temporal logics, e.g. (Herzog 1992); spatial logics, e.g. (Sablayrolles 1992); and geometrical reasoning, e.g. (Balbiani and del Cerro 1992).

3. AN EXAMPLE STORY

Consider the following subset of the restaurant script:[3] *John PTRANS John into restaurant; John ATTEND eyes to table; John MBUILD where to sit; John*

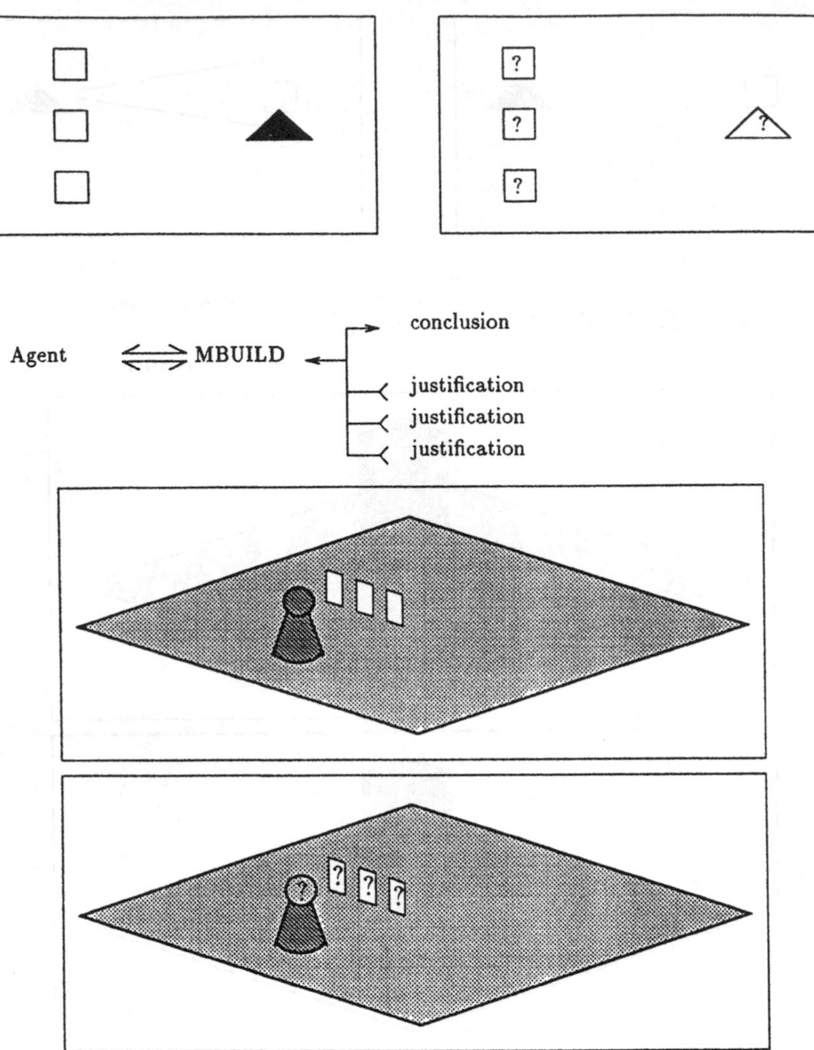

Fig. 4. 2-D and 3-D designs for the MBUILD primitive. The '?' in the agent is reflected in the '?' in the objects which are used for the act of MBUILD.

PTRANS John to table; John MOVE John to sitting position; Waiter PTRANS waiter to table; Waiter ATRANS menu to John; John ATTEND eyes to menu; John MBUILD choice of food (F); John MTRANS 'I want F' to waiter; Waiter PTRANS waiter to chef; Waiter MTRANS 'customer wants F' to chef; Chef DO (prepare F); Chef ATRANS F to waiter; Waiter ATRANS F to John; John INGEST F; John MTRANS to waiter (Waiter ATRANS bill to John); Waiter PTRANS waiter to John; Waiter ATRANS bill to John; John PTRANS John to cashier; John ATRANS money and bill to cashier; John PTRANS John out of restaurant.

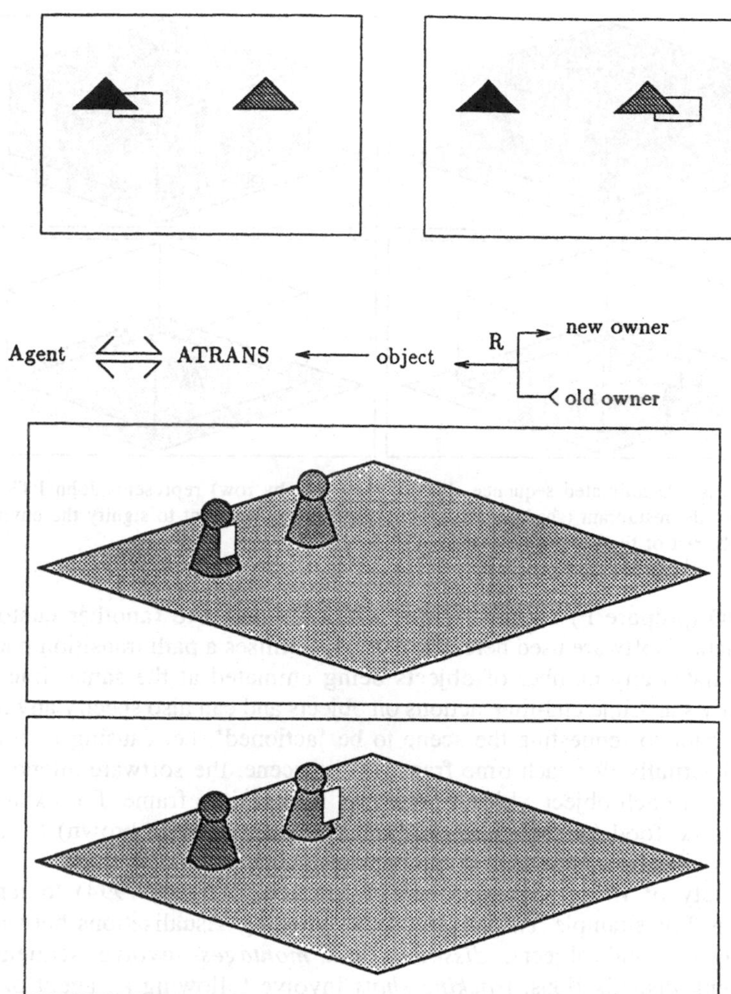

Fig. 5. 2-D and 3-D designs for the ATRANS primitive. The object (white rectangle) is transferred from one agent to another.

The visualisation of this sequence is provided in Figures 6–10. The process of moving from one expression to another is captured in a sequence of animations taking into account the roles and locations of individuals and objects, and the actions to be performed upon them. Visualisation primitives are linked to language primitives via a dictionary, and the re-occurrence of various agents and objects in the language primitives are used to generate bridging visualisations between visualisations explicitly representing individual conceptualisations. Objects and/or agents need not be moved in the animation unless the primitives require them to be moved.

Also, animations of different objects can occur concurrently. For example, if

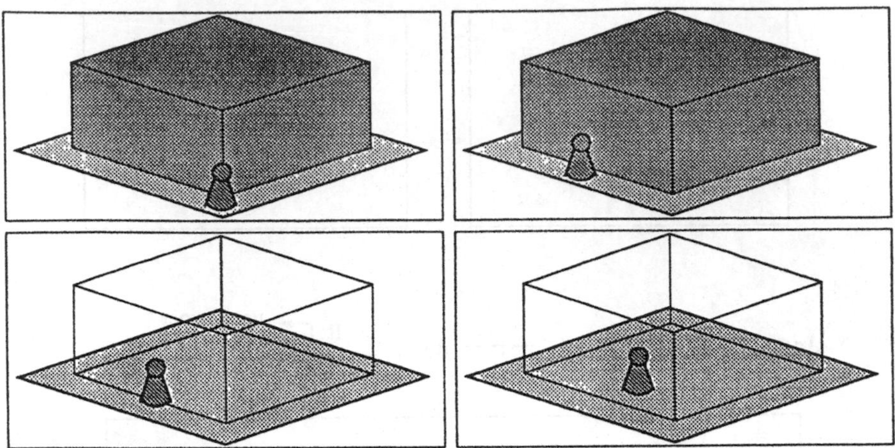

Fig. 6. This 3-D animated sequence (left-to-right, row by row) represents John PTRANSing himself into the restaurant (shaded cube), which becomes transparent to signify the environment in which the rest of the story takes place.

'Chef DO (prepare F)' while 'Waiter ATRANS menu to ⟨another customer⟩', the animation software used here (Ford 1993b) utilises a path transition paradigm that facilitates any number of objects being animated at the same time. Users can specify start-time/end-time actions on objects and can also specify any number of these prior to requesting the scene to be 'actioned', i.e. causing it to be displayed. Internally, for each time frame of the scene, the software attends to the animation of each object which is acted on in that time frame. For example, in Figure 9, the food (white rectangle) can change colour (to brown) to indicate cooking while the waiter serves another customer.

A variety of film techniques can be applied (Manuel 1994) to language animation. For example, *cutting* involves switching visualisations between different agents and objects, *dissolves* and *montages* involve sequences of overlapping visualisations, *tracking shots* involve following an agent or object through some complex scenario (such as following the customer), *establishing shots* involve setting the scene (as in Figure 6 where the restaurant is expanded), and *cut-away shots* involve a brief shot to clarify a link. Pauses can be introducd after explicitly stated events in the story so that these are distinguished from implicitly stated events. Current research is directed towards implementing these facilities using 3-D animations, where the perspective and magnification of the animations can be altered, including 'entering the head' of an animated agent to follow the action from the agent's point of view.

4. TOWARDS A BOTTOM-UP THEORY OF VISUALISATION

At present most visualisations tend to be specialised towards their specific tasks (e.g. knowledge representation for video (Davis 1994)). A number of common

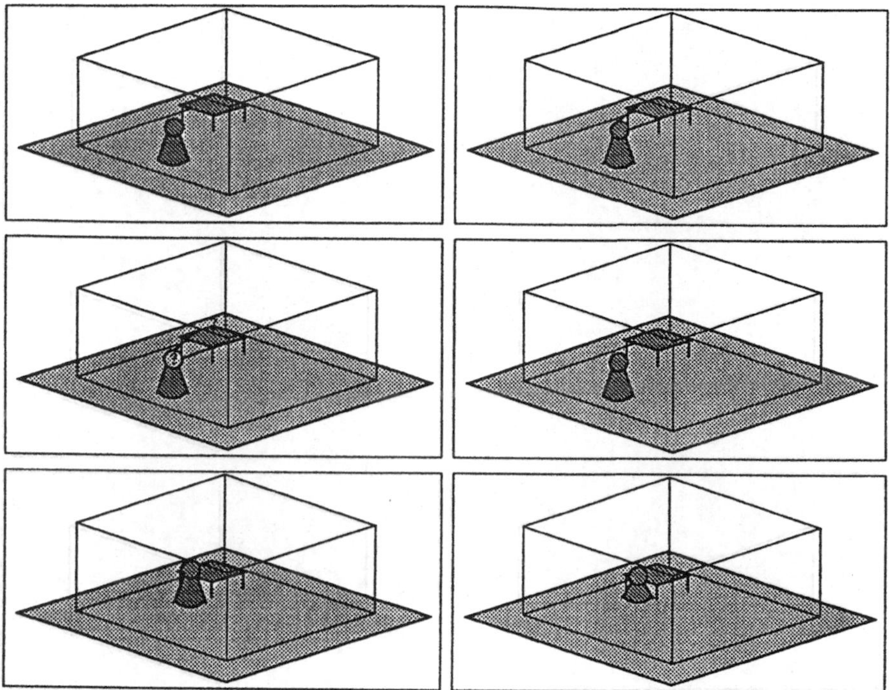

Fig. 7. This sequence animates the actions of John looking at a table and deciding whether to sit there. After moving towards the table, John sits down (the agent symbol is squashed).

visualisation techniques which occur in existing systems for program visualisation and which also appear in the visualisations described in this paper include (Price *et al.* 1993):

- The use of arrowed lines to indicate pointers and other forms of access to items.
- The use of boxes that are variable in size to indicate values of various kinds. The size of the box is proportional to the value of the variable represented.
- The use of objects that change colour (black to white) to show boolean values or changes of state (rather than value).
- The use of boxes to group together related items such as the fields of an objects, or array elements.
- The use of colour in an abstract way, so that an object's colour does not represent a value or state but is used to differentiate between different graphical objects (e.g. two actors in a single environment).

As more visualisation systems are implemented an increasing number of visual presentation techniques, perhaps based on visual data in psychology, will be identified as effective for different purposes. Such techniques can form part of a theory of visualisation as the number of applications grows. There are, however, two other ways in which such visualisation theory can be formed: through commonalities in (a) system architecture, and (b) system representation of visual information.

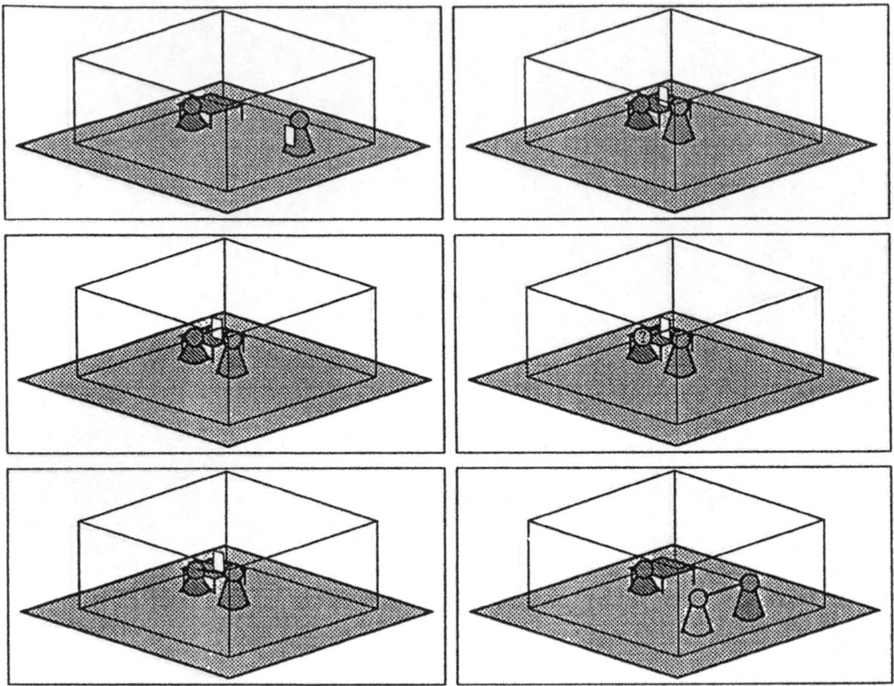

Fig. 8. The waiter, who possesses the menu (white object), moves towards John's table and hands the menu to John, who scans it, decides what to eat, and communicates his choice (arrow) to the waiter who then moves to the chef and informs the chef.

4.1. *System Architecture*

Our system of visualisation can be divided into three main parts (Figure 11):

- Writer: The system that generates the relevant system commands for the visualisation from the expressions to be visualised.
- Actors: The objects contained within the system that act upon the orders of the Writer to fulfil the requirements of the visualisation.
- Director: The system derivation that ascribes attributes to the various components of the system.

4.1.1. *Writers*

The Writer has the task of converting specific objects (and their specific commands) found in the source text (typically an event trace file or a story represented in a suitable primitive-based form) into the small number of general objects used by the system. The Writer must also make the relevant conversions of their single operations into a sequence of simple general operations as given by basic objects in a taxonomy of visual objects (Section 4.2), using any domain-specific knowledge in the process. The Writer states what the actions of the visual objects in the system are to be (rather than how an action is to be

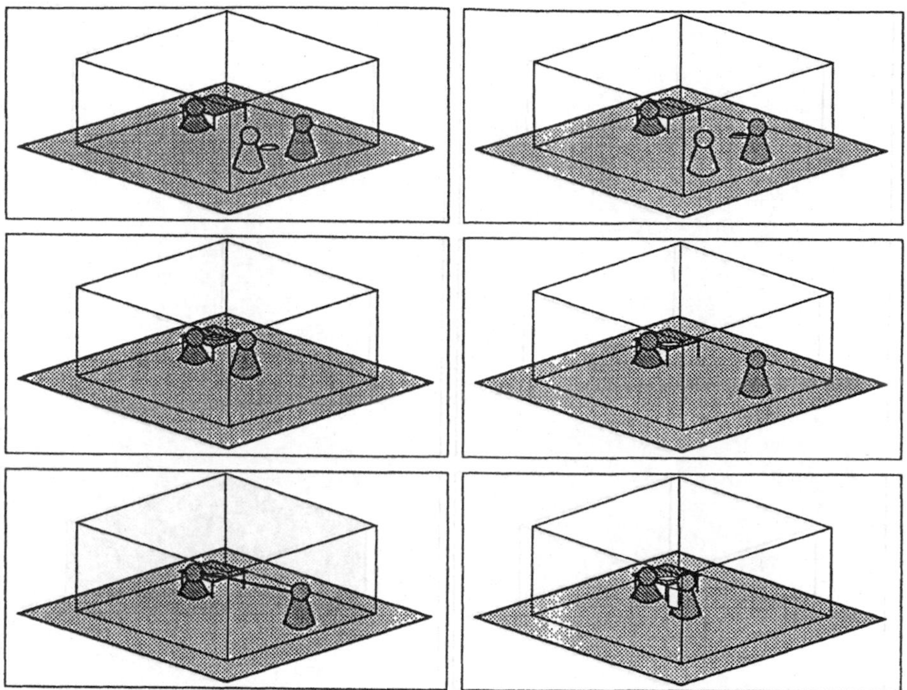

Fig. 9. The chef prepares the food (circular object) and hands it to the waiter, who puts it on John's table. After eating, John asks the waiter for the bill (white rectangle).

visualised). For example, a visualisation of an event (e.g. 'customer PTRANS customer into restaurant') is re-written as a sequence of Writer expressions which require the creation of an agent 'customer', an environment 'restaurant' and the movement of the agent into the environment. (An example of Writer output is presented in Section 4.3.)

In the case of visualising stories, the output sequence from the Writer is in the form of a Visual Script which contains information about the sorts of entities which have occurred in the story as well as the proper sequence of events. The Writer will need access to the general script of going to a restaurant so that it can check for the correct sequence of events in the input story against the general template of such stories. Implicit events need not be represented as completely as explicit events in the Visual Script (e.g. if the chef is not explicitly mentioned in the input story, there may be no need to visualise in detail the chef's preparation of food). In the case of software visualisation, the input to the Writer will typically be from an event trace file. For example, the addition of one variable to another may be visualised in any number of ways depending on the objects used to represent each of the variables. However, all that is created by the Writer is a request for *ADD A* to *B*, which is stored in the Visual Script. The sequence of commands in the general Visual Script events is passed to the Director.

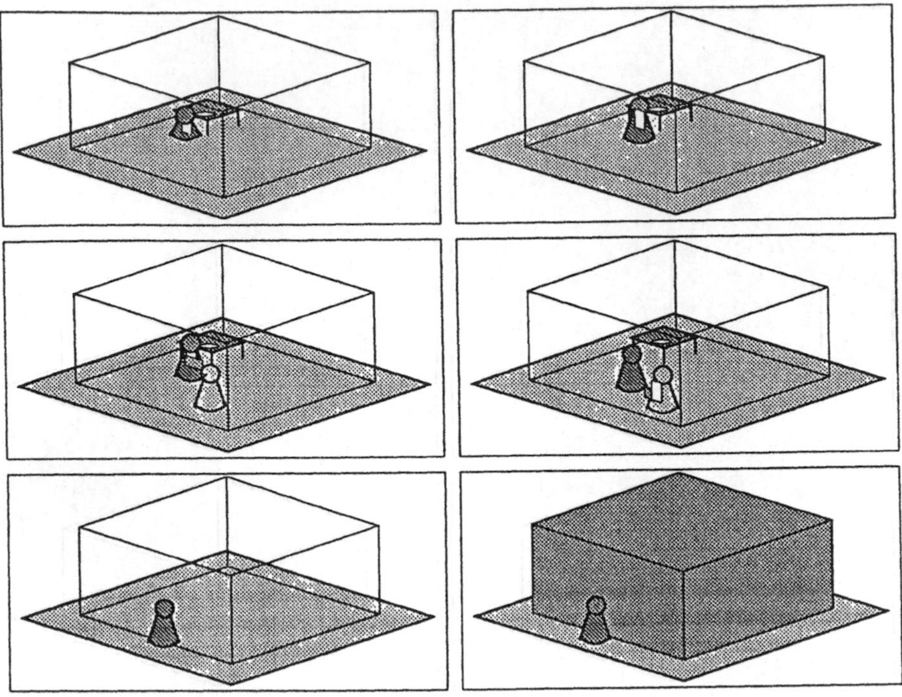

Fig. 10. John stands up with the bill, gets some money (second, small shaded rectangle), and hands the bill and money to the cashier (another agent) before leaving the restaurant.

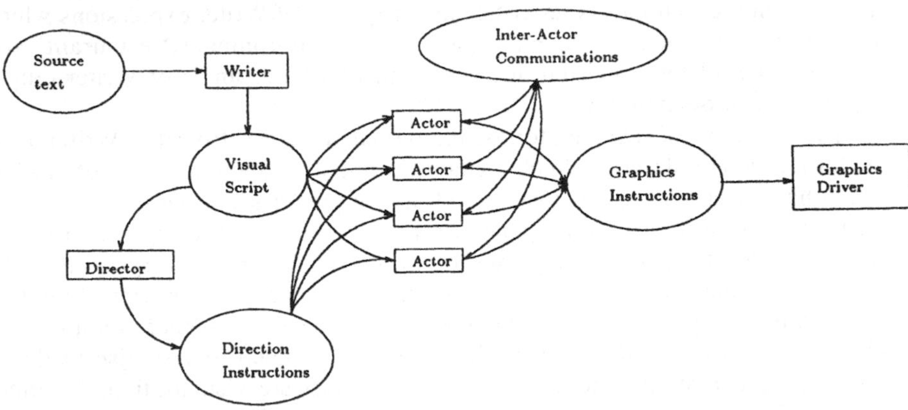

Fig. 11. The data flow diagram for the system architecture. The architecture assumes a script-based story as input, but an event file based on a particular program run can also be used. Although only four actors are depicted, there can be any number of actors. The graphics driver (i) converts the graphics commands produced by actors into actual visual displays, and (ii) manipulates these displays.

4.1.2. *Directors*

The Director takes the Visual Script and decides (i) what visual constructs are shown at any point in the visualisation, (ii) in what form they are used (e.g. used as a value or as a pointer), and (iii) what values their size, position, colour and any other attributes available should take. As a result of these decisions, the Director can associate particular and appropriate Actor objects from a library of previously used Actors. These decisions are expressed in the form of Director Instructions. It may also decide on the importance of each of the objects within the overall framework, so that it can then determine which actions should be performed the fastest or slowest, or whether they can be ignored due to lack of immediate relevance. These Direction Instructions are fed to the appropriate Actor which also contains knowledge from the Visual Script as to what its role and actions are.

The Director need not be an automatic program. The user can use an interface to the Director as a design tool. In this case users are Directors and form the structure of the visualisation themselves. The alternative is that the Director program uses automated reasoning to determine how much importance to place on each object and what form and size it should take. This can be done by some form of semantic analysis of the data being visualised. The Director can use the information sent to it by the Writer and Visual Script (a) to analyze the calls made on objects for an indication of semantic information, and (b) to cast the types of Actor available.

4.1.3. *Actors*

The Actors are individual self contained objects. This section of the system is object-oriented in the tradition of object-oriented programming (see (Strassmann 1994) for another object-oriented approach to visual Actors). Objects are created by Direction Instructions, and their roles are determined by the Visual Script. The objects represent variables, functions, literal values, Schank-like agents and props, and other such constructs. There will be a number of different object types, each representing either a different type of construct (e.g. string or integer) or constructs used in different contexts (the difference between an integer used to represent a value and one used to represent an array index, or two different props in a Schank-like script). These objects inherit characteristics from other object types and, via Inter-Actor Communications, have operations (e.g. requests for positional information) performed on them using only their own internal functions. They also contain values or states (in whatever form they may take, assuming that they have any form of value/state). This allows for different types of object to interact without the need for special-case instructions to deal with object type conflicts. Active Actors produce graphics instructions specifying graphical manipulations of themselves and other Actors. The information needed by an Actor is provided by the Direction Instructions as well as Visual Script events. Each Actor, via Inter-Actor Communications, will have knowledge of what its current object state is. These graphics instructions are in turn fed to a Graphics Driver of a GUI for display.

There may be a relatively large number of possible Actors and objects to choose from. The objects used in the visualisation of a 'going-to-a-restaurant' story will not necessarily be the same as those used in ordinary programs, but the interfaces to these objects will be of the same form. The use of object-oriented techniques allows the constant addition of new objects without the need for alteration of the original objects. As an example, imagine that the data being visualised is a program event file (for software visualisation) which includes a one-dimensional array and two integer variables, one of which is used as the index for the array. When these variables are visually represented it makes sense for the objects to signify that one of the three object is an array and one of the other objects is used with it in a particular way. By looking through the event file the Writer can determine that one of the objects is an array from the program/module declarations. This is cross-referenced by the Director with all objects that it knows of that can be used to represent arrays. For the index, the fact that it is always being used in conjunction with the array in the dereferencing operation should indicate its semantic meaning and a visual object representing an array index relevant to the visual array object is chosen. The positioning and scaling of these objects are then based on each other, as are any limits or guidelines suggested by the visual object definitions. Similar examples can be given for Schank-like scripts and other possible applications.

Summarising, Writers decide what should happen. It does this by mapping between input source text and an object hierarchy (to be described below), using any other domain-specific knowledge available. This information is stored in a Visual Script. Directors determine what form the events in the Visual Script should take. They do this by casting Actors and giving them specific attributes and values. Actors perform the relevant actions described in the Visual Script under Direction Instructions. They are driven by events in the Visual Script, the Direction Instructions and Inter-Actor Communications. Actors produce Graphics Instructions which in turn are fed to a GUI via a Graphics Driver.

Possible problems with this approach are:

1. Poor visual constructs: The hierarchy of visual objects used by the Writer, and the derived animations, do not provide an adequate basis for meaningful visualisation.
2. Poor Visual Script: The Writer commands are not sufficiently detailed to provide meaningful visualisations (because, for example, the domain-specific knowledge is not adequate). Objects and Actors are either too similar and so are difficult to differentiate, or are too different when they should be similar.
3. Poor casting: The Director issues Direction Instructions which fail to take into account the appropriate roles of Actors and values of objects.
4. Inappropriate display of Actors: The Director generates inappropriate Direction Instructions, leading to badly structured displays. For instance, Actors who are dormant for a lengthy period of time should be removed temporarily from the display, or there are too many Actors popping in and out of displays.
5. Poor Inter-Actor Communications: Communications between Actors are slow or inappropriate.

4.2. *System Representation of Visual Information*

From our empirical work in different applications a hierarchy of visual objects for use by Writers is beginning to emerge. Figure 12 shows a basic breakdown of objects. *General Object* forms the root class and contains basic information about properties of objects in general. There are two subclasses: *Active* and *Passive*. Active objects are objects which can ask other objects (passive or active) to carry out various functions. Passive objects receive requests and cannot activate other objects. So far, the only subclass of active objects used in our applications have been *Active Entities* (Agents). Such entities can be assigned tasks, can refer tasks to other objects (including themselves, as in 'John PTRANS John to . . .'), and can deal with conditions and other complex procedural requirements, such as task delegation and coordination. For example, 'John' and 'waiter' are active in 'John MTRANS signal to waiter', and 'John' is active and 'food' is passive in 'John INGEST food'. Passive objects can be *Fixed Objects* or *Variable Attribute Objects*. The former are objects which, once their values are set on initialisation, cannot be modified. They can only be created or copied. There are two subclasses: *Fixed Attribute Objects* are objects such as literals and constants (e.g. 'table' in 'John PTRANS John to table', where once the table object is created it will remain constant during the visualisation). Such objects will not move or be moved, nor will their properties (e.g. size) change.[4] The attributes of an *Environment* are also set at create time and can only be copied. The restaurant environment object, for instance, will consist of four walls, a floor and a ceiling, with fittings (e.g. lights), none of which will be subsequently modified. Variable attribute objects are objects which, while not active, can be modified. For instance, a chair is a variable attribute object, in that its

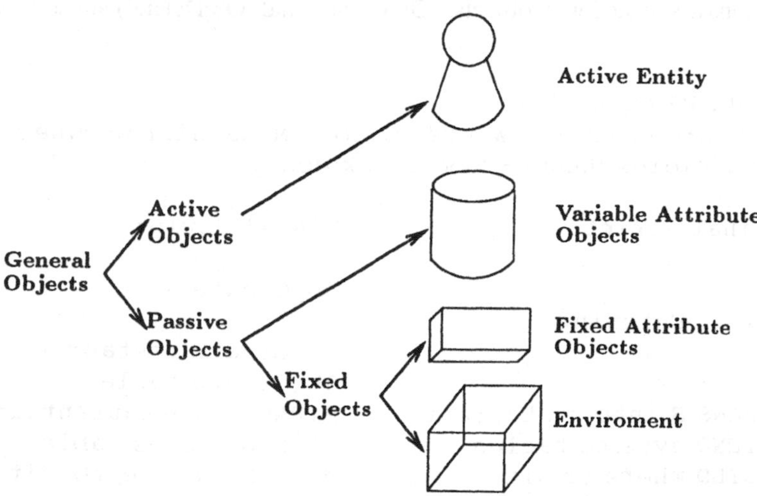

Fig. 12. A basic taxonomy of visual object types. Objects at lower levels become more specific to certain objects and tasks, but less capable of performing general tasks. Problems with object mapping could arise if objects are represented at the wrong level of the hierarchy.

location can change (it may be moved from one table to another) and its status can take one of two values ('empty', 'occupied').

The class into which individual objects fall within the taxonomy will be determined by the application. For instance, in one restaurant script tables may be fixed attribute objects and chairs variable attribute objects. However, in a student cafeteria tables may be variable attribute objects: Actors may move tables around to form bigger tables around which a group can sit and eat. The question of how to classify individual objects in the event file (for program visualisation) and a story (for visualising natural language) is a current research topic.

One way is to make a dynamic classification as the event file is processed (as the story unfolds) and then either reclassify if the initial classification is shown to be wrong, or set up an 'exception link' between the individual object and its parent object to signify that certain properties are not to be inherited from the parent object.[5] Another is to process the event file twice: first, to identify the objects and second, to identify their roles and thereby their classifications.

The hypothesis is that one system alone with a small set of objects can visualise a large number of domains. Increased generalisation may allow for the existence of systems that visualise many scripts or sets of instructions, provided that some way of systematically classifying entities in programs and scripts onto the basic taxonomy can be found. The only part of the system which then needs changing from one application to another is the Writer, with one Writer to each potential application.

4.3. *Application of Theory to a Schank-like Script*

The following is an example of how a Schank-like script is converted by a Writer into a Visual Script which uses objects taken from the taxonomy. The basic operations associated with objects ('ObjCreate' and 'ObjDelete') are self-explanatory.

```
Script: RESTAURANT
Roles: S-Customer W-Waiter C-Cook M-Cashier O-Owner
Props: Tables Menu F-Food Check Money

Original Script                     Visual Script

                                    ObjCreate S
Scene 1: Entering
                                    ObjCreate restaurant
                                    ObjCreate table
S PTRANS S into restaurant          PTRANS S restaurant.inside
S ATTEND eyes to tables             ATTEND S.eyes table
S MBUILD where to sit               MBUILD S where_to_sit
S PTRANS S to table                 PTRANS S table
S MOVE S to sitting position        MOVE   S sitting_position
```

```
Scene 2: Ordering
                                      ObjCreate W
S MTRANS signal to W                  MTRANS S.'signal' W
W PTRANS W to table                   PTRANS W table
S MTRANS 'need menu' to W             MTRANS S.'need menu' W
                                      ObjCreate menu
W PTRANS W to menu                    PTRANS W menu
W PTRANS W to table                   GRASP W menu
                                      PTRANS W table
W ATRANS menu to S                    ATRANS S W.menu
S MTRANS menu to CP(S)                MTRANS CP(S) menu
S MBUILD 'choice of food'             MBUILD S.choice_of_food
                                        menu
S MTRANS signal to W                  MTRANS S W
W PTRANS W to table                   PTRANS W table
S MTRANS 'choice of food' to W        MTRANS S.choice_of_food W
                                      ObjCreate C
W PTRANS W to C                       PTRANS W C
W MTRANS (ATRANS F) to C              MTRANS W.choice_of_food C
                                      ATRANS W.choice_of_food C
C DO (prepare F) to scene 3           ObjCreate F C

Scene 3: Eating
C ATRANS F to W                       ATRANS W F.C
W ATRANS F to S                       PTRANS W S
                                      ATRANS W.F C
                                      ObjDelete C
S INGEST F                            INGEST S F
                                      ObjDelete F

Scene 4: Exiting
S MTRANS to W                         MTRANS S W
  (W ATRANS bill to S)                ATRANS S W.bill
W MOVE (write check)                  ObjCreate S.check
W PTRANS W to S                       PTRANS W S
W ATRANS check to S                   ATRANS S W.check
S ATRANS tip to W                     ATRANS W S.tip
                                      ObjDelete W
                                      ObjCreate M
S PTRANS S to M                       PTRANS S M
S ATRANS money to M                   ATRANS M S.money
                                      ObjDelete M
S PTRANS S outside restaurant         PTRANS S restaurant.
                                        outside
                                      ObjDelete restaurant
                                      ObjDelete S
```

```
Definitions:
  ATRANS - Transfer of abstract relationship.
  PTRANS - Physical movement (transfer) of object.
  ATTEND - Focus sense organ on something.
  MTRANS - Transfer of mental information.
  MOVE - Movement of body part of animal.
  INGEST - Taking an object into an animal.
  MBUILD - Construction of new information from old.
```

An interesting additional item here is the need for the Writer to determine when objects must be created and deleted, with no explicit information in the script for guidance. For instance, tables must remain in the environment even though there may be no further reference to tables after the initial reference 'John looked at the tables', while the waiter can disappear while John is eating his food (Narayanan *et al.* 1994).

5. TOWARDS A TOP-DOWN THEORY OF VISUALISATION

Section 4.2 proposed a hierarchy of objects for visualising any domain. The mapping between objects and domain is made by Writers through an analysis of program event traces (artificial language) or stories (natural language). Writers may require domain-specific knowledge (e.g. a script) at this point. Another way to achieve a systematic and consistent mapping is to examine the whole program (rather than a specific event file which represents one path through the program) or the whole script (rather than an individual story which also represents just one path through the script) and use the information available in the program declarations and executable statements (script declarations and conceptualisations, respectively) to make an initial classification. The idea here is that once the complete and total artificial language structure (program) or natural language structure (script) is captured visually at some high enough level, all visual instances of that program (runs) or scripts (stories) are derivable from this high level structure, in the same way that program traces and stories are derivable from the program and script. There is then no need for detailed analyses of individual event trace files or stories: a visualisation is path through a high level, previously produced, visual representation. Writers can then just check whereabouts in this previously produced representation individual expressions in the input text occur, so that it can identify the path being taken through this high level visual representation by the actual story or event trace. Again, it makes sense to adopt a primitive-based approach here: if the source text can be broken down into text-based primitives, and the text-based primitives are associated with visual primitives which occur in the high level visual counterpart, identification of the path taken by the story or event trace will be facilitated.

For this idea to work, a definitive mapping must be found between program and script constructs on the one hand, and on the other the way that objects in the visual object hierarchy described in Section 4.2 can be constituents of expressions in the associated high level visual representation. The definitions must be sufficiently broad to encompass program as well as script constructs, without becoming so general that they have no practical purpose. In particular, the low level information which is present in event trace files and stories and which may provide critical information for visualisation is completely ignored by this approach. The provision of definitive mappings may require an examination of language grammars where, for instance, each syntax rule for a particular language has a visual counterpart in a visual system. The visual system, in other words, provides a visual interpretation of each syntax rule. The mapping between language constructs and the hierarchy of visual objects could be performed at the leaves of the parse-tree which describes the syntactic structure of the complete expression (program/script), or at other levels of the parse-tree, or both. As stated earlier, an accurate, consistent and systematic mapping onto the appropriate levels of the visual object hierarchy is critical for the success of a visualisation.

6. SUMMARY

The approach described in this paper is process-oriented with maximal continuity (language animation). A way of linking language to visual representations was first described where language primitives have a direct mapping onto visual primitives. This was followed by an example visualisation of a story taken from the script literature (Schank and Abelson 1977). Based on this and other applications, first, a visualisation architecture was proposed which is not application-dependent, and secondly a general taxonomy was identified which forms the basis of classifying visual objects for any application. This led to the issue of higher levels of description for both natural and artificial languages for the purposes of visualisation. Together, the architecture, taxonomy and possible higher level descriptions provide a conceptual foundation in the search for a theory of computational visualisation.[6]

NOTES

[1] The authors are grateful to Patrick Olivier, Irina Reyero-Sans, Paul McKevitt and anonymous referees for comments at various stages during the drafting of this paper.

[2] See (Mc Kevitt 1994) for an overview of the ways that language and vision can be integrated.

[3] Scripts (Schank and Abelson 1977) are knowledge organisation representations which describe stereotyped sequences of events in particular contexts. Scripts consist of entry conditions, a result, agents, objects, props, roles, scenes and conceptualisations representing events. Events within a script are causally ordered: if event x is before event y in the script, an agent must perform the action associated with event x before being able to perform the action associated with event y.

[4] Zooming in and out of a visualisation, and re-orientating a visualisation by, for instance, moving to the other side of a 3-D display, involve the movement and modification of passive (and active) objects for display purposes only. The graphical interface which changes the perspective of the visualisation according to user requirements does not modify any object attributes themselves. That is, it is important to distinguish the functions of the graphical interface from the functions of the visual objects displayed by the graphical interface. It is quite possible that, during a change of

perspective by the graphical interface, individual visual objects are moving around or are being manipulated by other visual objects, irrespective of the change of perspective.

[5] As long as the basic taxonomy of visual objects is hierarchical, there will be no problems concerning nonmonotonicity if an exception is introduced. See (Al-Asady and Narayanan 1993) for details of how exceptions might be handled in nonmonotonic multiple inheritance structures.

[6] Other aspects of such a theory, such as psychological and cognitive plausibility, aesthetics and HCI, while also important, have not been discussed here.

REFERENCES

Al-Asady, R. & Narayanan, A. (1993). More Notes on 'A Clash of Intuitions'. In Proceedings of *The 13th International Joint Conference on Artificial Intelligence (IJCAI93)*, 682–687.

Balbiani, P. & del Cerro, L. F. (1992). A Tableaux-Based Engine for Geometrical Reasoning. In Aurnague, M., Borillo, A., M. B. & Byas, M. (eds.) *Semantics of Time, Space, Movement and Spatio-Temporal Reasoning*, 407–418. Groupe LRC Toulouse. Working papers of the 4th International Workshop.

Beardon, C. (1992). CD-Icon: An Iconic Language Based on Conceptual Dependency. *Intelligent Tutoring Media* **3**(4): 111–116.

Beardon, C. (1995). Discourse Structures in Iconic Communication. *Artificial Intelligence Review* **9**(2–3), 189–203 (this volume).

Buschbeck-Wolf, B. (1992). A Semantic Approach to the Translation of Locative Prepositions. In Aurnague, M., Borillo, A., M. B. & Byas, M. (eds.) *Semantics of Time, Space, Movement and Spatio-Temporal Reasoning*, 53–67. Group LRC Toulouse. Working papers of the 4th International Workshop.

Cai, W., Pian, T. L. & Turner, S. J. (1994). A Framework for Visual Parallel Programming. Technical report, University of Exeter Department of Computer Science. Available through anonymous ftp (atlas.ex.ac.uk), Report Number 288.

Cox, K. C. & Roman, G. C. (1994). A Characterization of the Computational Power of Rule-Based Visualization. *Journal of Visual Languages and Computing* **5**(1): 5–28.

Davis, M. (1994). Knowledge Representation for Video. In Proceedings of *The 12th National Conference on Artificial Intelligence (AAAI-94)*, 120–127. American Association for Artificial Intelligence.

Ford, L. (1993a). Automatic Software Visualization Using Visual arts Techniques. Technical report, University of Exeter Department of Computer Science. Available through anonymous ftp (atlas.ex.ac.uk), Report Number 279.

Ford, L. (1993b). Goofy Animation System. Technical report, University of Exeter Department of Computer Science. Available through anonymous ftp (atlas.ex.ac.uk), Report Number 266.

Ford, L. (1993c). How Programmers Visualize Programs. Technical report, University of Exeter Department of Computer Science. Available through anonymous ftp (atlas.ex.ac.uk), Report Number 271.

Ford, L. (1994). Interactive Learning and Researching with Visualization. In Franklin, S. D., Stubberud, A. R. & Wiedeman, L. (eds.) *University Education Uses of Visualization in Scientific Computing (IFIP Transactions A-48)*. Elsevier Science.

Ford, L. & Tallis, D. (1993). Interactive Visual Abstractions of Programs. Technical report, University of Exeter Department of Computer Science. Available through anonymous ftp (atlas.ex.ac.uk), Report Number 273.

Gapp, K.-P. & Maass, W. (1994). Spatial Layout Identification and Incremental Descriptions. In *Integration of Natural Language and Vision Processing: Workshop Notes*, 145–132. American Association for Artificial Intelligence. AAAI-94 Workshop Program.

Herzog, G. (1992). Utilizing Interval-Based Event Representations for Incremental High-level Scene Analysis. In Aurnague, M., Borillo, A., M. B. & Byas, M. (eds.) *Semantics of Time, Space, Movement and Spatio-Temporal Reasoning*, 453–463. Group LRC Toulouse. Working papers of the 4th International Workshop.

Jayez, J. (1992). Some Problems About Hybrid Symbolic Representations Based on French Motion

Verbs. In Aurnague, M., Borillo, A., M. B. & Byas, M. (eds.) *Semantics of Time, Space, Movement and Spatio-Temporal Reasoning*, 89–103. Groupe LRC Toulouse. Working papers of the 4th International Workshop.

Manuel, D. (1994). The Use of Art Media Techniques in Computer Visualizations and the Creation of Partially Automated Visualization Systems. Master's thesis, University of Exeter Department of Computer Science, Exeter, EX4 4PT, UK.

Mc Kevitt, P. (1994). Visions for Language. In *Integration of Natural Language and Vision Processing: Workshop Notes*, 47–57. American Association for Artificial Intelligence. AAAI-94 Workshop Program.

Narayanan, A., Ford, L., Manuel, D., Tallis, D. & Yazdani, M. (1994). Animating Language. In *Integration of Natural Language and Vision Processing: Workshop Notes*, 58–65. American Association for Artificial Intelligence. AAAI-94 Workshop Program.

Narayanan, A. & Hashem, L. (1993). On Abstract Finite State Morphology. In Proceedings of *The 6th Conference of the European Chapter of the Association for Computational Linguistics (EACL93)*, 297–304. Available through anony-mous ftp (atlas.ex.ac.uk), Report 272.

Narayanan, A. & Hashem, L. (1994). Finite State Abstractions on Arabic Morphology. *Artificial Intelligence Review* **7**(6): 373–400.

Ó Nualláin, S., Farley, B. & Smith, A. G. (1994). The Spoken Image System: On the Visual Interpretation of Verbal Scene Descriptions. In *Integration of Natural Language and Vision Processing: Workshop Notes*, 36–39. American Association for Artificial Intelligence. AAAI-94 Workshop Program.

Olivier, P., Maeda, T. & Tsujii, J.-I. (1994). Automatic Depiction of Spatial Descriptions. In Proceedings of *The 12th National Conference on Artificial Intelligence (AAAI-94)*, 1405–1410. Association for Artificial Intelligence.

Olivier, P. & Tsujii, J.-I. (1994). Prepositional Semantics in the WIP System. In *Integration of Natural Language and Vision Processing: Workshop Notes*, 139–144. American Association for Artificial Intelligence. AAAI-94 Workshop Program.

Price, B. A., Baeker, R. M. & Small, I. S. (1993). A Principled Taxonomy of Software Visualization. *Journal of Visual Languages and Computing* **4**(3): 211–266.

Rajagopalan, R. (1994). Integrating Text with Graphical Imput to a Knowledge Base. In *Integration of Natural Language and Vision Processing: Workshop Notes*, 14–21. American Association for Artificial Intelligence. AAAI-94 Workshop Program.

Reyero-Sans, I. & Tsujii, J.-I. (1994). A Cognitive Approach to an Interlingua Representation of Spatial Descriptions. In *Integration of Natural Language and Vision Processing: Workshop Notes*, 122–130. American Association for Artificial Intelligence. AAAI-94 Workshop Program.

Sablayrolles, P. (1992). Spatio-Temporal Semantics in Natural language: The Case of Motion. In Aurnague, M., Borillo, A., M. B. & Byas, M. (eds.) *Semantics of Time, Space, Movement and Spatio-Temporal Reasoning*, 69–87. Groupe LRC Toulouse. Working papers of the 4th International Workshop.

Schank, R. C. (1972). Conceptual Dependency: A Theory of Natural Language Understanding. *Cognitive Psychology* **3**: 552–631.

Schank, R. C. & Abelson, R. P. (1977). *Scripts, Plans, Goals and Understanding*. Lawrence Erlbaum.

Sharkey, N. E., Jackson, S. A. & Partridge, D. (1994). Internal Report for Connectionists Technical report, Department of Computer Science, University of Exeter, Exeter EX4 4PT, UK. Available through anonymous ftp (atlas.ex.ac.uk), Report Number 312.

Strassmann, S. (1994). Semi-Autonomous Animated Actors. In Proceedings of *The 12th National Conference on Artificial Intelligence (AAAI-94)*, 128–134. American Association for Artificial Intelligence.

Turner, S. J. & Cai, W. (1992). The 'Logical Clocks' Approach to Visualization of Parallel Programs. Technical report, University of Exeter Department of Computer Science. Available through anonymous ftp (atlas.ex.ac.uk), Report Number 252.

Yazdani, M. (1991). LINGERing On: Steps Towards an 'Intelligent' Language Tutoring Environment. In Thompson, J. & Zähner, C. (eds.) *Proceedings of the ICALL Workshop*. CTI Centre for Modern Languages, University of Hull. Workshop held at UMIST.

Yazdani, M. & Mealing, S. (1995). Communicating Through Pictures. *Artificial Intelligence Review* **9**(2–3): 205–213 (this volume).

Artificial Intelligence Review **9**: 237–242, 1995.

Book Review*

Title: **Intelligent Multimedia Interfaces**
Editor/Author: Mark T. Maybury
Publisher/Date: AAAI Press/MIT Press/ Menlo Park / Cambridge / London, 1993
Price: US$39.95, ISBN 0-262-63150-4

This book, which goes back to a workshop held at AAAI-91 contains 15 papers on various aspects of multimedia interfaces. It is organized into three sections: Automated Presentation Design, Intelligent Multimedia Interfaces and Architectural and Theoretical Issues. In the following I will discuss each section in turn.

Automated Presentation Design

The first section begins with an introductory chapter (Steven F. Roth and William E. Hefley: *Intelligent Multimedia Presentation Systems: Research and Principles*) which gives an excellent overview of the various problems which have to be addressed when designing an intelligent multimedia presentation system; among the research fields identified by the authors are: interface concepts (in particular a definition of terms like media, modes, etc.), the architecture of intelligent multimedia presentation systems, domains, applications and information to be covered by the presentation, characterization of the information to be presented, characterization of the function of presentations, presentation design knowledge, and human-computer interaction using intelligent multimedia presentation systems. Additionally, for each of the topics state of the art approaches are discussed.

The following five chapters of the book deal with systems that extend and adapt ideas from text generation for the production of multimedia presentations; these systems are TEXPLAN (chapter 2), WIP (chapters 3 and 4) and COMET (chapters 5 and 6).

In Chapter 2 (*Planning Multimedia Explanation Using Communicative Acts*) Mark Maybury describes a plan-based approach for the generation of multimedia explanations and its implementation in the TEXPLAN system. He shows that the production of multimedia explanations can be considered a complex action which has to be carried out in order to achieve a communicative goal. This complex action is composed by single communicative acts of which five types can be distinguished: rhetorical acts (e.g., IDENTIFY, DESCRIBE), linguistic acts (e.g., INFORM, REQUEST; ASK, COMMAND), graphical acts (e.g., DEPICT), non-linguistic auditory acts (e.g., SNAP, RING), and physical acts (e.g., GESTURES). Each communicative act is formalized as a plan, which has constraints and preconditions that controls its application. An effects-slot specifies the follow-up actions to be carried out once the plan operator is applicable. Finally, a decomposition-slot describes subplans into which the plan can be decomposed. Examples are given to illustrate how the plan-based approach is applied for the generation of (1) a textual identification of a given location, (2) a multimedia explanation of a location, and (3) a complex multimedia explanation.

The WIP system is presented in the following two chapters: chapter 3 (Elisabeth André, Wolfgang Finkler, Winfried Graf, Thomas Rist, Anne Schauder and Wolfgang Wahlster: *WIP: The Automatic Synthesis of Multimodal Presentations*) describes architecture and functionality of the full WIP system while chapter 4 (Elisabeth André, Thomas Rist: *The Design of Illustrated Documents as a Planning Task*) focuses on a plan-based approach for the generation of illustrated documents, in particular on presentation planning. The research reported here is taking place in the area of multimedia instructions for use and maintenance of an espresso machine.

The first of the two WIP articles describes the various modules the WIP system is composed of (1) the presentation planner which is responsible for content determination and mode selection, (2) the layout manager which determines adequate text/graphics combinations using a constraint-based approach, (3) the text generator which is responsible for text design and text realization, and (4) the graphics generator which carries out design and realization operations for concepts to be expressed by non-textual media. The presentation planner attributes chunks of information to either text or graphics generator where they are finally realized. The results are then communicated back to the presentation planner for revision.

Presentation planning is discussed in more detail in the second WIP paper. The article first argues that well-known concepts from the area of natural language processing like speech acts and rhetorical relations receive an extended meaning in the context of multimodal communication. Consequently, not only the generation of pure text, but also the generation of multimedia presentations is considered a goal-directed activity which can be operationalized by a plan-based approach. The main point of the paper is a description of the inadequacy of a conventional hierarchical planner for the treatment of the interdependencies between content determination, mode selection and realization. To solve this problem planning has been designed in a way that allows interleaved processing; this is done by using uniform planning mechanisms (for content and mode selection) and by employing parallel processing techniques with the possibility to exchange information. Revision is done by output and structure sharing and by structure adding. The planning principle incorporated in WIP is then illustrated by means of an example.

In contrast to WIP the COMET system as described in chapter 5 (Steven K. Feiner and Kathleen R. McKeown: *Automating the Generation of Coordinate Multimedia Explanations*) is blackboard-based. It has been developed for application in the field of maintenance and repair of military radios. Unlike WIP the content planner of COMET fully determines the content to be visualized before realization takes place. The structure resulting from that phase is gradually augmented by information determined by the media coordinator, which increments parts of this structure with information about the media appropriate for their realization and later with the resulting realizations. This means that the interaction between the text and the graphics generator happens by using a blackboard technique. The interaction between these two components allows for the treatment of phenomena like e.g., the coordination of sentence and picture breaks and the generation of cross-references.

The second article related to the COMET project (Steven K. Feiner, Diane J. Litman, Kathleen R. McKeown, and Rebecca J. Passonneau: *Towards Coordinated Temporal Multimedia Presentations*) discusses future extensions of the system which have to be made in order to visualize temporal information like events and durations using "temporal media" as e.g., animation and speech. It is shown how Allen's temporal logic can be adapted for that purpose and which features of natural language and graphics can be exploited to foreground temporal aspects of multimedia presentations.

The last article in the first section (Bradley A. Goodman: *Multimedia Explanations for Intelligent Training Systems*) focuses on the automatic combination of video segments into longer animated instructions and their combination with speech, text and graphics in the framework of an intelligent diagnosis training system for Apple Macintoshes. Reuse of knowledge, in particular of small video-sequences showing basic actions, is an important aspect of the approach outlined in that chapter. The prototype VISUAL REPAIR allows the user to specify complex plans for the repair of a computer and to execute, i.e., to visualize, full or partial plans using combined media. If a plan specified by the user is incorrect the system interferes and corrects the user. Multimedia is also used for the generation of help information.

Intelligent Multimedia Interfaces

The second section of the book includes papers which are mostly concerned with interactive systems, i.e., with systems and prototypes that rely on feedback of the user. Many of these systems incorporate the hypermedia idea for information exchange.

The first of these articles (John D. Burger and Ralph J. Marshall: *The Application of Natural Language Models to Intelligent Multimedia*) reports about a system, AIMI, which supports the user in the task of devising cargo transportation schedules and routes. In order to fulfill this task the user is provided with maps, tables, charts and text, parts of which are sensitive to further interaction, i.e., to direct manipulation. The model takes both the user and the context into account to choose the adequate mode for information presentation. Nevertheless, the user can override automatic choices made by the system. It is envisaged that for a future implementation different system responses can be generated out of the same information tailoring the output directly to the user.

In Chapter 9 Oliviero Stock and the ALFRESCO Project Team[1] (ALFRESCO: *Enjoying the Combination of Natural Language Processing and Hypermedia for Information Exploration*) describe how an interactive system can profit from the combination of natural language and hypermedia: while prefabricated hypermedia texts can compensate for a lack of coverage in the natural language modules the on-demand generation of user-tailored texts can help to prevent disorientation in the hypermedia environment. This insight led to the development of the ALFRESCO system for accessing information about Italian frescoes of the 14th century which not only combines these two media but also adds the possibility to inspect and inquire pictures and video sequences using touchscreen technology. A special feature of this system is the integration of a model of the user's interest which is continuously adapted to the ongoing dialogue and to the information inspected. The interest model is exploited for the generation of answers to user requests: concepts relevant for inclusion in the system answer are determined taking the user's interest into account. Texts generated on the fly are available for further access as hypermedia cards, as are ready-made texts about artists' biographies, frescoes, etc. Additionally, further information about details of pictures and videos can be maintained by asking questions in natural language combined with direct pointing actions. This complex functionality is achieved by an integration of the following modules: a KL-ONE-oriented knowledge representation component (YAK), a chart-based parser for Italian (WEDNESDAY-2), a topic module for the treatment of focus and deixis, an interest model of the user, and a tactical and strategical generation component.

The Jet Engine Trouble Shooting Assistant JETA is described in the following chapter (Suhayya Abu-Hakima, Mike Halasz and Sieu Phan: *An Approach to Hypermedia in Diagnostic Systems*). The system is based on a representation of diagnostic troubleshooting networks. If the user's actions in maintaining a given device contain errors or inconsistencies the system initiates a dialogue with the user. The interaction proceeds in a menu-based fashion, taking the profiles of three distinct user groups into account. The system is able to provide context-dependent information explaining and defining concepts mentioned in the ongoing discourse. The module for the automatic generation of explanations, which will be extended significantly in the near future, will provide session-sensitive explanations (e.g., about events and actions) and also explanations which detail the facilities of the system (i.e., meta-information). The hypermedia-idea is realized in JETA insofar as hypermedia links exist between graphics and text.

The following paper (David B. Koons, Carlton J. Sparrell, Kristinn R. Torisson: *Integrating Simultaneous Input from Speech, Gaze and Hand Gestures*) shows how the integration of speech, eye tracking and gestures can be of benefit for systems which model the interaction with a map database or which are situated in the blocksworld domain. For each of the three input modalities a separate parser exists. All three of them parse into the same frame-based formalism. It is a specific requirement of the mode combination described here that information about time and duration of the single actions has to be taken into account so that simultaneous actions in different modes can be synchronized, combined and thereby interpreted together. The article also provides a detailed description of the parser for gestlets. This module first attributes features like posture, orientation and motion to sequences of hand data. Then an additional level of abstraction is added by grouping these features into complex gestlets (e.g., SWEEP).

Architectural and Theoretical Issues

The third section of the book collects articles that address topics like the identification of the knowledge needed to generate and control multimedia interaction, but also empirical aspects of multimedia interface design.

The work presented in the twelfth chapter (Yigal Arens, Eduard Hovy and Mira Vossers: *On the Knowledge Underlying Multimedia Presentations*) addresses the media allocation problem by discussing which knowledge types and processes are required for multimedia presentation. The authors determine the knowledge types by abstracting from observations made in multimedia document analysis. The four knowledge types identified are: (1) characteristics of the media; (2) characteristics of the information to be conveyed; (3) goals and characteristics of the document producer, and (4) characteristics of the perceiver/reader of the document and of the communicative situation. For each of the types a detailed discussion of various possible subtypes is given. Since many interdependencies exist between the various information types a representation form had to be chosen which takes this into account. Therefore, Systemic Networks as developed in Systemic Functional Linguistics have been used which describe the potential of all information types and their hierarchical organization. The interrelationships are accounted for by means of rules which determine the most adequate combination of information types in a given situation. Two examples are discussed to illustrate this approach.

The next article (Matthew Cornell, Beverly Park Woolf, and Daniel Suthers: *Using "Live Information" in a Multimedia Framework*) reports about the development of a multimedia environment to support the creation, organization and communication of knowledge. This environment allows the user to individually decide how the information is to be presented. The user can also prepare the information for sharing and reuse. This principle, called "Live Information" has been used in the field of tutorial systems, in particular in the domain of electricity and electrical networks. A future application in the area of intelligent text processing is envisaged. The basic concepts of the implementation in the IKit system are objects, displayers, actions and references. Each displayer stands for a certain medium, which can be used to realize the surface form of a given object. Depending on the displayer chosen a person instance, for example, can be visualized by a name or a picture. On the objects gestures can be performed in order to execute system or user-defined actions. References are created by combined dragging and dropping actions.

Chapter 14 (Jürgen Krause: *A Multilayered Empirical Approach to Multimodality: Towards Mixed Solutions of Natural Language and Graphical Interfaces*) is emphasizing empirical foundations and observations concerning multimedia interfaces. The author proposes to include empirical tests at any stage of the development of a multimedia system, using simulated prototypes in the early development stages and using the implemented system in later stages. This principle is illustrated by showing how natural language and graphics have been combined in a number of ways throughout the development process of the WING-IIR system and how empirical studies showed that a mixed graphical/direct-manipulation interface is most promising for a material database.

The final chapter of this book (Andrea Bonarini: *Modeling Issues in Multimedia Car-Driver Interaction*) reports about a system which handles the interaction between a driver and its artificial co-pilot (MIMa). The paper first describes the various parameters which have to be taken into account when planning content and media-combination of a message to be issued to the driver. These parameters are grouped into four classes: (1) features common to input and output tools, e.g., complexity of the message a tool can convey, communication channels available, (2) features of the input tool, e.g., attention needed to use the tool, quality of message reception, (3) features of the output tool, e.g., attention needed to understand, agitation induced when the message is issued, and (4) the driver model including features as e.g., psychological state, attitude, driver goals etc. Starting from default features at the beginning of the interaction the values are continuously adapted to the situation, attributing discrete values to the features, which are circumscribed in natural language. The appropriate combination of modalities is computed on demand i.e., when a message to the driver is to be issued. The principle described here is visualized by means of an example.

Critical Discussion

The book gives a good overview of state of the art research done in the area of multimedia interfaces. It provides many diverse views on the various problems in the design of multimedia interfaces and it contains relevant solutions. Theoretical and practical aspects are discussed ranging from empirical research in the area to the description of concrete applications.

The book continues a row of collections that describe the state of the art in multimedia interface design (Catarci *et al.* 1991 and Blattner and Dannenberg 1992). These books are based on workshops that took place in 1990 and in spring 1991. In that context also Sullivan and Taylor (1991), has to be mentioned, whose work is dedicated to the whole field of user interfaces but contains various sections addressing multimediality. In contrast to these collections Maybury's book emphasizes the linguistic aspects of multimedia interfaces.

Maybury's book contains about two thirds of the papers which were originally given at the AAAI-91 workshop on Intelligent Multimedia Interfaces (Maybury 1991). The articles not included in the book mostly deal with retrieval interfaces and applications. The papers in the book have been considerably extended and improved; unfortunately they do not address the progress made since the workshop took place. Also, a visionary article is missing indicating the various directions in which research in multimedia interfaces is developing at the moment.

Some critical remarks have to be made concerning the quality with which the book has been produced: throughout the book many layout errors can be found, as e.g., paragraph breaks in the middle of sentences. Most disturbing is the complete lack of a figure in chapter 12, which is crucial for understanding the explanation given in the text (thereby also giving a clear illustration that good text/picture combinations are crucial for document understanding). Other figures contain slight errors or include text that runs off the end of the page. I also missed a list of the authors' addresses and affiliations.

Despite these minor flaws the book is highly recommendable to people working in the field of multimedia, but also for people doing research in related areas, as e.g., human-computer interfaces or natural language processing. Also the book is appropriate as a text book for students or for researchers new in the field since most of the articles are written very clearly.

Notes

* This review was funded by the German Federal Ministry for Research and Technology (BMBF) in the framework of the Verbmobil Project under grant 01IV101K/1. The responsibility for the contents of this study lies with the author.

[1] G. Carenini, F. Cecconi, E. Franconi, A. Lavelli, B. Magnini, F. Pianesi, M. Ponzi, V. Samek-Lodovici, C. Strapparava.

References

Blattner, M. & Dannenberg, R. (eds.) (1992). *Multimedia Interface Design*. Addison-Wesley: Reading, MA. ACM Press: New York.

Catarci, T., Costabile, M., & Levialdi, S. (eds.) (1991). *Advanced Visual Interfaces – Proceedings of the International Workshop* AVI-92. World Scientific: Singapore/New Jersey/London/Hong Kong.

Maybury, M. (ed.) (1991). *Intelligent Multimedia Interfaces – Workshop Notes from the Ninth International Conference on Artificial Intelligence* AAAI-91. American Association for Artificial Intelligence.

Sullivan, J. & Taylor, S. (eds.) (1991). *Intelligent User Interfaces*. Addison-Wesley: Reading, MA. ACM Press: New York.

ELISABETH MAIER
German Research Center for AI – DFKI GmbH
Saarbrücken, Germany